Passions of the Voice

Passions of the Voice

Hysteria, Narrative, and the Figure
of the Speaking Woman,
1850–1915

CLAIRE KAHANE

The Johns Hopkins University Press
Baltimore and London

The Johns Hopkins University Press
2715 North Charles Street
Baltimore, Maryland 21218-4319
The Johns Hopkins Press Ltd., London

A catalog record for this book is available from the British Library.

Library of Congress Cataloging-in-Publication Data

Kahane, Claire.
Passions of the voice : hysteria, narrative, and the figure of the
speaking woman, 1850–1915 / Claire Kahane.
p. cm.   Includes bibliographical references and index.
ISBN 0-8018-5161-0 (alk. paper). — ISBN 0-8018-5162-9 (pbk. : alk. paper)
1. English fiction—19th century—History and criticism.
2. Hysteria in literature.   3. English fiction—20th century—
History and criticism.   4. Psychoanalysis and literature—Great
Britain—History.   5. Women and literature—Great Britain—History.
6. Sex differences (Psychology) in literature.   7. Modernism
(Literature)—Great Britain.   8. Speech in literature.   9. Voice in
literature.   10. Narration (Rhetoric)   I. Title.
PR878.H93K34   1996
823'.809353—dc20   95-18035

Contents

PREFACE   vii

ACKNOWLEDGMENTS   xvii

One
History/Hysteria: A Glance Backward   1

Two
Freud's Passion/Dora's Voice   14

Three
Invalids and Nurses: The Sisterhood of Rage   34

Four
Medusa's Voice: Male Hysteria in *The Bostonians*   64

Five
From Dream to Night-Mère: The Poetics of Hysteria
    and Masochism in *The Story of an African Farm*   80

Six
The Great Refusal: *The Voyage Out*   99

Seven
Male Modernists and the Ear of the Other in
    Heart of Darkness and *The Good Soldier*   127

NOTES   151

WORKS CITED   177

INDEX   189

Preface

―――――

A voice, a human voice.
—Olive Chancellor, in *The Bostonians*

A voice, a voice.
—Marlow, in *Heart of Darkness*

THERE IS ALWAYS a voice in a story; at the very least, what is said presupposes someone who has said it. Virginia Woolf provocatively extended this truism by insisting on the diabolical power of words to invoke the writer's presence even more than signification. "Why words do this, how they do it . . . nobody knows. . . . Even words that are hundreds of years old have this power; when they are new they have it so strongly that they deafen us to the writer's meaning" (1966, 2:248). Although Woolf did not pursue the reasons for this illusion of presence, narratologists have pointed out that such aspects of a text as the arrangement of sequence, the constellation of metaphors, the location of deictic centers, work to constitute the voice of an implicit speaking subject who tells the tale to which a reader listens.[1] Moreover, while this speaking subject is often centered in a particular character or even in a group of characters who function as authorial spokespersons with whom the reader identifies, traditional narrative has typically privileged what is said outside of quotation marks, the anonymous, omniscient third-person voice external to the story. Issuing from a transcendent and thus more authoritative subject position than that of any character or first-person narrator susceptible to the story's turbulence, this third-person voice is more insidiously introjected by the reader as the voice of truth; it is also presumably disinterested, belonging to a universal subject beyond the particular constraints of gender.[2]

This book explores a breakdown in these conventional sufficiencies of narrative voice in certain problematic texts of the late nineteenth and early twentieth centuries. Whether first-person or third-person, whether inside or outside the tale they narrate, the narrative voices of the texts I engage can be characterized by their inability to sustain a neutral and consistent subject position, by their anxious subjection to what I designate as the passions of the voice. Indeed, these voices manifest an anxiety about the voice itself, about who has it and what it can do, about who can speak and who can listen, which is especially provoked by a new nineteenth-century figure, the woman who speaks with a powerful voice. In using the word *figure*, I am not limiting myself either to a character within a fiction or to an actual historical personage. I intend, instead, to evoke the idea of a cultural trope that circulates within the discourse of a particular historical era, provocatively embodying its anxieties and desires. My use of *figure* in this sense leans on Roland Barthes' distinction between figuration and representation. As Barthes points out, nineteenth-century realism assumes a prior reality that is re-presented by a neutral observer outside the frame of action. Within such a frame of representation, desire circulates among the characters; "nothing leaps out" (1975, 58) to implicate the writer or the reader in that desire. With the more pervasive notion of figuration, on the other hand, objectivity yields to the effects of subjective desire, to the recognition that desire continues to circulate not only among the characters within the story's frame but also between text and reader, text and writer, text and time.

Barthes, of course, is thus a principal contemporary commentator on the shift in the nature of the textual voice, from a "classic" voice which is by and large attached to an origin that we can identify— either a character or a consciousness—to a modern voice that has no parentage, in which reference to origins is impossible, an illusion at best. But as Barthes notes in *SZ* (1974), there are some instances of classic texts in which the voice "gets lost, as though it had leaked out through a hole in the discourse . . . leaving a gap which enables the utterance to shift from one point of view to another, without warning" (41–42). This "tonal instability" is analogous to what I define in this book as the hysterical voice.

I begin with a historical premise that has been elaborated by a number of feminist critics: that the conventional delineation of sexual difference and desire that predominated in Victorian discourse—and by "Victorian" I mean to signify the prevailing rule of bourgeois social proprieties in the second half of the nineteenth century rather than the literal geotemporal boundaries of Queen Victoria's reign—was increasingly challenged by the rise of feminism and the appearance of the "New Woman."[3] I focus on a particular figuration of the New Woman: the woman as speaking subject, a figure actualized in the wave of feminist orators who, from midcentury on, took the platform in the cause of women's suffrage. Both a disquieting internal imago and an external social reality, the figure of the speaking woman had a profoundly unsettling effect on nineteenth-century cultural discourse. By claiming discursive authority and the legitimacy of a public as well as a private voice and performing that claim, the figure of the speaking woman disturbed not only the patriarchal structure of social relations but also the gendered conventions of nineteenth-century domestic fiction.

Although both men and women are constructed as sexual subjects through discursive practices that vary historically, women and men have always been positioned differently within those practices. Teresa DeLauretis (1984) has astutely elaborated the ways in which Western narrative has been dominated by an oedipal paradigm, which constructs the questing subject as masculine, a hero who, like Oedipus, seeks his desire in a maternally inflected object. In oedipal narrative, as Freud also maintained in "Creative Writers and Daydreaming" (1908 [1907], *SE* 9), it is the masculine hero whose ambition and desire drive the action while the woman longs to be the object of his love, the mirror of his achievement. The nineteenth-century domestic novel flourished within a version of this paradigm, typically restricting the heroine's sphere of action to the arena of heterosexual romance and directing her desire toward marriage.[4] Even when, like Austen's Emma or Brontë's Jane Eyre, the heroine claimed her own desire and insisted on being the subject rather than object of the narrative action, the plot eventually—albeit uneasily—inserted her into a marriage which formalized her submission to the patriarchal ordering of that desire.

Through the latter half of the nineteenth century, that fictional resolution was increasingly problematized by the newly emergent figure of the speaking woman as an articulate, desiring subject; her appearance cast doubt not only on the inevitability of this plot but also on the very laws of sexual difference that constituted it. By subverting an implicitly gendered narrative syntax that marked the speaking and desiring subject as male, the figure of the woman with a potent voice augured a sexual anarchy in representation that threatened the narrator's ability to tell a coherent story. Because the voice was itself construed as a fetishistic object of presence and power, the woman with a potent voice figured a kind of vocal Medusa both fascinating and fearsome, arousing apprehension in the very narrative voice that imagined her.[5] Hysteria as theorized and exemplified in Freud's Dora case is my interpretive paradigm for reading that apprehension and its textual effects.

Hysteria reached epidemic proportion in the late nineteenth century, but it had a long and varied history before Freud made it the founding neurosis of psychoanalysis. In chapter 1 I briefly sketch its historical trajectory, foregrounding those features of its history and structure that have some bearing on the relation between voice and gender. Whatever its variants through time, however, as the very etymology of the term indicates, hysteria has been primarily associated with female sexual disorder. Even though male hysteria was an acknowledged category of neurosis by the nineteenth century, the very name linked the condition to the feminine qualities of the man in question. Certainly by the 1880s, male as well as female hysteria was an intense subject of medical study, most notably by Freud's predecessors Janet and Charcot in France, whose contributions to the elucidation of hysteria sparked Freud's radical rethinking of psychic structures. But it was Freud's qualitatively different intervention in hysteria's history that made a psychopathology relevant for contemporary hermeneutic studies. Elaborating a meaning for hysteria, insisting on the symbolic sense of its symptoms, Freud converted a descriptive disorder in the realm of physiology to a dynamic disorder in the realm of psychology, and specifically, a disorder of representation. Thus, for example, he could read the symptomatic, dysfunctional speech in both Breuer's Anna O. case (*Studies of Hysteria* [1895], *SE* 2) and his own case of Dora (1905 [1901], *SE* 7), as symbolic representations of specific dysfunctional desires.

Freud defined hysteria as the somatic representation of a repressed bisexual conflict, an unconscious refusal to accept a single and defined subject position in the oedipal structuration of desire and identity ("Hysterical Phantasies and Their Relation to Bisexuality," 1908, *SE* 9). For Freud hysteria comprised, and performed in bodily symptoms, two sexual identities—masculine and feminine—which contended with each other for dominance. Thus, for example, Freud interpreted the symptomatic behavior of a patient who tried to pull off her dress at the same time that she tried to resist that act as an example of a sexualized psychic double play, in which bisexual identifications were performed through the body's mimicry of a sexual seduction (1908, *SE* 9:166). Moreover, Freud argued that although sexual difference is culturally located in genital difference, hysterics, in a defensive refusal of difference, displace that site of conflict upward, playing out their sexualized contestation of identity in a more ambiguous register of the body. Thus, hysteria is frequently marked by disturbances of voice, vision, hearing, and even breathing—disturbances involving the earliest bodily zones of exchange between inside and outside, between incorporation and projection, between a subject in the process of becoming and a libidinally invested object world. Hysteria records a conflict in these zones, a confusion about who does what to whom, about who is supposed to do what to whom, which makes itself felt also in a confusion between body and language.[6]

Indeed, the centrality of the body rather than verbal language as the site of representation and the simultaneous rejection of sexual difference in the typical etiology of hysteria suggest that hysteria refuses any concept of lack; nothing is given up. Paradoxically the hysteric refuses the body, or more accurately, refuses its symbolic limits and laws, yet continually interrogates those limits through a projective other. In Lacanian reformulations of this drama, the subject poses the question of sexual difference to an other, demanding that the other produce an answer: Am I a man? Am I a woman? How are these identifications embodied? How are they signified? How do they determine a relation to the speaking subject? Not surprisingly, in an era that constructed sexuality as a predominant gauge of psychosocial identity, these insistent questions became increasingly prominent and are symptomatically articulated in the narrative voices of the texts I explore.

Freud's focus on ambivalent desire and identifications as the primary source of hysterical symptoms, however, is extended in my readings to include the effects of repressed rage. Although Freud recognized the importance of rage as a factor in hysterical conflict—for example, he points out that Dora's unconscious rage against her father provoked death wishes and negative transference—his comments on rage remain relatively untheorized, scattered throughout various texts.[7] For my purposes his most relevant remarks on rage occur in his description of feminine psychosexual development and its inevitable promotion of the daughter's rage against the mother. Recontextualized recently within a feminist problematic by Juliet Mitchell, Julia Kristeva, and Luce Irigaray, the daughter's rage as a significant feature of hysterical symptomatology is central to my argument, especially in chapter 3. I rely also on the earlier writings of Melanie Klein, who makes oral rage the centerpiece of her theory of infantile anxiety and its relation to aesthetic structures.[8] Indeed, for Klein it is rage rather than erotic desire that provokes the fiercest unconscious conflict, rage that is the strongest factor in repression and its symptomatic consequences.[9]

In this context, it seems especially noteworthy that however common rage is in the psychic life of men and women, the cultural demand for its repression is clearly gender-inflected. For while the expression of rage can be easily integrated into culturally acceptable forms of masculine identity and desire, Freudian theory and the cultural order it describes allow little place for the integration of rage in women's libidinal development unless those women are first defined as "virile," "castrating," or "phallic";[10] the alternative is to turn rage inward, to convert it into "feminine" masochism or melancholia. Given such antinomies of affect and identity, it is not surprising to find rage and its vicissitudes a pervasive feature of hysterical conflict in texts written by women, as I suggest in my readings of such diverse texts as Florence Nightingale's *Cassandra,* Charlotte Brontë's *Villette,* and Alice James' *Diary.* Nevertheless, such sudden outbursts of rage as deflect Henry James' narrative voice in *The Bostonians* or Ford Madox Ford's in *The Good Soldier* make clear that internal prohibitions on rage are not restricted to one sex.

In thus viewing hysteria as a consequence of both repressed rage and repudiated desire, I inevitably raise certain questions that have not received previous critical attention: What are the determining links among rage, gender, and narrative voice? How is rage represented as textual symptom? What happens to the rage of those "new women" who newly claim the power of the voice in a text? of those who are newly compelled to occupy the position of listener to the woman's voice? Can one who has been accustomed to the authority of speech become a listener without evincing aggressive retaliation? To address these questions, my readings pay close psychoanalytic attention to the permutations of the textual voice, to its gendered tensions and its defensive strategies.

By this point it should be clear that in reading the voice of a text, I move beyond questions of voice as a formal literary category to the psychosocial function of the speaking voice more generally, both as the material vehicle of speech and as a psychic object of desire. Writing, of course, inscribes the absence of the speaking voice, whose place is represented by the words of the text. Even this concept of "representation" has been made suspect by current theories that cut the cord between language and any notion of prior presence. For Freud, however, the prior presence of the speaking voice was implicit in the power of language; as he pointed out, "Verbal residues are derived primarily from auditory perceptions. . . . A word is after all the mnemic residue of a word that has been heard" (1923, *SE* 19:10–11).

While the general poststructuralist dismissal of authorial presence discourages us from hearing a voice in the text, I assume also that whether spoken or written, words bear the weight of audition; they are "heard" with the third ear even when there is no actual speaking voice present.[11] Moreover, as Garrett Stewart argues, "inner audition need not in any sense subscribe to the myth of an originary Voice before the letter" (1990, 3) in order to acknowledge the phenomenality of the voice in reading and writing.[12] Interestingly in this regard, Stewart contends that the act of reading itself evokes a silent voicing in the reader, who involuntarily mimes in the body his or her identificatory reception of the text, and that this unconscious corporeal mimicry includes the organs of vocal production. Thus, the reader comes literally, perhaps even hysterically, to embody the voice of the text's speaking subject, including its fractures, its implicit conflicts, its points of pleasure and danger.[13]

There is always a special risk in reading for the symptomatic in discourse, a risk not only of miming the hysterical fragmentation of the text, but of projecting too much into the text in writing out an analysis, as Freud's own "Fragment of an Analysis of a Case of Hysteria" (1905 [1901], *SE* 9) illustrates. I have attempted to be sensitive to this danger, recognizing that the Dora case foundered as case, story, and case history precisely because Freud did not take into account the countertransference, the effects of Dora's voice on his desire and its articulations. But I admit to also using the countertransference, to taking silent note of the effects of a textual voice on my response as I construct an analysis. Appropriately then, after presenting a historical context for my emphasis on the figure of the speaking woman in hysterical representations (chap. 1), I begin with Freud's narrative of Dora (chap. 2). Written on the cusp of the century, this is the text in which Freud as analyst develops the concepts of both hysterical narrative and transference by acting out and in a postscript analyzing his own hysterical discourse as he unfolds the meanings of Dora's. Because my understanding of hysterical fictions and their historical moment comes out of my reading of Freud's performative analysis, this case history becomes my exemplary text for exploring the problematics of desire and identification in hysterical narration.

In the chapters that follow, I develop a virtual psychopoetics of hysteria, anatomizing its different psychic components as they structure a number of male- and female-authored texts. Each of these texts exhibits features of a discourse in crisis: excessive splittings and displacements of the subject of the story, frequent paralyses of plot, phonemic rather than semantic continuities, and seemingly gratuitous and often bizarre disruptions of narrative sequence. Against these textual instabilities, the narrative voice struggles to find a form that will contain the confusions of its utterance. Chapters 3 and 4 highlight the effects of hysterical rage in Florence Nightingale's *Cassandra,* Charlotte Brontë's *Shirley* and *Villette,* Alice James' *Diary,* and Henry James' *The Bostonians.* Chapter 5 develops the effects of masochism and melancholia on the hysterical structure of Olive Schreiner's *Story of an African Farm.* These various elements of hysterical representation are incorporated in the discussion in chapter 6 of Virginia Woolf's *The Voyage Out,* the novel that initiated Woolf's lifelong experimentation with narrative voice. I conclude in chapter 7 with the strategic use of the hysterical voice in T. S. Eliot's breathless prose poem "Hysteria," Joseph Conrad's *Heart of Darkness,* and Ford Madox Ford's *The Good Soldier,* using these texts to indicate the implication of hysteria in modernist poetics.

Ultimately, my readings construct my own narrative, in which late Victorian texts are unconsciously captured by an anxiety about the breakdown of difference that came to a climax around the turn of the century. By the end of the first decade of the twentieth century, my narrative suggests, hysteria had lost much of its unconscious currency. Indeed, by the end of the second decade, hysteria was both self-consciously thematized as a trope of literary modernism as well as formalized as a poetics that could more adequately represent the dislocations of the modern subject. In this sense one can say that hysterical narrative voice not only preceded literary modernism but made it possible. For modernist writers, hysteria was not a psycho-pathology subject to cure but a sign of the time.

Yet this formal reconversion of hysteria into textuality, which suggests a degree of acknowledgment, did not mean that the hysterical tensions around issues of gender and voice had been eradicated. While the fragmentation of the speaking subject and the dispersions of consciousness that characterize modernist syntax have come to be seen as a mimetic representation of the way a "normal" mind works, of a kind of normative hysteria, modernist texts often present a disorder of voice that goes beyond ordinary modern nervousness. Certainly they manifest an anxiety about "feminine" vulnerability and self-fragmentation that would be exacerbated by the Great War and its mass deconstruction of the illusion of male heroism.[14] Especially in texts written by male authors who are conflicted about the parameters of male subjectivity, indeed, who are at times captured by a terrifying desire to lose it, the woman with a big mouth remains a familiar locus of anxiety. By developing a strategy of mimicry, like Hamlet's antic play with madness, a strategy congenial to hysterics, modernist texts can both indulge and contain the anxiety of the speaking subject as it continues to struggle with the passions of the voice.

A number of recent studies have already set up a context for this book, indeed, have even called for it. Elaine Showalter's *Sexual Anarchy* (1990) and *The Female Malady* (1985) both describe the fin de siècle crisis in sexual identity and its cultural consequences. Ann Ardis's *New Women, New Novels* (1990) convincingly argues that the historical New Woman led to a new literary genre, the New Woman Novel of the 1880s and 1890s, which was a precursor of modernism. Sandra Gilbert and Susan Gubar's *No Man's Land* (vol. 1, 1988), elaborating the antagonistic relation between feminism and the male modernist establishment, also shows the influence of feminist writers on modernist experimentation. Susan Lanser's *Fictions of Authority* (1992) more closely addresses my own interests in narrative voice by pointing out that while "voice" has been an especially resonant trope for contemporary feminist critics as well as a crucial term for narratologists, feminist criticism and narratology have remained virtually separate, even antithetical, areas of inquiry. Joining the two, Lanser develops a materialist-historical analysis of texts by women writers from the seventeenth century to the present and examines the crisis of authority in the voice. These studies have established a necessary conversation into which my more psychoanalytic readings of hysteria and narrative can enter.

The particular relation between narrative and hysteria has been also addressed by Katherine Cummings' *Telling Tales: The Hysteric's Seduction in Fiction and Theory* (1991), a comparativist study that devises a deconstructionist dialogue between three male theorists and three male-authored European novels and plays with their representations of sexual difference and seduction across three centuries. Most recently, *Hysteria beyond Freud,* edited by Sander Gilman et al. (1993), has convincingly argued not only for the need to reconsider hysteria, but to bring together history and representation, medicine and ideology. While that collection begins that project, this study hopefully continues it, attempting to answer its call for an "illumination of the linguistic representations of hysteria" (xvi) by paying attention to the passions of a narrative voice disordered by its own productions.

Acknowledgments

THIS BOOK HAS been in the making for a good number of years, and it is difficult to single out the many voices of friends and colleagues who have contributed to its evolution. Without question, however, it was the members of my feminist writing group who were most supportive, and most responsible for my being able to turn abstruse thought and psychoanalytic intuitions into communicable prose. Without the general good sense, encouragement, and patience of Betsy Cromley, Elizabeth Kennedy, Hester Eisenstein, Carolyn Korsmeyer, Suzanne Pucci, and Carol Zemel, who read numerous muddy drafts of this project and helped me clarify my ideas, it would probably still be an ongoing project.

I would like also to thank Elizabeth Abel, Amy Doerr, Marilyn Fabe, and Rosemary Feal for their helpful readings of parts of the work-in-progress in its earlier stages, and William Warner for his sustained colleagial encouragement. Charlotte Pressler, who rescued me at the end by tidying up my documentation, and Joan Cipperman, whose good humor over the years while she patiently photocopied numerous versions of the manuscript, were also indispensable to the book's completion.

Finally, I thank my husband, Ronald Hauser, for his domestic support, which gave me the requisite time and private space to write over many a weekend, and my son Lukas, for putting up with the more vexatious effects of my absorption in this project. And thank you, Arlene, for demonstrating the truths of psychoanalysis, which I continue to discover in my own voice.

Sections of this book have been previously published in different versions. Parts of chapter 2 appeared in "Hysteria, Feminism, and the

Case of *The Bostonians*," in *Feminism and Psychoanalysis,* ed. Richard Feldstein and Judith Roof (Ithaca: Cornell University Press, 1989), 280–97. Chapter 3 contains a revised and extended discussion of "The Aesthetic Politics of Rage," *Literature/Interpretation/Theory* 2 (1991):19–31. A version of chapter 4 first appeared as "*The Bostonians* and the Figure of the Speaking Woman," in *Psychoanalysis And,* ed. Richard Feldstein and Henry Sussman (New York: Routledge, 1989), 163–74. Chapter 7 includes a revised version of "Seduction and the Voice of the Text: *Heart of Darkness* and *The Good Soldier*," in *Seduction and Theory,* ed. Dianne Hunter (Urbana: University of Illinois Press, 1989), 135–53.

Passions of the Voice

Chapter One

History / Hysteria
A Glance Backward

———————

Wherever the hysteric goes, she brings war with her.
—Moustapha Safouan, "In Praise of Hysteria"

CHANGE IS THE matter both of history and of narrative, but as historians have remarked, England in the second half of the nineteenth century seemed to experience its mutability with extraordinary intensity. The sense of cultural transformation that dominated both event and discourse in the Victorian era has been repeatedly chronicled; within one generation a technological revolution perhaps unparalleled until our own fin-de-siècle computer age gave rise to material transformations that radically altered the boundaries of the geosocial landscape. The rapid expansion of industrial capitalism and its promotion of shifts of population, the emergence of large urban centers with newly exploding populations and new social classes, the invention of telegraph and telephone, the expansion of railroads and steam power, created a vertiginous sense of social and economic acceleration to which Victorian discourse bore frequent witness.[1]

Clearly such swift change breeds anxiety as well as expectation, breeds a diffuse sense of being subject to forces beyond one's comprehension or control, a sense that went against the dominant Victorian ideal of progressive mastery and dominion in both politics and culture. Thus, for example, Walter Bagehot in *Physics and Politics* cannot quite remove the quasi-paranoid intimations of invisible presences in his voice even as he celebrates the new knowledge in physics: "One peculiarity of this age is the sudden acquisition of much physical knowledge. There is scarcely a department of science which is the same, or at all the same, as it was fifty years ago. A new world of inventions . . . has grown up around us which we cannot help seeing, a new world of ideas is in the air and affects us, though we do not see it."[2] As Bagehot's text testifies, the very word *new* emerges as a frequent incantation in the discourse of the late nineteenth century—the New Hedonism, the New Fiction, the New Realism, the New Drama, the New Sciences, and, not least for my purposes, the New Woman—undermining the old certainties that subtended the cultural order.[3]

What especially characterized this nervous age was that a generalized anxiety about change became increasingly linked to a particular anxiety about the change in and by women, a change that, as Peter Gay points out, was brought about in great part by the very successes of the bourgeois culture that was nervous.[4] If, for example, the speedy development of late-nineteenth-century capitalism called for a rapidly expanding workforce, women in ever greater number participated in that expansion. In the England of 1851 there had been almost no women clerks; in 1861 there were 2,000; and, by 1911, the number had mushroomed to 157,000. Moreover, the growth of crowded urban centers, inevitably attended by poverty, unemployment, illness, and crime, called for new social competencies and new professional qualifications. Although women remained a small minority in the professions—by 1897 there were only 87 women doctors in all of England—middle-class women took the lead as crusaders for social and spiritual reform. Precisely in the name of those female virtues conventionally attributed to them, women established reform societies, settlement houses, and educational alliances to address the needs of an expanding new mass population. Even religion, the conventional stronghold of patriarchal authority, was invaded by these newly public women, who, newly inspired, used the pulpit with millennial zeal to envision utopias in which women prevailed as arbiters of morality and the law. By the 1880s a new and increasingly vocal woman had emerged in both England and America, confident in her singularity, outspoken in the public arena, calling vociferously for suffrage and a legitimate voice in the affairs of state.

Much like the response of many conservatives to the second wave of feminism in the late 1960s, the social critics of the time responded to the emergence of this New Woman by predicting the end of Western civilization. Ann Ardis points to an anonymously authored article in the *Westminster Review* that claimed that the New Woman was "intimately connected" with "the stirrings and rumblings now perceivable in the social and industrial world, the 'Bitter Cries' of the disinherited classes, the 'Social Wreckage' which is becoming able to make itself unpleasantly prominent, the Problems of Great Cities,' the spread of Socialism and Nihilism" (1990, 1). Certainly this link between rebellion in the working class and the increasingly militant calls for women's liberation was not without precedent. In mid-nineteenth-century America Harriet Beecher Stowe's *Uncle Tom's Cabin* drew an analogy between black slavery and the economically servile position of bourgeois white women; similarly, in England Charlotte Brontë's *Shirley,* specifically structured as a double narrative of political struggle and individual domestic conflict, depicted both working-class men and middle-class women as oppressed by a powerful male gentry indifferent to their claims, each barely containing a resentment that had no legitimate outlet. Increasingly, British discourse of the late nineteenth century identified women and labor—the title of Olive Schreiner's pioneering study—as the two great problems of modern social life. Both were represented as cauldrons of unrest, twin sources of a Pandora's box just waiting to be opened.

Thomas Laqueur has remarked of the French Revolution that "wherever boundaries were threatened arguments for fundamental sexual differences were shoved into the breach" (1986, 14); both England and America in the mid-nineteenth century seemed to require that supplementation. As Mary Poovey points out, a binary model of sexual difference had begun to dominate European culture by the late eighteenth century, but it reached its zenith in the mid-nineteenth century. Significantly, it took the body as the natural site of social as well as sexual difference, and as Poovey notes, that meant reproduction: "Emphasizing the incommensurability of male and female bodies entailed foregrounding the role of the reproductive system, effacing other kinds of differences" (1988, 6). By midcentury woman's maternal function was ubiquitously taken as the foundation both of her social identity and of her sexual desire. Late-eighteenth-century medical treatises, for example, had unselfconsciously described women as having large sexual appetites, but by the second half of the nineteenth century, most doctors deemed frigidity more natural for women, whose sensual pleasure was assimilated to their maternal function, appearing as tenderness rather than lust.

Of course, such a conflation of woman's desire with maternity was not new; woman's role as mother had long been propounded as a religious ideal. With the increasing valorization of the sciences in the bourgeois century (Gay 1984), however, medical discourse, as if appropriating the social authority previously deemed divine, defined and prescribed what was "natural" as a biocultural imperative. Between 1875 and 1900 a considerable number of physicians claimed that female emancipation would inevitably cause gynecological disease (Sensibar 1991).[5] Women were constantly warned by doctors about the horrendous physical consequences of the unnatural use of their minds: education would shrivel up women's reproductive organs; thinking robbed the ovaries of energy. Not surprisingly, hysteria, a pathology whose very name implicated women's reproductive system, was adduced as the inevitable consequence of this perverse intellectual and political transvestism.[6] As one American medical expert wrote,

> The nervous force, so necessary at puberty for the establishment of the menstrual function, is wasted on what may be compared as trifles to perfect health. . . . Bright eyes have been dulled by the brain-fag and sweet temper transformed into irritability, crossness and hysteria, while the womanhood of the land is deteriorating physically. (William Edgar Darnell, quoted in Smith-Rosenberg 1985, 259)

In the context of this pervasive medical legislation of woman's reproductive identity, the figure of the mother became not only an idealized trope of female nature and destiny but a site of psychic conflict as well.

It would be reductive to conclude that such arguments were universally accepted, however; certainly one can find dissenting opinions that encouraged the emancipatory project of young women, and even some conservative doctors relented in their pronouncements as more women entered institutions of higher education without ill effects.[7] Women doctors especially, although few in number, were among the most vocal in countering the assertions of male physicians; they blamed not education for women's illness but the class hypocrisy of a medical establishment that could argue simultaneously both for the working woman's greater powers of endurance and for the natural frailty of women. Nevertheless, blatant contradictions in the representations of women continued to circulate in Victorian discourse. Thus, for example, as Smith-Rosenberg remarks, at the same time that "the True Woman was emotional, dependent, and gentle—a born follower . . . the Ideal Mother, then and now, was expected to be strong, self-reliant, protective, an efficient caretaker in relation to children and home" (1985, 199).

Both meanings were fused into what has been called "the Cult of True Womanhood" (Welter 1966). Widely promulgated in mid-nineteenth-century fiction and poetry, this cult, with its doctrinaire insistence on separate spheres of action for men and women, had spawned perhaps the most tendentiously feminine-maternal figure, the "Angel in the House" who circulated in Coventry Patmore's popular tract-poem of that name (1854). Thirty years later Charles Darwin's *The Descent of Man* gave this essentialist separatist doctrine a scientific history by arguing that women had evolved differently from men, that their nurturant capacities naturally fitted them for home and hearth, while men had evolved aggressive abilities that suited them for competition in the public arena. Like Patmore's versified representation, Darwinian law represented woman as both nurturant and self-sacrificing, and thus the natural conservator of Victorian morality and civilization.

What seems obvious in retrospect is that the Victorian scripture on gender difference was being urgently disseminated at the very time that socioeconomic conditions, historical forces, and cultural representations were increasingly undermining it. Nina Auerbach's reading of the contradictory meanings of the Victorian woman, who was old maid, fallen woman, and angel in the house rolled into one, captures the complicated effects of the era's attempt to control the representation of women's nature. As Auerbach points out, "woman's very aura of exclusion gave her imaginative centrality in a culture increasingly alienated from itself. Powerful images of oppression became images of barely suppressed power, all the more grandly haunting because, unlike the hungry workers, woman ruled both the palace and the home while hovering simultaneously in the darkness without" (1982, 188). By the 1880s the Angel in the House was challenged by the appearance of "Novissima" (Ardis 1990, 1), the New Woman who rejected marriage and motherhood and provocatively contested the boundaries of those separate spheres.[8]

Yet clearly the very term *New Woman,* appearing ubiquitously in the popular press, had stirred up the demons of uncertainty not only about women's proper place, but about men's proper place as well. Elaine Showalter remarks that the New Woman "threatened to turn the world upside down and to be on top in a wild carnival of social and sexual misrule" (1990, 38).[9] Showalter's metaphor of sexual reversal, a common image for the cultural consequences of women's liberation in the popular iconography of the time, indicates the implicit challenge to heterosexual positioning that the New Woman conveyed, but nowhere more so than by mounting the platform and speaking, by putting herself actually on top. For it was particularly the feminist orators, who claimed an equal place in a *fraternal* order of culture, who took their political demands to the public platform, that most raised the hackles of the public about women's proper sexual place, if we can judge from the vehemence of popular critical reaction. From midcentury onward, antifeminist literature, cartoons, sermons, and caricatures increased in circulation. Typically, they took the form of questioning the gender identity of women who spoke in public; that is to say, they made the woman's public voice the primary signifier of her problematic sexual being. American feminist conventions like those at Seneca Falls (1848) and Rochester (1852) had provoked fierce denunciations in the popular press, which represented the feminist orator as an unsexed woman. The *New York Herald* denounced feminist orators as "mannish women, like hens that crow" (September 12, 1852). Similarly, in England, *Punch* joined with the House of Commons to caricature women who took the podium as masculine harridans. "My hair is dark chestnut; my moustachios are rather lighter," *Punch* quipped, mimicking the voice of a female candidate for office (21 [1851], 157).[10] The mannish woman orator became an increasingly familiar figure in satiric novels; in *The Rebel of the Family,* the antifeminist writer Eliza Lynn Linton, who coined the phrase "shrieking sisterhood," referred to one "specimen of a female public orator" whose "case-hardened self sufficiency was as ugly as a physical deformity," and described another with suspiciously "close-cropped hair, a Tyrolese hat . . . a waistcoat and a short jacket" (quoted in Showalter 1990, 24).[11]

Paradoxically, feminist orators were portrayed not only as hermaphrodites but also as prostitutes, acting out a vulgar and suspect exhibitionism, which offended womanly proprieties. "There is something repugnant to the ordinary Englishman in the idea of a woman mounting the platform and facing the noisy, gaping, vulgar crowd of an election meeting," writes Mary Jeune in the 1890s ("English Women in Political Life," *North American Review* [1895]:453, quoted in Showalter 1990, 24). It is particularly ironic that not only does Jeune herself confound boundaries by speaking in the name of the English-*man*, but her "repugnance"—an affect associated with hysteria—itself suggests the hysterical ground of her response to the feminist orator. If these ubiquitous images of the woman orator pointed to the sexual anxieties of an aroused public, they also unveiled the cultural fantasy that provoked them: the freakish man-woman with a voice was the woman with a phallus, a vocal Medusa, to be suppressed for the sake of the social order, repressed for the sake of the psychological one.

It was no mere coincidence that at the same time that the woman orator became an increasingly audible and visible figure in the pulpit and on the podium, female hysteria, with its characteristic symptoms of aphonia and paralysis, swept across Europe and America in epidemic proportion.[12] Neil Hertz (1983) describes male hysteria in the eighteenth century as a response to the image of the anarchist woman of the French Revolution and its arousal of male castration anxiety. The nineteenth-century woman orator was also a kind of woman warrior, and it is not surprising that she provoked similar fears of being unmanned in her male audience. What is remarkable, however, is that this figure of the speaking woman also provoked women's anxiety—about the propriety of possessing the power of the voice, about having the phallus rather than being it, an anxiety whose effects are still evident in women's continued ambivalence about public speaking. To approach that ambivalence and its relation to hysteria, I want first to note that while feminist critics often conflate the feminist and the hysteric, seeing them as two sides of a singular political heroine—the revolutionary feminist-hysteric[13]—there is a significant distinction to be drawn between them as historical figures. The feminist and the hysteric presented mirror images of women's relation to the public voice: the feminist orator claimed an active subject position and the power of the voice; the hysteric passively acted out through her body what her voice could not speak.

If this mirror relation serves to describe an essential antithesis between the feminist and the hysteric, it also figures a psychic split *within* the hysteric, an internal division between active speaking subject and passive spoken object that inhibited if not totally suppressed her public voice.[14] Joan Rivière's well-known article "Womanliness as Masquerade" (1929; rpt. Burgin et al. 1986), although written in and about a later period, offers a useful point of entry into that division by its interrogation of a particular case of anxiety over the issue of public speaking. Rivière cites the case of a woman who seemed to have it all: a professional life that satisfied her ambitions, a family, a good sex life. As Rivière writes, "She had a high degree of adaptation to reality and managed to sustain good and appropriate relations with almost everyone with whom she came in contact" (36). There was a problem, however:

> She was an American woman engaged in work of a propagandist nature which consisted principally in speaking and writing. All her life a certain degree of anxiety, sometimes very severe, was experienced after every public performance, such as speaking to an audience. . . . She would be excited and apprehensive all night after, with misgivings whether she had done anything inappropriate, and obsessed by a need for reassurance. This need . . . led her compulsively on any such occasion to seek some attention or complimentary notice from a man or men at the close of the proceedings in which she had taken part or been the principal figure. (36)

Noting the "incongruity of this attitude with her highly impersonal and objective attitude during her intellectual performance" (36), Rivière locates its source in a doubled conflict familiar also to the etiology of hysteria: identification and rivalry with her mother (which implies desire for the father) and identification and rivalry with her father (which implies desire for the mother).

It is her rivalry with her father for the phallus, as Rivière describes it, which seems especially relevant for understanding why the feminist orator would provoke hysteria in women. For Rivière's patient public speaking "signified an exhibition of herself in possession of the father's penis, having castrated him" (39); her retreat to feminine behavior, her "womanliness as masquerade," was thus meant to ward off a feared punishment for appropriating the father's power.[15] The feminist orator could also be said to have stolen the father's phallus; but unlike the hysteric, she claimed her *right* to the phallus, her right to exceed the strictures of femininity, to compete with the father as an active, desiring subject. Circulating that claim in the expanding movement for women's suffrage, the feminist orator provoked a wishful identification among a good number of women auditors at the same time that she provoked an unconscious dread—an ambivalence that had mixed effects. While, as Judith Butler claims, the daughter's "rivalry with the father is not [necessarily] over the desire of the mother, but over the place of the father in public discourse as speaker" (1990, 51), it is virtually impossible to separate transgressive desire from rivalrous identification in this contestation with the father, which, at its worst, results in the kind of hysterical mutism that Henry James probes in *The Bostonians*. As with Rivière's early-twentieth-century patient, who was unable to either acknowledge the claim to the phallus and its oedipal ramifications or give it up, the hysterical woman of the nineteenth century kept silent her fantasmatic rivalry, and dissimulating by simulating femininity, spoke her divided desire in symptoms.

HYSTERIA HAS ALWAYS been associated with femininity, from the Greek depiction of hysterics as lazy women with wandering wombs, through the demonically possessed women of the Middle Ages, to the nineteenth-century hysterics that fascinated Freud (Bernheimer 1990a). Moreover, as Ilza Veith (1965) points out in her extensive survey of the disease, historically "the symptoms were modified by the prevailing concept of the feminine ideal."[16] The relation between hysteria and the feminine ideal in the nineteenth century is further elucidated by Alan Krohn's (1978) observation that passivity has been a consistently central component of hysteria. The hysteric, Krohn argues in his cross-cultural study, uses the dominant myth of passivity in her or his culture to represent internal conflict. Since passivity, and particularly passive desire, came to define a normative and ideal femininity in the nineteenth century, the Victorian feminine ideal itself became a privileged site of hysterical ambivalence. Freud's opinion that what is repudiated in both sexes is femininity (1937, *SE* 23:250), specifically defined as passive desire, foreshadows the conclusions of these historical and cross-cultural studies. All suggest that both female and male hysterics were—are—involved in conflictual feminine identifications that they both desire and abhor.[17]

Even before the nineteenth century, femininity and passivity had been joined in the medical discourse on hysteria. "This disease attacks women more than men," wrote a Dr. Sydenham in the seventeenth century, "because they have a more delicate, less firm constitution, because they lead a softer life, and because they are accustomed to the luxuries and commodities of life and not to suffering" (quoted in Bernheimer 1990a, 12). Sydenham is credited with promoting the modern liberation of hysteria from its biological basis as a female disorder (Rousseau 1993, 144).[18] For Sydenham, hysteria was a common "affliction of the mind" induced by a passive lifestyle and thus a function of an increasingly affluent civilization. His female hysterics, all wealthy women, were especially suspect, however; leading "a softer life," they embodied more fully the social ills of the time. Sydenham's liberating definition of hysteria still cast the woman, "less firm" in constitution, as more "naturally" prone to hysteria.

Although men increasingly entered the ranks of hysterics throughout the eighteenth century, their susceptibility to hysteria was defined by their being "tender, nervous, brittle . . . either mentally or morally of feminine constitution" (Rousseau 1993, 170). Representations of male hysterics as "timid and fearful" or "coquettish and eccentric" (Showalter 1993, 289) reinforced the relation between hysteria and women, particularly women of a stereotypically fragile feminine constitution. Thus, although Enlightenment medicine continued to move away from the literalization of hysteria as a wandering womb to its being a more general signifier of a nervous disorder that afflicted both men and women, hysteria remained effectively tied to cultural definitions of a denigrated femininity. By the nineteenth century, hysteria had proliferated as a diagnosis. Covering a wide spectrum of physical disorders of uncertain origin, it remained doubly tainted both by its link to femininity and by a suspicion that it belonged to the realm of the imaginary.[19]

In the early nineteenth century the French physician Philippe Pinel, known as the "Liberator" for literally removing the chains from institutionalized patients, had proposed that some unacknowledged sexual transgression was part of the etiology of hysterical symptoms. Because hysteria resulted from deviant sexual conduct, Pinel recommended as a cure marriage and the family, a return to the sexual fix that was itself often an instigating factor in the etiology of the illness. If Pinel thus chained the hysteric to a suspect morality, he did make two significant contributions to the modern history of hysteria: (1) he empirically severed hysteria from biology, and therefore from an essential female nature, by demonstrating clinically that disorders associated with hysteria could not be traced to any organic changes in the brain or nervous system; (2) he used conversation to explore the source of his patients' disturbance, a method of treatment that antedated the talking cure of psychoanalysis (Bernheimer 1990a, 5).

Perhaps more than any nineteenth-century figure before Freud, Jean Charcot contributed to a change in the perception of hysterics by extensively studying hysteria in men as well as women and delineating it as an actual pathology with precise laws.[20] Yet in spite of his categorization of hysteria as a non-gender-specific disorder, Charcot's most dramatic public representations of hysterics were of women. At his famous Leçons du Mardi, weekly lectures that took place in a hall beneath a picture of Pinel having the chains taken off the madmen in the Salpetrière, Charcot used hypnosis to produce, catalogue, and remove hysterical symptoms from women of different classes (Bernheimer 1990a, 6–7).

In composing the features of a mysterious behavior into a coherent, structured symptomatology, Charcot catalogued four phases in the hysterical attack that Freud records: (1) the epileptoid phase—convulsive attacks preceded by "aura sensations," especially the *globus hystericus* (spasms of the pharynx, "as though a lump were rising from the epigastrium to the throat"); (2) the *grands movements* phase—movements of wide compass, which Freud notes are elegantly performed; (3) the hallucinatory phase—the famous *attitudes passionelles,* "distinguished by attitudes and gestures which belong to scenes of passionate movement, which the patient hallucinates and often accompanies with the corresponding words"; during this attack consciousness is often lost; (4) the terminal delirium phase—the *grand attaque* (*SE* 1:42–43, 151). Although this description of the stages of intensification of a pathology has the structure of spectacle—indeed, Charcot made extensive use of photography in documenting and cataloguing hysterical symptoms[21]—its diachronic movement offers the rudiments of a sequenced story told through the hysterical body. That story moves from blocked orality to its liberation—from a lump coming up from within to an oral site of conflict at the throat, where it remains unexpressed; to the dissemination of that "lump" that blocks expression into a sexual scenario performed by body parts; and, finally, to orgiastic delirium. Charcot's ordering, which situates its initial conflict in the oral zone, would be elaborated by Freud, who gave the formal symptoms a particular content as the representation of an individual history, and joining temporality to meaning, foregrounded the importance of hysterical narration in finding a path to the cure.

In this regard, what proved most germane for the emergence of Freud's psychoanalysis was Charcot's demonstration through hypnosis that the hysteric's very consciousness was beyond her control, that she could speak and act from another place without being present as a subject of consciousness, that an erotic scenario unknown and unacknowledged was being articulated through her body and could be read. Writing of Charcot's patient and the *attitude passionelle,* Freud had remarked: "In many cases it is quite obvious that this phase comprises a memory from the patient's life. . . . Even when *attitudes passionelles* are lacking, hypnosis provides proof of psychical process such as is revealed in the phase *passionelle,* ie. a sexual scenario" (*SE* 1:151–52). Charcot's patients provided Freud with evidence of a disjunction among memory, sexuality, and consciousness, a disjunction in the very temporal reality of the subject that became the founding premise of his new science of the unconscious. Moreover, by reading the symptom as a linguistic representation of an unconscious conflict not available to the conscious subject, Freud challenged also the Enlightenment assumption of a unitary subject of language.

The move from Charcot to Freud, as Stephen Heath first remarked, is a move from the metaphorics of vision to voice, a move that subverted the distance between subject and object (1981, 202–4). If Charcot's careful visual charting had distanced and isolated the hysteric in the manner of objective science, Freud's method of listening to the speaking voice promoted proximity and the inevitable ambiguities associated with language. It also promoted a more permeable boundary between speaker and listener through the circulation of a disembodied voice. Indeed, the shift from vision to voice can also be seen as a shift in the aesthetics of narrative form, from a realism that makes extended use of objective description—those material details that so irritated Virginia Woolf in her critique of Arnold Bennett and John Galsworthy ("Modern Fiction" [1953])—to a modernism that insists on blurring the boundaries between the subject and object of representation through the permutations of an emphatically subjective narrative voice.[22] The case history, Freud's own new narrative genre, exemplifies the problematic consequences of this shift.[23]

Chapter Two

Freud's Passion /
Dora's Voice

Hearing is a physiological phenomenon;
listening is a psychological act.
—Roland Barthes

To LINK HYSTERICAL representation to the term *passions* may seem paradoxically perverse, since hysteria is more often associated with a refusal of passion. Yet *passions* is an apt signifier for the hysterical object of psychoanalytic as well as feminist interpretation. Derived etymologically from *passus,* meaning "suffered," the word *passion* is the antonym of action and denotes a passive relation to desire and agency, the very subject position of the Victorian woman and the position that Freud concluded provoked hysteria. It is this sense of passion as a subjection *to* an insupportable desire, and moreover, a subjection accompanied by a rage too infrequently acknowledged, which is represented in Freud's narration of the Dora case. Whose passion is it? And how is it transmitted?

André Green has called passion "a derangement of the senses," suggesting a prior arrangement or organization of the sensorium, an ordered regimen of the body, presumably "de-ranged" by what Green calls an "erotic madness" (1986a, 223). The primary "derangement" that Freud identified in himself and in Dora was a "pétit hysteria," a derangement of heterosexual imperatives that was symptomatically played out in a derangement of the body.[1] Because repression, the dissociation of word-presentations from thing-presentations, foreclosed verbal articulation,[2] the hysteric acted out both the active/masculine and passive/feminine parts of a repressed sexual scenario, dramatizing its tensions across the body rather than in words.[3] Giving as example the patient who tried to pull off her dress at the same time that she tried to resist that act, a performance of bisexual identification that unconsciously mimicked both roles in a scene of sexual seduction, Freud ultimately concluded that "the hysterical symptom is the expression of both a masculine and a feminine unconscious phantasy" (1908, *SE* 9:166).

Since hysteria was a malady of representation, the cure was worked through representation. If the hysteric converted verbal symbol into corporeal symptom, the talking cure would return her to the spoken word. The hysteric's speech, however, also proved to be symptomatic —fragmentary, digressive, contradictory, punctuated by reproaches and self-reproaches, full of gaps that signified continued repression. What is more, in attempting to construct a reasoned explanatory narrative of hysterical etiology, Freud's new genre, the case history, seemed itself inevitably to mime the deranged discourse of the hysteric. As Freud prophetically remarked, "No one who, like me, conjures up the most evil of those half-tamed demons that inhabit the human breast, and seeks to wrestle with them, can expect to come through the struggle unscathed" ("Fragment of an Analysis of a Case of Hysteria" 1905 [1901], *SE* 7:109).

Certainly neither Freud nor Breuer—his colleague in the early pursuit of the passions called *Studies on Hysteria* (1893–95, *SE* 2)— came through unscathed. Breuer ran from Anna O. when he could no longer ignore her passion for him, when her body dramatically enacted a hysterical pregnancy as a fulfillment of her desire. Anna O. embodied her conflict in the materiality of language as well. Cutting up her mother tongue into disjunctive fragments, forgetting the grammar and syntax of German and replacing it with a grotesque synthesis of foreign languages, Anna O. symptomatically announced her self-alienation through speech (Hunter 1985). Indeed, in a voice fissured by "absences," Anna O. explicitly acted out a dissociation of the subject from its action by substituting infinitives for the normal logical syntax of subject and verb. If, as Julia Kristeva suggests (1986c), the enunciation of noun plus verb places the subject in linear time, Anna O.'s enunciation through the infinitive refused both the particularity of agency and the temporality of history, asserting instead the hovering stasis of potentiality in a linguistic version of hysterical paralysis.

Breuer ran from this derangement of the body and language. Freud remained with his hysterics, indeed, identified himself as one of their company, and found a way to restrain, retrain, their passion and his by containing and homeopathically deploying it in language. Compelling his hysterics for the sake of the cure, but even more for his stake in his new science, to enter a conversation about the erotic body and its secrets, Freud discovered that a conversation about sexual matters itself evoked desire, that especially the embodied dialogue between a masterful doctor and a vulnerable patient generated erotic and aggressive effects through and in the circulation of the speaking voice. Indeed, Freud's case histories are exemplary texts for illustrating that enunciation is itself a form of passion, and the talking cure a libidinally compelling oral/aural exchange between voice and ear, speaker and listener.

In the psychoanalytic dialogue, the intersubjective relation between analyst and analysand is constituted by the voice, which, circulating between two interiorities, functions as a kind of transitional object, binding speaker and listener in an imaginary dual-unity. This binding function is reinforced by the archaic place of the voice in the construction of subjectivity. As Kaja Silverman notes, the primal speaker is typically the mother; the primal listener, the child (1988, 80). The mother's voice is usually the first object to be isolated by the infant from its environs, the first object to be internalized. Recognized by the baby before the mother herself is perceived as an object, the maternal voice precedes the mirror stage in the constitution of the infant as a separate subject. Thus, Silverman points out, the female voice functions as a fetish, conveying a sense of presence that has been lost (38). As Michel Chion writes,

> For the child after birth, the Mother is more an olfactory and vocal continuum than an image. One can imagine the voice of the Mother, which is woven around the child, and which originates from all points in space as her form enters and leaves the visual field, as a matrix of places to which we are tempted to give the name "umbilical net." (1982, 57)

The maternal voice has been called a "blanket of sound," "a sonorous envelope" that surrounds and sustains (Guy Rosolato 1974, 81), "a bath of sounds" (D. Anzieu 1976, 173). These tropes of the voice are analogous to Winnicott's (1967b, 111) "holding environment" and to Julia Kristeva's (1980, 6–7) "chora," a field of sound and gesture comprising the earliest mother-child relation. Whatever the variations in metaphor, these theorists postulate a primal, amorphous infantile experience of the maternal voice as a vehicle for the experience of plenitude.

Yet the voice also ruptures plenitude; coming from elsewhere, the voice is also an intrusion, invading the open ear of a vulnerable listener, breaking an imaginary fullness that compels recognition of separation, that initiates the infant into human subjectivity through loss and language.[4] Indeed, the heterogeneous field of the voice very quickly takes on the discriminations and differentiations that mark its relation to language. Because language preexists the infant, the speaking voice functions as the site of a division that is in language, which bears both the heterogeneous traces of maternal presence through its particular materiality (tone, timbre, rhythm)—what Roland Barthes (1977, 66–67) calls the "grain of the voice" and Kristeva (1984) the "semiotic"—and the symbolic system of meanings predicated on absence into which the infant-subject is born.[5] Edith Lecourt provocatively describes the maternal voice as a "musico-verbal envelope" comprising two indissociable faces: "The verbal face, more linear (in time), univocal and a visible thread in the texture, is turned toward the outside. The musical face, in thickness, woven of voices (in space as in time) and plurivocal, is turned more toward the inside. . . . One sounds, sings, vibrates . . . the other is articulatory and more abstract. One is 'us,' the other is 'I' " (1990, 225). These two modalities of the voice, which conform to Kristeva's useful formulation of the "symbolic" and "semiotic" (1984), are culturally identified with paternal and maternal functions and are exploited in the psychoanalytic dialogue. Privileging the analyst, this dialogue typically situates her or him as a combined parent-figure, an imaginary ideal ego/other, father-mother, who has it, knows it all.[6]

Clearly, in "Fragment of a Case of Hysteria" Dora as hysterical analysand was the ostensible speaking subject, but she told a piecemeal story to a privileged ear, a custodian of meanings whose very silence could operate as a site of knowledge and authority. Moreover, her voice issued from a body that was under scrutiny, controlled by the gaze and read as a text for its symptomatic acts, its unwitting self-revelations. She, on the other hand, spoke to an unseen interlocutor, whose disembodied vocal interventions could be easily experienced as an internal demand.[7] Thus empowered, the analyst's voice could serve as the bridge to a passionately desired identification with an ideal other or could be experienced as an intrusive and undesirable violation of boundaries.[8]

Psychoanalysis did not begin as only a talking cure, however. In its earliest stages it used not only the voice but also the hand as a libidinal bridge between analyst and analysand. Freud began his sessions with the pressure of his hand on the head of the hysteric, who was thus induced to speak. The image—a familiar one to the nineteenth century —is that of the healer, the mesmerist, a less than respectable image that Henry James had called upon in *The Bostonians,* in which the father's laying on of hands loosens the daughter's eloquent tongue. By the time of the Dora case, however, Freud had exchanged the laying on of hands for the talking cure. Especially since hysterics told stories of paternal seductions, Freud kept his hands off and relied on the technique of free association.

Yet the liberated tongue of the hysteric and the listening ear of the analyst did not constitute a neutral intercourse. Although Freud defensively insisted on keeping his aural/oral technique dry,[9] he realized that often the fantasies were themselves a production of the talking cure, of the embodied relation between doctor and patient: as he wrote, "I was at last obliged to recognize that these scenes of seduction had never taken place, and that they were only phantasies which my patients had made up or *which I myself had perhaps forced on them*" ("On the History of the Psychoanalytic Movement" [1914], SE 14:34, italics mine). In other words, Freud's own vocal interventions could constitute the fantasy of seduction, or even of rape, and thus further contribute to the symptoms of the hysteric. His voice could seduce or overwhelm hers, if she listened; but hers could also have its seductive and aggressive effects.

Freud and Dora both spoke, both listened; while the analyst's voice was especially empowered to influence the internal script of the analysand, he remained also subject to the analysand's voice. Indeed, he was paid to shut up and listen with what Theodor Reik called "the third ear."[10] What does it mean to listen with the third ear? Where is this third ear situated? What can it hear? Like the ear of the poet or musician, who "has a good ear," the third ear of the analyst signifies a sensitivity to the semantic and phonemic play of the spoken word. Freud had a good ear for pursuing the disguises and dispersions of the subject in language. Reading his case histories, one can hear him on the track of those switchwords that would lead him toward the hysteric's secret center; one can also hear not only the mastery he initially claimed for analysis, but his submission to his own unruly passions as he pursues those of his analysands. For to listen to their stories with the fantasmatic third ear, Freud had to be literally receptive, to be open, to allow an empathic identification with the speaking subject, to assume the passions of the speaker's narrative voice as his own. Thus, Freud could not avoid participating in what the hysteric was telling him. In the analytic dialogue, the permeable boundaries of the ear became the zone of exchange for the introjection of mobile fantasies carried by the voice of the speaker and the tale it told.

If the very act of listening to the hysteric's voice and probing its secrets destabilized Freud's subject position, Freud complicated the effects of listening by theorizing that listening had an inevitable history. Doubling the temporality of the listening act, Freud linked listening in the present to a prior fantasy of listening, a primal scene in which a hapless passive subject "discovers" sexuality by overhearing sounds in the night. Early in his speculations, Freud took note of an aural source of hysterical fantasy, of voices heard in preoedipal infancy, articulations whose meaning was deferred. "The point that escaped me in the solution of hysteria lies in the discovery of a new source from which a new element of unconscious production arises. What I have in mind are hysterical phantasies, which regularly, as it seems to me, *go back to things heard* by children at an early age and only understood later. The age at which they take in information of this kind is very remarkable—from the age of six to seven months onwards" ("Letter 59," *SE* 1:244–45).

These "things," heard before the child understands language, leave a memory trace that is activated at a later moment, when voiced sound "means," by a repetition that strikes a chord over the interval. Thus, mnemic traces of primal sounds are later narrativized into a drama of parental intercourse by a listener, who inhabits the various parts of that drama through projective identifications. This resonance, however, can be experienced as a profound dissonance. Although Freud's subsequent focus on the sight/site of castration directed subsequent attention to the importance of vision—as Stephen Heath reminds us, in psychoanalytic discourse there is no auditory counterpart to the term *voyeur* (1981, 176)[11]—the trace of the voice and the importance of auditory phenomena continued to play a key part in Freud's elaboration of hysteria.[12]

Recent interpretations of the imaginary construction of the primal scene agree that it is less what is seen and more the mysterious sounds in the night that encourage the putative listener to imagine a sexual scenario.[13] In this context, listening acquires the value of mapping one's way into a subject position through an enigma. What is going on? Who is doing what to whom? These are the questions of the primal scene listener; these are also the questions that Freud pursues in the case histories, as he traces the analysand's secrets through the disguises and displacements of language. Not surprisingly, in listening for the hysteric's secret story, Freud as analyst/auditor often finds himself in the middle of his own primal scene. Listening to the voice is thus for the analyst as well as analysand an experience of anxious potentiality and self-dispersion.[14] In short, the passions of the voice in analysis emerge from an imaginary scenario in which the intersubjective dimension is multiplied; the speaking voice of the analysand narrating a story of identification, desire, and transgression acts as a medium for analogous ambiguous identifications and desires of the analyst.

This transference and countertransference is especially provoked by the demands of narrativization in Freud's case histories. For, like the analytic dialogue, narrative depends for its power on transgressive identifications that are not encouraged in Freud's more theoretical papers. Thus, in his case history of Dora, Freud continually defends himself against an inner voice that accuses him of various breaches of propriety, of being a writer of fiction rather than a scientist, of titillating his readers rather than illuminating his subject. Witness his reiterated construction of an imaginary hostile reader imputing his motives in speaking about sexuality to a young woman; his defense, as Neil Hertz points out, is to insist on the technical nature of his scientific discourse as opposed to the prurient thrills of literary narrative (1990, 221–42). If readers were aroused, they were the wrong readers, looking for pleasure rather than knowledge. In hysteria, however, pleasure and knowledge could not be kept separate: the desire to know was itself pervaded with an erotics of mastery and submission, as the Dora case revealed.[15]

If, as I have been suggesting, the analytic dialogue depends for its effectiveness on transgressive identifications, what did it mean for Freud to assume the passions of the voice when it belonged to an eighteen-year-old hysterical girl, the only female subject of a major case history? The past decade has seen a multiplicity of readings of the Dora case, which answer that question in richly complex formulations, many collected in *In Dora's Case* (1990). Critics have remarked upon the defensive digressions and linguistic displacements of the narration, have analyzed Freud's identification with Dora, the hysterical daughter, while at the same time attempting to preserve his discrete boundary as analyst-father. Moreover, Freud's suppression of any interrogation of the maternal relation has also been pointed out as an index of his own repression.[16] Yet the case continues to fascinate for what it does and does not do. Like an analysis interminable, readings of the Dora case continue to proliferate, opening the *mis-en-abyme* of vexed relations that comprise the oedipus complex and the sexuation of subjectivity. At the same time, the case is an exemplary illustration of the structural facets of hysteria as it configures narrative voice through reversal, denial, digression, fragmentation, imagined reproaches, and compulsively repeated self-justifications. All indicate the persistence of Freud's own passions in his attempts to give a reasoned narrative account of Dora's.

By now we know the story Freud wants to tell: a nineteenth-century oedipal narrative of heterosexual romance, of the exchange of a daughter from one family to another, ending in an appropriate marriage that will resolve all the contradictory tensions let loose in the course of that exchange. The principal facts of the case are as follows. Dora's father, engaged in an affair with Frau K., had handed Dora over to Herr K. in return for his complicity. Dora had raised no objections to this arrangement, even suppressing information about a sexual advance by Herr K., a kiss that he had forcibly impressed upon her when she was fourteen. Although Dora refuses to continue her role in this sordid melodrama, she develops symptoms—loss of voice, fainting fits, a mysterious limp, a nervous cough—that, in the logic of the psychoanalytic symptom, mark her own conflict and complicity.

Dora must have a secret desire as well as an overt demand, a desire Freud names: Dora unconsciously desires the virile—and, in Freud's eyes, entirely "prepossessing"—Herr K. Voicing his own attraction to the object he desires *for* her, through a series of compelling interpretations, he presses Dora to recognize his desire as hers. Indeed, in a neurotic confusion of fantasy and reality, he asks her to consider *marrying* Herr K. as the perfect resolution of this domestic romance.

Freud's failure with Dora compelled him to modify both his understanding of hysteria and to rewrite in a series of footnotes the conventional heterosexual plot on which it had been based. Dora revealed that the secret of the hysteric was not only an unacknowledged desire for the father—the core fantasy for the conventional female oedipal complex and the determining factor in the assumption of femininity —but also an unacknowledged *identification* with him. Dora felt not only rivalry with the woman who was her father's love object and Herr K.'s wife, but sexual desire. As Freud concluded in a digression, her love for Frau K. was "the deepest unconscious current in her psychic life" (*SE* 7:120, n.2). By leading Freud to infer the essential bisexuality of hysteria, Dora problematized the conventional oedipal narrative with its fixed heterosexual scenario and revealed instead an essential instability of gender, a fluidity of aim and object in the erotic life of men and women.

What is particularly noticeable in this narrative structure is its emphasis on orality, a privileged zone of hysterical displacement.[17] Freud constitutes Dora's history as a series of seductive oral exchanges, ranging from eroticized conversations that have actually occurred— Herr K. and Dora, Frau K. and Dora, the governess and Dora—to the primal fantasy of the case, his analytic construction of an imaginary act of fellatio, an embodied oral exchange that reverberates with the dynamics of the talking cure in which he and Dora were engaged. Freud isolates a conversation with Herr K. at a resort as the crucial scene that provoked Dora's most recent hysterical attack. Herr K. has propositioned her in words that repeat a phrase that Dora had heard before—"I get nothing out of my wife"—the very phrase she knew Herr K. used to seduce a governess before her (*SE* 7:26, 98). It is this repetition that provokes her to slap his face and flee. Significantly, Freud writes virtually this same phrase as a direct quotation of Dora's father: "I get nothing out of my own wife." (The differential modifier *own* constitutes an admission of an already enacted adultery lacking in Herr K.'s use of the phrase to seduce.) Indeed, in "The Clinical Picture," the only voice assigned direct discourse aside from Freud's own is the voice of Dora's father, who speaks these words of self-justification. In this passage Freud both foregrounds the sentence that will recur at several junctures in his interpretation and makes it the trigger of Dora's conflict. In a later footnote (*SE* 7:106), he ascribes Dora's recognition of an adulterous analogy between Herr K. and her father to her having heard both men speak this sentence. In thus attributing virtually the same sentence to Dora's father and Herr K., Freud makes both men linguistic subjects of a complaint that is also a justification of paternal seduction and at the same time inserts himself into this chain of suspect fathers.

Certainly, Freud also wants something out of Dora that he doesn't get from his wife: he wants her to open herself to his collection of picklocks, to satisfy his theoretical desire to know in an erotics of interpretation that he must continually justify. Indeed, the phrase "I get nothing out of my wife" is a nodal point in Freud's narration, an overdetermined phrase of oral desire, deprivation, and impotence that resonates with ambiguity about who can "get" and who has something to give, who is allowed to get and who to give. Reappearing in Freud's text at significant junctures, this paternal complaint also resonates with the fellatio fantasy that Freud constructs for Dora, an imagined scene of sexual relations between "a man without means" (*SE* 7:47) who can get nothing out of his wife (Dora's impotent father) and the idealized sexual mother of Dora's family romance who gives him the means (Frau K.). In constructing a scene of paternal sexuality as fellatio, Freud reifies a metaphor that informs his own transgressive oral demand that Dora accept his "interpretations." Freud's fellatio fantasy can thus be read as an overdetermined linguistic reversal of the repeated phrase, moving from paternal lack to fulfillment. The question of who has the means, however, still remains open.

Lacan was the first to point out that when confronted with Dora's claim that she knew sexual satisfaction could be achieved by means other than genital intercourse, Freud assumed she was referring to fellatio rather than cunnilingus ("Intervention on the Transference," 1952; rpt. *In Dora's Case*, 1990). That Freud imagines fellatio as the answer to the question, "Who does what to whom when the male is impotent?" suggests that female desire and *jouissance* are an absence to him—the sign of a repression. Moreover, repression in hysteria is also marked by disgust. While Freud's interrogation of Dora uncovers her symptomatic disgust with sexuality, his own imaginative leap away from female genital sexuality to fellatio points to an operative structure of hysterical disgust in his voice as well. As Monique David-Ménard points out, sexual disgust is "a passionate denial," symptomatically marking a desire that cannot be swallowed but constantly returns as a demand (1989, 103).[18] One can find numerous examples of this demand in Freud's chains of association, as when, in explaining Dora's disgust after the traumatic embrace of Herr K. in the kiss scene, Freud's text takes a bizarre turn in its logical sequence:

> Such feelings seem originally to be a reaction to the smell (and afterwards also to the sight) of excrement. But the genitals can act as a reminder of the excremental functions; and this applies especially to the male member, for that organ performs the function of micturition as well as the sexual function. Indeed the function of micturition is the earlier known of the two, and the only one known during the pre-sexual period. Thus it happens that disgust becomes one of the means of affective expression in the sphere of sexual life. The Early Christian Fathers' "inter urinas et faeces nascimur" clings to sexual life and cannot be detached from it in spite of every effort. (*SE* 7:31)

Note that while he attributes Dora's disgust to the smell of the male member because of its double function, both excretory and sexual, in his evidentiary quotation he slips without remark from male to female sexual organs: "inter urinas et faeces nascimur." To prove Dora's disgust with Herr K.'s male member, he offers the example of a "typical" disgust with women's genitals, the site of the smell of sex.

Repeatedly in his writings Freud singles out the importance of smell, his own imp of the perverse, and a concomitant disgust in the development of human sexuality. In *Civilization and Its Discontents* he even leaves his central text and in long digressive footnotes narrates a primal myth that begins with the male response to the menstrual smell of women, lingers on a generalized confusion of sexual and excretory functions, and concludes with sublimation.[19] As Ned Lukasher argues, "disgust is not simply disgusting, it is also intensely pleasurable" (1989, xxiii). For Freud sexual arousal has its origin in the olfactory field and thus remains inextricably intermixed with a sexual repugnance that paradoxically threatens eros itself.[20] In this later essay, Freud speculates that this sexual repugnance is universal, and explains it by quoting the same adage ("inter urinas et faeces nascimur") on which he leaned to explain Dora's disgust. As with "I get nothing from my wife," the recurrence of the same phrase at such widely spaced temporal junctures in Freud's own writings indicates its significance as a nodal point of his unconscious distress. In short, Freud's texts suggest that it is the intolerable confusion of sexual and excretory organs in the maternal body, a confusion out of which the human subject is born, which causes hysterical conflations in his own discourse.

At the same time, Freud's elaboration of Dora's disgust foregrounds another important component of hysteria: the desire to keep the site of sexual difference ambiguous. For example, as Freud explains, Dora's disgust is linguistically elaborated around the word *catarrh,* an ambiguous term Dora uses to signify both respiratory and genital discharges. Reflecting an ambiguity about which bodily site is disgusting, the word sustains her ambiguous identification with both mother and father since both suffer disgusting discharges associated with her father's venereal disease as well as the more innocent head colds and respiratory infections. By its very ambiguity of signification, the word *catarrh* allows her to displace her own disgust with genital sexuality to the oral zone: thus, Dora suffers from coughs, respiratory infections, and aphonia. As David-Ménard describes this symptomatology, "Dora's mouth and throat are thus the theatre where she tries to articulate the way things are between the sexes" (1989, 90–91).

Freud's own argument also keeps the site of disgust and thus the site of sexual difference ambiguous. The negation of sexual difference is typically read as a defense against castration anxiety, but Freud's text suggests more is at stake than a defense. It suggests an active *desire* for a nondifferentiating eroticism that marks a relation to a homosexual economy. In an often quoted later passage, for example, Freud defends himself from the accusation of a perverse oral exchange with an innocent girl by a long digression that moves from heterosexually charged French puns—"je m'appelle un chat un chat" (48) or "pour faire une omelette il faut casser des oeufs" (49)—through an erotically inflected diction to conclude with a contiguous association to homosexuality, which he calls that "perversion most repellent to us" (50). That "perversion most repellent" immediately becomes the subject of another digression in which he defends the value of homosexual contributions to culture. The text thus performs a hysterical transmutation of a forbidden heterosexual object, the innocent girl, into a forbidden homosexual object of desire, which is in turn converted into an object of disgust ("the perversion most repellent to us"), which is finally recuperated both by its psychic universality ("we are all originally perverts") and its potential cultural value.

In this context of sexual ambiguity, it is not surprising that Freud forecloses female genital sexuality by constructing Dora's sexual fantasy as fellatio, a fantasy in which there is no female genital sexuality, in which as he literally remarks, the "sexual organ proper" is the penis (*SE* 7:52). Paradoxically, however, he also virtually eliminates this male "sexual organ proper" from the imagined sexual scene by interpreting fellatio as a repetition of the erotics of sucking at the breast. By thus transforming Dora's impotent father into a nursing phallic mother, Freud reconstitutes a primal scene in which the phallic male is the phallic mother, and thus, at the very least, sexually ambiguous.[21] Indeed, at the climax of Freud's discussion of fellatio is an image of the sexual indeterminacy of the phallus itself that is not only characteristic of hysterical representation and its anxious question, "Who has 'it' to give?" but also the question "What is 'it'?" "It [fellatio] is a new version of what may be described as a prehistoric impression of sucking at the mother's or nurse's breast—an impression which has usually been revised by contact with children who are being nursed. In most instances the udder of a cow has aptly played the part of an image intermediate between a nipple and a penis" (*SE* 7:52). This sexual indeterminacy at the very site of the primal scene of sexual difference is covered over by an insistent plotting of heterosexual cause and effect which, as Madelon Sprengnether (1985) convincingly argues, defends against Freud's own orality, passive desire, and femininity—a hysterogenic triad animated by the intersection of Freud's and Dora's voices.

If the analytic dialogue generates a symptomatic discourse of digressions and contradictions in "The Clinical Picture," another kind of symptomatic revelation is performed through the difference in narrative voice between "The First Dream" and "The Second

Dream," both of which constitute the double structural center of Freud's story. In "The First Dream," Freud uses direct discourse, thus textually embodying the dialogic relation between himself and Dora in order to invoke the dialogic construction of meaning that is psychoanalysis. As in the novelistic use of direct quotation, which implies a reality external to the narrator's voice, here Freud allows Dora's voice to enter his text even though he directs its unfolding. In "The Second Dream," however, after the presentation of Dora's dream, direct discourse is eclipsed; there is no dialogue, no mimesis of his technique nor of Dora's voice, which is withheld from representation. Instead, Freud narrates in the first person both his interventions and Dora's associations, using indirect discourse to maintain monological mastery. Here Freud's narration functions to obscure technique, to bind Dora and her dream to his own purpose. Why this difference in narrative voice?

In elaborating the first dream, Freud allows Dora as the other to speak because what he hears represented is Dora's desire for the father, for Herr K., for him. Recall, for example, his interpretation of Dora's longing for a kiss from a smoker, Herr K., and its olfactory stimulus:

> The thing which I had to go upon was the fact that the smell of smoke had only come up as an addendum to the dream, and must therefore have had to overcome a particularly strong effort on the part of repression. . . . That is, concerned with the temptation to show herself willing to yield to the man . . . the addendum to the dream could scarcely mean anything else than the longing for a kiss, which, with a smoker, would necessarily smell of smoke. (*SE* 7:73–74)

Connecting this smell of smoke to Dora's desire for Herr K.'s kiss, Freud puts himself in Herr K.'s place: "Taking into consideration . . . the indication which seemed to point to there having been a transference on to me—since I am a smoker too—I came to the conclusion that the idea had probably occurred to her one day during a sitting that she would like to have a kiss from me" (*SE* 7:74). Dora's first dream, in which her father saves her from danger, confirms Freud as the good and powerful father-analyst as well as the erotic object of her desire, the figure upholding oedipal law and sexual difference.

The second dream is more problematic, however; it presents a maternal letter that announces the death of the father. It is, as Freud points out, a dream of rage rather than love, of Dora's desire for revenge rather than submission. More significantly, Dora's associations to this dream lead to women: to the governess, to an aunt, to the adored Madonna, to Frau K. with her "adorable white body" (*SE* 7:61)—all maternal figures of desire, identification, and disappointment. Rather than trace these displacements by means of which Dora attempts to recuperate a denigrated maternal object, Freud instead asks Dora and the reader to follow a different track: his associations to the material of analysis, which he presents, as he writes, "in the somewhat haphazard order in which it recurs to my mind" (*SE* 7:95), since suddenly he can no longer reconstruct the sequence of Dora's associations. Thus, it is his associations that lead to a medical discourse that, as he himself points out, "is known to physicians though not to laymen" (*SE* 7:99). With such phrases as "There could be no doubt," "it was easy to guess" (*SE* 7:96), "a certain suspicion of mine became a certainty" (*SE* 7:99), Freud's rhetoric effectively forecloses any difference between his story and hers. Authorizing the attribution of his knowledge to her, he insists on Dora's active desire to enter a woman's body, and marks her subject position as masculine in a fantasy of "defloration" (*SE* 7:100).

Freud does not stay with this narrative of a homoerotic desire that takes the form of a fantasized heterosexual intercourse; he switches the tracks of his reconstruction back to Dora's heterosexual feminine desire for Herr K. and for the child that would be its consequence. In a retrospective footnote, Freud even literally inserts a question into her dream as logically necessary to its meaning: "Which way to Herr K.'s house?" (*SE* 7:104, n. 2). The question. like his narrative, shifts the resolution of the quest from mother to father, from the body of a woman to the house of a man, and reasserts the heterosexual paternal figure as object of desire. In its symptomatic confusion about the sequence of Dora's revelations, in its shifting from maternal to paternal quests, in its suppression of direct dialogue, Freud's narration of "The Second Dream" increasingly reveals its own resistance to Dora's different voice.

What is perhaps most significant in this regard is that whether Dora's subject position is defined as masculine or feminine, in both instances desire as the passion *for* an object, that is to say, active oedipal desire, is foregrounded, and identification, the passion to be the object, to which Freud's later texts would devote increasing attention, is minimized.[22] Yet Dora's dream interrogates identification as well as desire, indeed, literally questions the complex relation between identification and desire that Freud would develop later as the complete oedipus complex, a structure in which ambivalent identification is an essential component.[23] A question mark is the primary figure of the second dream, a literal diacritical mark disrupting the normal syntax of a sentence, in the phrase "if you like?" that appears both in her mother's dream-letter and in her own association to a letter from Frau K. inviting her to the lake. Although Freud questions the appearance of the question mark, he does not question it as a signifier. It is precisely the question of Dora's desire, however, which is at issue. The dream's question—if you like?—posed as a desire made possible by the father's dream-death, is the familiar question of the hysteric's desire, which is a desire *to be* as well as *to have*. How is sexual identity assumed? How is it represented? Is "gynecophilic" (Freud's initial term for Dora's desire) the same as "masculine"? Freud's interpretation, that underlying Dora's dream is a fantasy of a *man* seeking to force entrance into a woman, not only erases the question mark of the dream, but also compounds hysterical conflict by constituting heterosexuality as a forced entrance of an active man into a passive woman, fixing passivity as the position of femininity and thus obliterating the active female subject.

Freud's reading also brings to the surface of the text a metaphor of rape that pervades his interpretive stance in this case. A fantasy ubiquitously implicated in the hysterical anxiety of late-nineteenth-century texts, the rape of an innocent young woman by a sexually brutal male was the staple of Victorian melodrama. That trope is unwittingly echoed in Freud's reconstruction of the tyrannous demands of the father-daughter relationship.[24] Insistently trying to open Dora up, Freud both hears a fantasy of defloration in Dora's description of wandering lost in a wooded area with an obscure goal and enacts it by appropriating Dora's voice and dream as his own. In this context it is of more than passing interest to note that Freud used an analogous metaphor for the structure of his dream book: an imaginary walk into a dark wood, "where there is no clear view and it is very easy to go astray. There, there is a cavernous defile through which I lead my readers . . . and then, all at once, the high ground and the prospect and the question: Which way do you want to go?" (*SE* 4:122, n.1). Representing his quest for knowledge here through an image that he describes in the Dora case as the body of a woman, Freud not only raises a similar specter of the labyrinthine female body and the proto-typical question—"which way to go?"—which informs the hysteric's dream but reveals the intricate relation between his ambitious quest and his appropriation of Dora's dream.

Thus, when Freud inserts his own question into Dora's dream, answers it, and then informs Dora of his conclusions—"I informed her of my conclusions. The impression upon her mind must have been forcible"—Freud's own diction resonates with these intrusive impli-cations of paternal violence and desire. Dora's immediate response to this "forcible" impression is to recall another dream detail, to open herself still further: "she went calmly to her room and began reading a big book that lay on her writing table" (*SE* 7:100). As Freud points out, Dora's odd words here are "calmly" and "big"; their emphatic presence as markers suggests that both are to be questioned. Thus, Freud notes that "calmly" suggests a linguistic cover-up of its oppo-site, and that Dora later added "not sadly" to clarify the meaning of "calmly." Although there is no "No" in the unconscious, he does not question her negation—"*not* sadly"—or indicate its significance. If "not sadly" is a negation of "sadly," "sadly" points to a grief, to a loss associated with reading the big book that links hysteria to melancholia.

In discussing Freud's theory of feminine development, Luce Irigaray points out that "if all the implications of Freud's discourse were followed through, after the little girl discovers her own castra-tion and that of her mother—her 'object,' the narcissistic representa-tive of all her instincts—she would have no recourse other than mel-ancholia" (1985a, 66). Irigaray concludes that the girl's repression of her previous masculinity results in an inhibition of activity and a fall in self-esteem, and ultimately in a melancholy that derives from having radically lost the mother both as erotic object and as narcissistic object of identification. "This devaluation of the mother accompanies or fol-lows on the devaluation of the little girl's own sex organ. Thus . . . the relationship to the (lost) object is not simple, but complicated by conflict and ambivalence that remain unconscious . . . which may re-

sult in . . . their being 'remembered' in the form of 'somatic affections' that are characteristic of melancholia? and also of course of
hysteria" (68).[25]

In thus foregrounding the girl's inevitable loss of the maternal
object through prohibition and devaluation and the consequent im-
brication of melancholia in hysteria for women, Irigaray points to
another meaning in Dora's turn to the big book in her dream. Although Dora's dream reading of the "big" book confirms for Freud
his speculation that an encyclopedia was the source of Dora's sexual
knowledge, we can also read her reading of the *big* book on *her* writing
table as a trope of her situation as a woman who must read her inscription as Woman in the "big book" in order to answer the question,
"What does a woman want?" Could the big book she reads be also
Freud's own big book, *The Interpretation of Dreams,* to which her
subjectivity as case history was both a supplement and an exemplum?
Did Dora experience the imposition of his paternal word as a definition that she would resist? Where would her support for this resistance
come from?[26] Is there a maternal book, a metaphorics of sexual differences, which authorizes the mother's letter?

Certainly there is a maternal letter, literally, in Dora's dream, but it
is not a dominant dream-trope in Freud's reading. Nor does the
maternal letter itself signify when, in a notable association, Freud tells
us that Dora hides a letter from her grandmother when he enters the
waiting-room of his office: "I believe that Dora only wanted to play
secrets with me," he writes, "and to hint that she was on the point of
allowing her secret to be torn from her by the physician" (*SE* 7:96).
Negating the letter's content, he focuses only on its function in the
game between physician and patient as a "secret to be torn from her."
The violence of his metaphor mirrors the violence of the game
of heterosexual pursuit called "playing doctor" that he plays with
Dora. Indeed, Freud's sadomasochistically toned representation of
the doctor-patient relation, a representation that governs his descriptions of heterosexual relations throughout his writings, suggests that
sadomasochism more generally defines the erotic power-politics of
heterosexuality, that it is ineluctably linked to the cultural posi-
tionalities of masculine and feminine as constructed in nineteenth-
century discourse.

What is more, this erotic ordering inevitably represses the maternal metaphor. "The enactment of sadomasochistic fantasies," Irigaray writes, "is governed by man's relation to his mother: the desire to force entry, to penetrate, to appropriate for himself the mystery of this womb where he has been conceived, the secret of his begetting, of his origin" (1985b, 351). Irigaray's analysis of the patriarchal construction of female desire and its occlusion of maternal power speaks forcefully to the issue of Freud's obsession with the source of Dora's knowledge —Was it oral or written? Did it come from the mother's voice or the father's text?—and to his own rhetorical turn from the maternal letter to the big book. Ultimately, it suggests that Freud's rivalry and envy of maternal procreative power fuel his desire to promote the primacy of his own written word.[27]

Yet Freud did not—perhaps could not—exclude references to the maternal letter from his story or eliminate its effects from the psychoanalytic exchange. The corporeal remainder of the voice continued to assert the body's presence in the utterance, and especially when a woman was speaking her secrets, to remind Freud of the mother, to indicate her centrality as the primary figure of repression and loss in hysteria.[28] The speaking voice thus led him as the receptive ear through evocative articulations into an unconscious where the line between his and hers was obscured. Through what Garrett Stewart calls "the verbal stream in which otherness mutters to us" (1990, 33)— mutters, mutter, matter, mother—the vocative, provocative, and evocative, of the analytic dialogue and its hypercathexis of the voice repeatedly opened into a radical otherness, a feminine alterity that required a filling in as well as a covering up. Thus, Freud writes of his narrative, "Part of this material I was able to obtain directly from the analysis, but the rest required supplementing" (SE 7:80). Narrativization enacted that supplementation, but as we have seen, such a supplement filled in, covered up too much. Perhaps especially because the Dora case, originally to be called "Dreams and Hysteria," was meant to substantiate *The Interpretation of Dreams,* Freud seems especially compelled to fill in the gaps of her story, to ground his metaphysics in her physics. In Dora's case, however, one story led to another; the ground kept shifting as Freud attempted to discover the "true" object of Dora's passion. Ultimately, Freud's narrative unveiled the voice itself as the passionate object of the hysteric and of psychoanalysis. Who has the voice? Who does what with it? To whom does it belong? These become the primal questions of the texts I address in the following chapters, texts in which voice and ear, speaker and listener, become fantasmatically gendered positions generating hysterical rivalry.

Chapter Three

Invalids and Nurses

The Sisterhood of Rage

Hysteria is the daughter's disease.
—Juliet Mitchell

Daughter of the father? Or daughter of the mother?
—Julia Kristeva

IN READING FREUD'S case history of Dora for its illumination of hysterical narrative voice, I have explored Freud's desire more than Dora's, his symptomatic use of language more than hers. Yet, as Juliet Mitchell remarks, hysteria has been particularly the daughter's disease.[1] What does it mean to be a daughter in the narrative of psychoanalysis? Why is it so problematic? Freud's initial answer was that the daughter signifies the oedipal child who not only desires the father, but more specifically desires to be the object of the father's desire. It was a scene of passive submission to another's desire that Freud had first defined as the traumatic experience in the etiology of hysteria, and although he moved from the seduction theory, in which an early external trauma causes hysteria, to the theory of infantile fantasy, in which the subject's own transgressive desire is the origin of the symptom, even in fantasy the pleasure of being done to rather than doing, the proper feminine position, remained perilous for Freud as well as for his analysands. Desire in this form, as an eroticized submission as object, is the desire that Freud ultimately located in the death drive, in a primary masochism in which the subject seeks pleasure in a return to nonbeing, to nondifferentiation, to silence. Masochism is thus a primary temptation in hysterical conflict, a seduction into objectification that erases the active subject of desire.

As the Dora case revealed, however, the hysterical daughter did not rest easy as a silent object. In conflict with that masochistic pleasure, she simultaneously struggled to assume the position of subject, to speak her desire. Since within the patriarchal ordering of subjectivity that dominated nineteenth-century discourse, to speak as an active subject was to occupy a masculine position, the voice of the female hysteric became a favored site of an ambivalence that troubled her speech. As we know, in the Dora case Freud analyzed this ambivalence as a matter of unconscious desire and identification: the hysteric was caught between an unacknowledged desire for the father—the core fantasy of the conventional female oedipal complex—and an acknowledged rivalrous identification with him that took a maternal figure as erotic object. Yet implicit in this formulation of sexual ambivalence is an aspect of hysteria that needs more attention: its spawning of rage. For at the heart of the daughter's oedipal oscillation was a more primal engagement with a maternal fantasm, an archaic figure of power and pleasure whose inevitable loss and social devaluation persisted as a burr in the daughter's psyche. Dora was a classic example of the daughter's ambivalent rejection of a devalued mother that inevitably provoked rage.

Although Freud's theorization of the function of rage remains slight and scattered among various texts,[2] he explicitly remarks upon the daughter's rage in his theorization of female psychosexual development, explaining her greater hostility toward the mother as deriving from her recognition of maternal lack ("Femininity," in *New Introductory Lectures,* 1933 [1932], *SE* 22: 112–35). In Freud's narrative, the daughter, enraged at the mother for having deprived her of the valued phallus, repudiates her as a love object, a repudiation encouraged by patriarchal demands that she transfer her love to the father. More recent feminist reformulations expand this explanatory narrative to include the daughter's relation to the symbolic order and language. In Kristeva's account, in order to emerge as a subject of language, the daughter must disavow her primary identification with the maternal body and move toward an imaginary and symbolic identification with the father. This maternal disavowal generates a narcissistic crisis, resulting in a chronic melancholia and its concomitant, repressed rage.[3]

Luce Irigaray, as I remarked above (chap. 2), describes a similar dilemma: "The girl's relationship with her mother is not lacking in ambivalence and becomes even more complicated when the little girl realizes that the phallic mother to whom—according to Freud—she addressed her love, is in fact castrated. This devaluation of the mother accompanies or follows on the devaluation of the little girl's own sex organ" (1985a, 68). This oedipal turn from devalued mother to father initiates both a self-devaluation and a hysterical melancholia, a loss of the mother as loved and idealized object that is withdrawn from consciousness.[4] What is more, as Irigaray argues, girls lack access to "representations [that] will replace or assist this 'unconsciousness' in which is grounded the girl's conflictual relationship to her mother and to her sex organ. Which may result in their being 'remembered' in the form of 'somatic affections' that are characteristic of melancholia? And also, of course, of hysteria" (1985a, 68).[5] Since this maternal loss cannot be recuperated symbolically, the daughter must inscribe her desire through an alienating phallic signifier.

If Freud and French feminist psychoanalysts derive the daughter's rage from a recognition of maternal lack, Klein, a major theorist of infantile rage, locates its origin in a fantasy of maternal plenitude.[6] In Klein's view, this fantasy provokes oral-sadistic wishes to rob those parts of the mother where a fantasized fullness lies (her breasts, her body), to incorporate them in a totality that is the essence of primary narcissism. As Klein theorized, because such rage has as its aim the oral incorporation of the maternal body as well as its destruction, rage threatens to destroy the subject as well in a fusion that respects no boundaries. Thus, rage must be contained and loss gradually acknowledged as the subject moves through a primal mourning into what Klein called the depressive position.

Whatever their differences, these psychoanalytic theorists make a common point: the first lost object, which is also the first object of identification and the first object of rage, is the mother, the most ambivalently constructed other, who bears at the same time the traces of self. Certainly for an ambitious Victorian daughter, the stark disjunction between a paternal identification that validated her as speaking subject and a body that compelled her to identify with a devalued maternal object is repeatedly shown to provoke an unutterable rage.

One thinks of Maggie destroying her doll in *The Mill on the Floss* in a paradigmatic repudiation of the maternal role that destroys the child-doll as well; or Dora, contemptuously negating her mother's importance in her story but in the process losing her own voice. Indeed, the daughter cannot negate the mother without also negating herself. Suspended at the oedipal moment in all its ambiguous and paralyzing potential, the daughter who succumbed to hysteria typically turned her rage against herself in a kind of masochistic biting of her own tongue instead of using it aggressively against the other and silently mimed in her body the script that had entrapped her.[7]

What would it mean for the invalidated daughter to have valid speech? to have a tongue? What would be said? and in what form? In asking these questions, women writers frequently transform the conventional figure of the patriarchal daughter into the rebellious sister in a discourse of equal rights—of liberty, equality, and fraternity—which values sorority as well. Yet although such writers as Charlotte Brontë and Olive Schreiner variously challenge fraternal privilege and paternal prohibitions in their fictions, their textual voices frequently betray their own bondage to those very prohibitions and the rage that is their affective complement. In what follows I want to look at the effects of rage on the narrative voices of three women whose writings represent three different genres: the *Diary* of Alice James; the polemical essay, *Cassandra,* of Florence Nightingale; and the novels *Shirley* and *Villette* of Charlotte Brontë. It is of perhaps more than passing interest that two of the three women were declared hysterics. James wrote her *Diary* during the final years of her life while sequestered in London with hysterical ailments until she succumbed with relief to a "real" one. Florence Nightingale, also housebound by hysterical debilities after her return from the Crimean War, began *Cassandra* as an autobiographical fiction meant to reveal the pathogenic nature of women's position in culture, but it became a long and digressive essay that found no public audience during her own lifetime. In contrast, Charlotte Brontë became a professional writer, successfully able to represent as writing her ambivalent relation to cultural authority and narrative law. Yet the written discourse of all three can serve to illuminate the effects of rage on narrative voice.

ALICE JAMES HAD no public presence during her life, nor was she a writer by profession or self-proclamation. Unlike her famous brothers, who in spite of hysterical phenomena in their histories, inscribed themselves into public discourse, Alice James remained essentially the silent sister.[8] Hysterically invalided from the age of nineteen, she spent her life as the quintessential patient, her body the medium through which she covertly represented the problematics of her identity.[9] During the final years of her life, having followed Henry to London, housebound from ailments no doctor could diagnose as real, and cared for by her loyal friend and intimate companion, Katherine Loring, she took up the pen to record her life. Not surprisingly, her writing took the form of a diary, a private voice.

Yet clearly James intended her *Diary* to be read; Leon Edel notes that in 1894 she had four copies of the *Diary* printed, one for each of her brothers, and that she intended to publish the book if they approved ("Introduction" to *Diary*, 1964 [1982], vii). Moreover, in a number of comments she imagines herself exercising a public voice heard by others. In several entries she addresses an imaginary reader, who, significantly, was gendered male, an inflection especially striking since she dictated the better part of the *Diary* to Katherine Loring. But in this perversely gendered address, James' voice speaks the very contradiction of the hysteric: the imaginary ear of the listerner/reader who confirms the speaking subject belongs to a man even when James is speaking literally to a woman. James herself comments on this incongruous imaginary male ear in her entry of January 1891, shortly before her death: "I am as much amused, dear Inconnu (please note the sex? pale shadow of Romance still surviving even in the most rejected and despised by Man) as you can be by these microscopic observations recorded of this mighty race" (166).

What strikes this reader is that the *Diary* seems unnecessarily narrow in the field of its attention: even in James' comments on reading—an area in which her observations could have transcended the confines of her domestic space—her thoughts are not allowed the expansion of significant reflection. Her remarks are crabbed or conversationally elliptical, her voice characterized more by biting commentary than by probing analysis or meditation.

Certainly although James writes in that most private of literary forms, the diary, the actual passages of introspection or self-reflection are few. When she does occasionally cast a cold eye on herself, what she reveals is a torturous self-division, as in this well-known passage in which she describes the aftereffects of her own first hysterical attack:

> As I lay prostrate after the storm with my mind luminous and active and susceptible of the clearest, strongest impressions, I saw so distinctly that it was a fight simply between my body and my will. . . . Owing to some physical weakness, . . . the moral power pauses . . . and refuses to maintain muscular sanity, worn out with the strain of its *constabulary* functions. As I used to sit immovable reading in the *library* with waves of violent inclination suddenly invading my muscles, taking some one of their myriad forms such as throwing myself out of the window, or knocking off the head of the benignant pater as he sat with his silver locks, writing at his table, it used to seem to me that the only difference between me and the insane was that I had not only all the horrors and suffering of insanity but the duties of doctor, nurse, and strait-jacket imposed upon me, too. Conceive of never being without the sense that if you let yourself go for a moment . . . you must abandon it all, let the dykes break and the flood sweep in, acknowledging yourself abjectly impotent before the immutable laws. When all one's moral and natural stock in trade is a temperament forbidding the abandonment of an inch or the relaxation of a muscle, 'tis a never-ending fight. (149)

The two forms of her violent inclination—self-destruction or the destruction of the father (and here a particularly archetypal father, the "benignant pater" writing)—and the totalistic either/or syntax speak a deeply regressive desire to break down the boundaries between self and other, here self and father, a desire to destroy the gendered polarities of the subject that confine her in the identity of the good daughter.

Appropriately, the setting of this melodrama is the father's library—the repository of patriarchy, where the daughter can read the script but not write it, a scene repeatedly invoked in late-nineteenth- and early-twentieth-century texts. Recall the provocative Maggie—a character James loved—reading her father's books, or Lucy Snowe in *Villette,* given instructional texts by M. Paul Emmanuel, or even Dora's dream of reading a big book. While Eliot's Maggie outdoes her brother in intellectual prowess, James' leading symptom is an intellectual inhibition. "Cerebration is an impossible exercise and from just behind the eyes my head feels like a dense jungle into which no ray of light has ever penetrated," she writes of her inability to study or think concentratedly without great anxiety (149). Given the phallic marking of intellectual activities—activities in which her particularly brilliant brothers excelled—it is not hard to loosen the knot of meanings in her inability to think, by which she avoids the domain of her brothers and performs a conventional femininity she also despised. "How sick one gets of being 'good,'" she writes. "How much I should respect myself if I could burst out and make every one wretched for 24 hours" (64). In a very real sense, Alice was "sick" of being "good."

This restriction of language and consciousness—a form of defense against knowing—was no doubt fostered by Alice's relation to William, who as Jean Strouse points out, played the flirtatious rake with his sister, his letters provocatively sprinkled with erotic double entendres (1980, 52–55). "If you had taken your pills last summer," William writes to her during one of her treatments for hysteria in New York, "you'd now be at home with my arm around you and the rich tones of my voice lingering in your ear" (110). Such amorous ambiguities between brother and sister were a staple of nineteenth-century discourse. If William's advances provoked forbidden desire, his advantages encouraged envy and rage as well in his less fortunate sister, that is to say, encouraged her narcissistic identification with a male counterpart and its inherent aggressive rivalry. It was such an intermingling of desire and rage that George Eliot represented in the climactic brother-sister *liebestod* of Maggie and Tom, who are found reconciled to the extreme, drowned in an embrace in *The Mill on the Floss,* a novel especially dear to Alice James. One can even hear its final scene embedded in James' articulation of her own struggle to contain "the flood" within her, a trope of excess that took its toll on her body.

In this regard, it is especially striking that the most vigorous eruption of rage and energy in the chatty surface of James' prose is provoked by her reading of George Eliot's letters:

Read the third volume of George Eliot's Letters and Journals at last. I'm glad I made myself do so for there is a faint spark of life and an occasional remotely humorous touch in the last half. But what a monument of ponderous dreariness the book! Not one outburst of joy, not one ray of humor, not one living breath in one of her letters or journals, the commonplace and platitude of these last, giving her impressions of the Continent, pictures and people, is simply incredible! Whether it is that her dank, moaning features haunt and pursue one through' the book, or not, but she makes upon me the impression, morally and physically, of mildew, or some morbid growth—a fungus of a pendulous shape, or as of something damp to the touch. I never had a stronger impression. Then to think of those books compact of wisdom, humor, and the richest humanity, and of her as the creator of the immortal *Maggie,* in short, what a horrible disillusion! Johnnie seems to have done his level best to wash out whatever little color the letters may have had by the unfortunate form in which he has seen fit to print them. (40–41)

The physical image by which she characterizes Eliot here is singularly repulsive and recalls the disgust at corporeality common to hysteria. What is it about Eliot that gives James the impression of a fungus, of something damp to the touch? If we follow the logic of the imagery, the morbid growth, the mildew, and fungus all share the quality of a repugnant and invasive parasitic dependence represented by tropes of abjection that are the antithesis of idealization. Certainly James' words, "I never had a stronger impression," suggest some very affective root has been tapped, and what follows next is its radical exposure: "On the subject of her marriage it is of course for an outsider criminal to say anything, but what a shock for her to say she felt as if her life were renewed and for her to express her sense of complacency in the vestry and church! What a betrayal of the much mentioned 'perfect love' of the past!" (41).

This sequence of associative enunciation, from Eliot as a damp fungus to her traitorous remarriage, suggests that her repulsion is associated with Eliot's indulgence of the body, imaged as a parasitic need for corporeal coupling at the expense of the ideal. Repeatedly James censures second marriages as an infidelity, a betrayal of an imagined "perfect love," and an unworthy craving for sensation.[10]

January 23, 1891: How surprised and shocked I am to hear that Ellie Emmet, whose heart, I had been led to suppose, was seared by sorrow, is contemplating marriage again. . . . 'Twould seem to the inexperienced that one happy "go" at marriage would have given the full measure of connubial bliss, and all the chords of maternity have vibrated under the manipulation of six progeny, but man lives not to assimilate knowledge of the eternal essence of things, and only craves a renewal of sensation. (172)

As with her response to Eliot's remarriage, James here criticizes remarriage as a "renewal of sensation," censuring these women for taking pleasure in the body with which she was continually at war.[11]

The body as enemy is a pervasive trope of the *Diary*—and a trope that makes remarriage a virtually criminal act. Moreover, voicing the familiar dichotomy between European guilt and American innocence that informs her brother's fiction, James describes remarriage as an act that characterizes British women more than American, who sustain more loyally the Puritan ideal:

> The women seem to do here constantly what so rarely happens at home, marry again. 'Tis always a surprise, not that I have any foolish young inflexibility about it, for I am only too glad to see creatures grasp at anything, outside murder, theft or intoxication, from which they fancy they may extract happiness, but it reveals such a simple organization to be perpetually ready to renew experience in so confiding a manner. (102)

This sardonic juxtaposition of remarriage with murder, theft, and intoxication is followed by a startling synecdoche in which the moral integrity of the women who remarries is analogized to the female flesh having been torn, with its connotations of sexual violation:

> As they do it [remarry] within a year or two the moral flesh must be as healthy as that pink substance of which they are physically compact, the torn fibres healing themselves by first intention, evidently. The subjective experience being what survives from any relation, you would suppose that the wife part of you had been sufficiently developed in one experiment, at any rate that you would like to contemplate the situation a bit from the bereft point of view—but, no, they are ready to plunge *into love again* at a moment's notice— as if 'twere quantity, not quality, of emotion that counted. (103)

The trope of the daughter as a potentially torn fiber occurs again in her retelling of a familiar narrative paradigm: a daughter who dies from grief at her father's remarriage, "a little maid" who "passed with peaceful joy from amidst the vain shadows. Will there be no stirrings of remorse in her father's bosom for the brutalities which rent that

delicate fibre?" (195–96). James' representation of the daughter as a
delicate fiber torn by the father's brutalities recreates a perverse Gothic family romance in which the renewal of paternal desire results in the
daughter's violation.

Given this representation of the inimical, vulnerable, or criminal
body, it is intriguing to find that when James represents her parents'
ideal marriage, she frames it by an association to her own body's
vulnerability. Having just remarked on her "devilish headache," she
first makes reference to the influenza epidemic and the danger of
microbes invading her chamber. Immediately James' text converts the
invasive material potential of actual microbes to "ghost microbes," a
trope for old letters from her parents that have had a profound effect
upon her, as she writes, "one of the most intense, exquisite and profoundly interesting experiences I ever had" (78). Although "ghost
microbes" implies an infection by the past, the text quickly transforms
this trope of the past as disease to the past as a fountain of perpetual
nurturance:

> It seems now incredible to me that I should have drunk, as matter of
> course, at that ever springing fountain of responsive love and bathed
> all unconscious in that flood of human tenderness. The letters are
> made of the daily events of their pure simple lives, with souls un-
> ruffled by the ways of men, like special creatures, spiritualized and
> remote from coarser clay. Father ringing the changes upon Moth-
> er's perfections . . . and Mother's words breathing her extraordi-
> nary selfless devotion as if she simply embodied the unconscious
> essence of wife and motherhood. What a beautiful picture do they
> make for the thoughts of their children to dwell upon! How the
> emotions of those two dreadful years, when I was wrenching myself
> away from them, surge thro' me. (79)

While her parents are represented as "remote from coarser clay,"
the physical underpinning of the image of her mother "breathing"
selfless devotion is striking, especially if one recalls that the very dress
of women in the mid-nineteenth century bound their respiration un-
naturally. Certainly James seemed stifled in representing her mother,
for aside from the above passage there is no anecdotal recall of her
mother in the *Diary*. While her father and brothers are frequently remembered in writing, her mother remains an absence, the maternal
voice and figure virtually effaced from representation. In its place are

substitute women who, by virtue of their bodies, can in no way approach the disembodied ideal.

It is this very de-realization of the mother, her disembodiment and virtual absence from representation, which implicates her as a primary object of James' hysterical repression. Idealization as such eliminates the material presence of the mother; it obliterates the maternal body as well as the maternal voice. It is notable that her mother's voice is not embodied in dialogue, as is her father's and her brothers', and as are the voices of a host of minor characters. Indeed, in the *Diary,* her father's voice is all too present; in the above passage, James recollects her father's voice ringing the changes on a maternal perfection James could not dare dispute or equal.

One of the final entries is a more disquieting memory of her father's voice, this time ringing the changes on her own character in a manner that perhaps illuminates her earlier impulse to smash the paternal pate. Using a metaphor that discloses a nodal point of self-conflict, she recalls the disapproving "ring of Father's voice, as he anathematized some short-comings of mine in Newport one day: 'Oh, Alice, how hard you are!' and I can remember how penetrated I was, not for the first time, but often, with the truth of it, and saw the repulsion his nature with its ripe kernel of human benignancy felt—alas! through all these years, that hard core confronts me still" (192). Since this "hard core" signifies precisely those qualities that are her strengths, she is paradoxically confronted with an image of self that negates her; her very core identity becomes a wound induced by internalization of the condemnatory paternal voice. Close upon this recollection of paternal judgment is another memory that further elucidates her father's place in her internal script. Interestingly, it is a scene that reenacts Freud's theorization of the joke structure—a scene in which Alice listens passively, while two men, figures of patriarchal authority, tell a joke involving her. Emerson, her father's friend, asks another friend: "'And what sort of a girl is Alice?' . . . 'She has a highly moral nature.' . . . 'How in the world does her father get on with her?'" (193). The punch line, so to speak, is the difference between her and her father, a moral difference in her favor. Yet she denies that difference by literally erasing herself as signifier in the next sentence: "But who shall relate that long alliance, made on one side of all tender affection, solicitous sympathy and paternal indulgence!"

Finally, then, it is a disturbing conflict about self-erasure in the name of the father—a self-erasure that also erases the mother—which inhibits self-representation in James' *Diary*. That erasure was extended to her body image, inducing a rage at the body that was paradoxically articulated through it.[12] At the same time, to undo that erasure, James makes herself a writing subject; but to avoid the implicit rivalry and aggressivity of that position—toward the father, toward her brothers—she writes a private text, a diary, and writes herself out of it as its primary subject. Only as the *Diary* closes on her last year, assuming what she called "a certain mortuary flavor," does she give voice to a greater self-reflexivity. "I would there were more bursts of enthusiasm, less of the carping tone through this, but I fear it comes by nature" (218). References to nature, to the body she could no longer ignore, increase, sharply etched by rage and self-loathing, while at the same time she continues to disclaim its significance:

> If the aim of life is the accretion of fat, the consumption of food unattended by digestive disorganization, and a succession of pleasurable sensations, there is no doubt that I am a failure, for as an animal form my insatiable vanity must allow that my existence doesn't justify itself, but every fibre protests against being taken simply as a sick carcass . . . for what power has dissolving flesh and aching bones to undermine a satisfaction made of imperishable things? (183)

Even as she approached the end and allowed herself to be the subject and object of her writing, she distanced her body by assuming the stance of pure percipient of its outline. "Of what matter can it be whether pain or pleasure has shaped and stamped the pulp within, as one is absorbed in the supreme interest of watching the outline and the tracery as the lines broaden for eternity" (232).

In spite of this self-representation as neutral observer, the lines that broadened were the lines she herself penned in the *Diary*, her textual voice giving her the only outline she still historically retains—as writer of the *Diary*. Not surprisingly, then, James continued to make manuscript corrections to the last, as if more than her life depended upon her words, so that, as Katherine Loring remarked, "although she was very weak and it tired her much to dictate, she could not get her head quiet until she had it written: then she was relieved" (232–33). While one must be very cautious about attributing psychological causality to physical events—cautious, that is to say, about privileging the imaginary as source of the real, especially given the very real suffering of Alice James—it remains an uncanny piece of James' history that she ultimately succumbed to breast cancer, a final physical symptom that exceeded the limits of the symbolic in its repudiation of the maternal signifier, and brought her a death she welcomed with relief.

IF ALICE JAMES was the archetypal patient, Florence Nightingale has come to signify the archetypal nurse. Yet scratching the surface of this representation reveals a historical irony, since Nightingale, like James, lived the life of the patient, bedridden for most of her life. The figure of the nurse and its inversion, the patient, has dominated histories of hysterics—from Anna O.'s nursing of her father, which was followed by her own need to be nursed (now inscribed as a contemporary myth of the origins of psychoanalysis), to Freud's remembered relation to his nurse, constructed as an origin of his own hysterical proclivities.[13] That Nightingale chose nursing as her field—and battlefield—of action, concerned as it is with mastery of the passive and vulnerable body, but through the body of the other, is certainly not without relevance to the battles of her inner world. Yet, Nightingale thought of herself not as a practicing nurse, but as an administrator, as a fabricator of the nursing system, a role more symbolically coded as masculine. Nightingale's biographers indicate that she was disdainful of Victorian femininity and its domestic concerns and rejected being characterized as a nurse.[14] Nevertheless, in virtually creating the profession of the modern nurse and becoming that symbolic figure as well as a lifelong patient, Nightingale acted out in her own life a bifurcated identification with both a powerful maternal imago and its passive counterpart that was to plague both her writing voice and her body.

The youngest of two daughters, Nightingale grew up in a divided family constellation in which her father, who had rigorously educated her, was her intimate ally against the more conventional social demands of her mother and sister. This family friction took its toll: in her autobiographical writings she describes the dreamlike trances and religious hallucinations of her childhood, her sense that "she was a monster," and the voices she heard at traumatic moments in her adolescence calling her to a special destiny (Showalter 1977, 62). Defying her mother's strong censure for not marrying, Nightingale chose to commit herself instead to the vocation of nursing. Yet after her phenomenal success in the Crimean War, she returned to London with a host of symptoms—including heart palpitations and an extreme nausea when presented with food—and at the height of her reputation, she retired to her bed for almost half a century. That her illness was a hysterical one is dramatically rendered by the fact that shortly after her mother's death, Nightingale, having been invalided for forty years, suddenly recovered, as if released from some magical entrapment.[15] Even invalided, however, she remained one of the most influential women in Europe, the founder of nursing as a respectable profession for middle-class women, and a prolific writer in the cause of health care reform.[16]

Although she was always writing—letters, reports, essays—writing is not what we associate with Nightingale. What she wanted to write—her own life story as admonitory narrative—she apparently could not. Among her papers is the fragmentary prose piece *Cassandra*, which began as an autobiographical novel but which she was unable to complete. Eventually, after many revisions, it metamorphosed into a long fractured essay, part of which has been published as a monograph by The Feminist Press. First written in 1852, before she took to her own bed, *Cassandra* was Nightingale's most persistent attempt to articulate her perception of the pathogenic conditions of women's lives. It is also a text that bears the classic marks of a hysterical discourse, riven by contradictory passions, digressive, fragmentary, inconsistent in its voice and subject position, a text that Lytton Strachey aptly characterized as a *cri de coeur* even though it had undergone repeated revisions (1918, 189).[17]

Nightingale's process of revising and rewriting from the early manuscript "novel" with its stilted artifice to the passionate cry of the essay instructively illuminates the nodal points of conflict that inhibited her ability to write a life-fiction.[18] In its first version *Cassandra* is framed as a third-person narrative but is "told" primarily in the first-person voice of its tragic heroine Nofriani, a Venetian princess who, in a series of long dramatic dialogues with little action, complains of her situation as a woman to her brother Fariseo, whose function is to listen and confirm her concerns. Making use of what Marianne Hirsch calls "the man who would understand,"[19] a male double who is both self and other, this early version used the device of a social conversation between brother and sister to embed a critique of the social condition of women and its ill effects.

Yet in a gesture that seems to contradict her polemical intent, Nightingale places Nofriani in a conventionally romantic setting and makes her a romantic heroine who expresses from the outset a conventional melancholy and a desire for death:

> The night was mild & dark & cloudy. . . . All was still. "I alone am wandering in the bitterness of life without," she said. She went down where on the glassy dark pond the long shadows of the girdle of pines the tops of which seemed to touch heaven were lying. The swans were sleeping on their little island. Even the Muscovy ducks were not yet awake. But she had suffered so much that she had outlived even the desire to die. (Add.MS 45839, f.237; quoted in Snyder 1993, 26)

What is significantly different in this awkwardly artificial fiction is that it is a woman who articulates this conventional melancholy. As Juliana Schiesari argues, melancholy is a gendered affect, traditionally an affliction of great but tormented men. Certainly for the nineteenth century, the privileged melancholy subject was male, a Keats or a Byron but not a Dorothy Wordsworth, a Rochester but not a Jane Eyre. Moreover, melancholy was considered not merely an affect, but a form of male creativity; it was precisely the ability of the subject to speak his melancholy in language that gave it cultural value (Schiesari 1993, 1–7). In contrast, women were typically represented not as melancholic but as depressed, a difference signified by their absence of speech, by their withdrawal into silence. Nightingale's heroine, then, in being primarily a melancholy first-person voice, already transgresses the place of the woman in the nineteenth-century literature of melancholia. Nevertheless, her destiny is classically feminine: after complaining of the social thwarting of women's desires, Nofriani dies, welcoming death in a gesture not unlike Alice James'. Significantly, it is the male voice of her brother that recounts her final words: "Free, free, oh! divine Freedom, art thou come at last? Welcome, beautiful Death!" (Add.MS 45839, f. 287; quoted in Snyder 1993, 26).

This conclusion, the declamation of a dying woman, was retained at the end of the final essay version as well, but in the essay the words are attributed to an anonymous dying woman by a voice external to the action. With the quotation marks of Nofriani's dialogue removed, the limited female voice and its melancholy romanticism are depersonalized and made into a general statement about women's unhappiness. Thus, Nightingale attempts to transform the romantic fantasy of a particular female subject into a generalized social criticism; failed novel is meant to be redeemed as political essay in great part through the transformation of the voice. To take another example, in the novel, Nofriani says that she is "too much ashamed of my dreams, which I thought were 'romantic' to tell them where I knew that they would be laughed at"; in the later essay version this embarrassment is made into a third-person description of a general condition: "thus women live—too much ashamed of their dreams, which they think 'romantic,' to tell them to be laughed at." Both cases, however, describe the inhibiting effects of shame—"too much ashamed of their dreams"—on women's narrative voice.

In this context the novel was obviously an inappropriate genre for Nightingale, for the novel requires a certain shamelessness, a scandalous exposure of dreams, a certain submission to fantasy, a letting go of the authorial first person. In her own attempted novel, that submission to fantasy had led Nightingale's heroine to a problematic flirtation with passivity and death. The essay, however, foregrounds authorial control and the authority of the first-person writing subject, and indeed, for that reason has been considered a male genre.[20] Paradoxically, the novel version of *Cassandra* insisted on the dominance of the first-person voice but at the same time too rigidly controlled it. Although the voice of the essay version is given more freedom, that, too, becomes problematic; the essay inconsistently shifts between third-person and first-person plural voices, digressing, obsessing, too often fracturing the focus of its argument. Significantly, in an intermediate stage, Nightingale excised the specifically feminine and thus culturally devalued narrative voice altogether; in this mediate version, the voice vacillates between a masculine first-person narrator, Fariseo, the brother who tells his sister's story, and an anonymous third-person narrator.

In the final essay, however, both Nofriani and Fariseo, brother and sister, are absorbed into another kind of splitting, an anonymous but gendered first-person plural and an authoritative third-person narrative voice, both of which eliminate the individual speaking subject and the potential shame at its revelations. The disembodied omniscient third-person voice can then speak with the authority of its transcendence, while the first-person plural "we" identifies with and explores the common concerns of women. Critiquing the detrimental effects of fantasy on women's psyches,[21] Nightingale uses the first-person plural to represent it as a dangerously seductive substitute for action: "We fast mentally, scourge ourselves morally, use the intellectual hair shirt, in order to subdue the perpetual day-dreaming, which is so dangerous!" (1979, 27). Fantasy itself becomes the object to be repressed rather than available for fiction. Thus, through critique, Nightingale excises the exotic passages that had plagued the novel. The move from novel to essay thus shifts attention from inner desire to outer determinants in order to uncover and proclaim those social conditions that predispose women to invalidism and passivity, and to call for action.

Perhaps the most vivid of *Cassandra*'s warnings about the danger of the passive position is Nightingale's description of being "read aloud to," which she calls "the most miserable exercise of the human intellect": "It is like lying on one's back, with one's hands tied and having liquid poured down one's throat. Worse than that, because suffocation would immediately ensue and put a stop to this operation. But no suffocation would stop the other" (34). The violence of the metaphor in which listening to the voice of the other is the equivalent of being force-fed, a metaphor that would become a violent reality for militant suffragettes a generation later, and its oral site of conflict point again to a familiar hysterical fantasy of an intrusive and suffocating maternal body. (Nightingale actually suffered from a symptomatic and recurrent nausea, the most corporeal symptomatic rejection of maternal intrusion.)[22]

That the maternal voice is commonly experienced as an intrusive violation of boundaries (see chap. 2) lends a special resonance to Nightingale's representation of listening as an oral menace, as a violation of both her bodily limits and her psychological integrity.[23] Her response is to propose an antithetical image of desire: the daughter's passionate desire to talk. While mothers taught their daughters that women were not passionate, Nightingale writes, in fact, passion swells their imaginations. Given the straitjacket of femininity, romantic passion is displaced into a passion for sympathetic conversation, a passion for the voice. Thus, Nightingale represents the fantasy of a vocal interchange with an imaginary male double—recall Alice James' "Inconnu"—as the fulfillment of the daughter's desire:

> That, with the phantom companion of their fancy, they talk (not love, they are too innocent, too pure, too full of genius and imagination for that, but) they talk, in fancy, of that which interests them most; they seek a companion for their every thought; the companion they find not in reality they seek in fancy, or if not that, if not absorbed in endless conversations, they see themselves engaged with him in stirring events. (26)

Romantic fiction, Nightingale suggests, appeals to women for the same reason: it encourages a fantasy of liberation through conversation with a sympathetic male other:

> What are novels? What is the secret charm of every romance that ever was written? The first thing . . . is to place the persons together in circumstances which naturally call out the high feelings and thoughts of the character, which afford food for sympathy between them on these points—romantic events they are called. The second is that the heroine has generally no family ties (*almost invariably no mother*), or, if she has, these do not interfere with her entire independence. (28, italics mine)

Note the barely disguised wish to eliminate the mother, primary figure of interference with her independence, which appears in parentheses that restrain it. Simultaneously, the parentheses interrupt the linearity of the sentence by pointing to another track of association. Just as in this passage, the mother is displaced by the imaginary counterpart with whom the heroine can share "food for sympathy" rather than be force-fed, so in her own life Nightingale displaced her mother with actual counterparts, significant figures upon whom she depended for sympathy and whom she ruled as narcissistic extensions of her will and desire. When ultimately the exigencies of life caused an intimate to leave her, she responded to this separation with rage and symptoms.

In *Cassandra* Nightingale recognized that invalidism was a perverse form of aggressivity that both corrupts the individual life and impoverishes the symbolic order. In one of her formidable insights into the paralysis induced by a rage with no outlet she writes: "The great reformers of the world turn into the great misanthropists, if circumstances . . . do not permit them to act. *Christ, if he had been a woman, might have been nothing but a great complainer*" (53, italics mine). The paradox is rich: if Christ had been a woman, he would only have complained rather than acted. But also, if Christ had been a woman, his discourse would have been impotent; his audience would have heard and dismissed his message as only a complaint. Christ would have been Cassandra, the enraged prophet-daughter who speaks but is destined not to be heard, whose voice is stripped of any claim to authority. Like a number of women in conflict with patriarchal femininity, like Alice James hearing her father's voice, her brother's voice, writing to her male Inconnu, Nightingale here establishes the discursive potency of the male voice, and finds her imaginary counterpart, her ego ideal, in Christ—the prophet-*son*—who is empowered to speak as a woman never is.

In moving from fiction to essay, Nightingale was attempting to lend more urgency, immediacy, and authority to her voice. Just as the voice without quotation marks is more privileged in narrative as a source of authority, so the essay as a form is presumed to be more "true" than fiction. *Cassandra*'s fragmentation of the voice subverted the authority it attempted to claim: not surprisingly, it found no welcoming audience until recently. It is especially telling and historically prophetic, then, that Nightingale chose to name her writing voice and alter ego Cassandra, the mad prophet-daughter to whom no one listens. (Nightingale referred to herself as "poor Cassandra" in her letters and notes.) Ironically, Nightingale's own proper family name was itself a fiction, a name her father had appropriated in order to claim an inheritance. Was its allusion to the myth in which a woman's complaint is silenced by cutting out her tongue a constant reminder of her problematic place as speaking subject? Did Nightingale hear herself as Philomela as well as Cassandra? The excision of the woman's tongue is meant to destroy the female voice as logos, as meaning.[24] The voice of the woman in patriarchal discourse must remain the voice of the nightingale, a vocal image of pleasure rather than knowledge, sound without meaning, without pain. If the myth of the nightingale represents silence as the form of women's suffering at the hands of the patriarchal order, Nightingale's Cassandra managed to give suffering a voice and made pain a spur to social action: "Give us back our suffering, we cry to heaven in our hearts—suffering rather than indifferentism, for out of nothing comes nothing. But out of suffering may come the cure. Better have pain than paralysis!" (29). Although Nightingale herself refused the label *feminist, Cassandra* turned rage into outrage and thus turned the hysterical complaint to political account.

CHARLOTTE BRONTË can also be said to have turned the romantic complaint to political account by shifting from fiction to essay, but in Brontë's case, the political essay was typically embedded within the romantic fiction. Thus, for example, the narrator of *Jane Eyre*, in a sudden textual turn from narrative to argument, interpolates a passage on the need for action in women's lives:

> It is vain to say human beings ought to be dissatisfied with tranquility; they must have action; and they will make it if they cannot find it. . . . Women are supposed to be very calm generally; but women feel just as men feel; and it is narrow-minded in their more privileged fellow-creatures to say that they ought to confine themselves to making puddings and knitting stockings, to playing on the piano and embroidering bags. . . . It is thoughtless to condemn them, or laugh at them, if they seek to do more or learn more than custom has pronounced necessary for their sex.
> When thus alone I not unfrequently heard Grace Poole's laugh. (1960, 112–13)

Virginia Woolf cited this text as an example of a disturbance in the narrative voice caused by an uncontrolled eruption of Brontë's anger into her story (1957, 104). While a number of critics have censured Woolf for that critique and justified Brontë's digression on both political and narrative grounds,[25] clearly, there is an awkward break. In an interpolation that ruptures the narrative flow of the moment, Brontë's narrator temporarily leaves the story to make an eloquent and passionately felt first-person appeal for her right to the active subject position and then returns clumsily to her story. Significantly, it is an imaginary derisive *male* laugh that creates this division within her narrative voice, momentarily moving the voice away from the story and its mad-woman into a first-person complaint that exceeds the diegetic boundaries to implicate Brontë's authorial voice.

Similarly, in *Shirley*, in the midst of the narrator's description of the heroine's romantic disappointment, rage takes over the voice and diverts it, in a digression that, as in *Cassandra,* is spurred on by Brontë's outrage at the suppression of women's speech:

> A lover masculine so disappointed can speak and urge explanation; a lover feminine can say nothing: if she did, the result would be shame and anguish, inward remorse for self-treachery. Nature would brand such demonstration as a rebellion against her instincts, and would vindictively repay it afterwards by the thunderbolt of self-contempt smiting suddenly in secret. Take the matter as you find it; ask no questions; utter no remonstrances: it is your best wisdom. You expected bread, and you have got a stone; break your teeth on it, and don't shriek because the nerves are martyrized: do not doubt that your mental stomach—if you have such a thing—is strong as an ostrich's—the stone will digest. You held out your hand for an egg, and fate put into it a scorpion. Show no consternation: close your fingers firmly upon the fight; let it sting through your palm. Never mind: in time, after your hand and arm have swelled and quivered long with torture, the squeezed scorpion will die, and you will have learned the great lesson how to endure without a sob. (1974, 128)

The flood of affect that courses through this passage is more fervent than in Jane Eyre's speech. It recalls the more impassioned passages of Alice James' *Diary;* one hears the resentment at the freedom of the male voice to speak its desires, the shame of self-exposure that Nightingale articulated, features that identify this enraged third-person voice as a woman's. The metaphors of negative nurturance accuse the mother of deprivation; the lesson of martyrdom and silence accuses the patriarchal culture of oppression. If the voice vents its rage in an imperious staccato syntax, it also commands the female reader and the writer, both here temporarily merged into the second person, to endure without a sob.

Significantly, the admonition to endure without a sob, spoken in passionate irony by the narrative voice, is spoken in all seriousness by a maternal figure within the plot:

> "Rose, don't be too forward to talk," here interrupted Mrs. Yorke, in her usual kill-joy fashion; "nor Jessy either; it becomes all children, especially girls, to be silent in the presence of their elders."
>
> "Why have we tongues, then?" asked Jessy, pertly; while Rose only looked at her mother with an expression that seemed to say, she should take that maxim in, and think it over at her leisure. (172)

That maxim is precisely at the core of Brontë's fictional conflict, as she explores and tries to explode the patriarchal restrictions on the woman's tongue here transmitted by a "kill-joy" mother. Significantly, in *Shirley* both heroines fall ill precisely because they cannot "endure without a sob." Indeed, not only the heroines but also the hero succumbs to a mysterious illness, a ubiquitous trope in *Shirley* that is used to indicate not only the psychosomatic effects of repression on the characters, but a more extensive causal relation between repression and social disorder.

There are two plots in *Shirley:* a romance plot and a political plot. Both converge in making demands on a hero who becomes the antagonist of both. Caroline Helstone in the romance plot and the disaffected weavers in the political plot are shown to be subject to the callous indifference of the new phallic-capitalist hero Robert Moore and his cohort of fellow mercantilists. Caroline, rejected by Moore for materialist reasons—she is too poor to do him good in his obsession with rebuilding his family estate—and unable to articulate her anger, falls ill; the weavers, about to be supplanted by more efficient machines and refused recognition of their legitimate grievance, give voice to a resentment that turns into a violent action. Although Brontë's text recognizes the heroine's feelings of thwarted desire, her rage remains unacknowledged; repressed by both character and narrative voice, that rage is displaced into the political plot, where it is voiced by the disaffected workers. Only occasionally does rage break through directly in the narrative voice, as in the above passage, where it reveals a disruptive demand for women's speech.[26]

Shirley is Brontë's most explicitly feminist and political novel; it is also the most diffuse and disjointed one. Its narrative voice swings ambivalently between polarities we have discerned in Nightingale's text as well: between a conventional romanticism and its ironic subversion, between a pragmatic political discourse of equal rights and a more suspect appeal to the delights of mastery and submission, between a desire for dependence and a longing for autonomy. The plot is also riven by contradiction, veering between the sketchily conceived political plot of labor unrest and the romance plot that ambivalently heroizes the dominant master Moore. This division between the political and the romantic also suggests a conventionally gendered difference in narration, the former concerned with the public realm of

rivalrous male power and the production of goods, the latter exploring the private province of women's desire. As other critics have also
remarked, Brontë's uneven and fragmentary handling of the political
plot makes it seem more an unsuccessful projection of the primary
romance plot onto the historical stage than a developed political scenario in its own right.[27]

Within the romance plot, the narrative point of view is again split
between the two heroines: Caroline Helstone, the virtuous and intel-
ligent but docile and silent Victorian daughter, and her wealthy and
feisty friend Shirley Keeldar, whose economic independence allows
her a social freedom of speech unavailable to Caroline. Abandoned by
her mother and reared by her misogynist uncle, Caroline has been
trained to be silent, and thus suffers the familiar Brontëan torment of
suppressed passion. In contrast, Shirley, who literally appropriates
masculine authority by renaming herself Captain Keeldar, occupies a
more privileged position, even demanding only half jokingly that she
be addressed as a young lord. Under the protection of the masculine
name and the social place it signifies, Shirley argues with the elders
about female authority, brazenly defies her uncle in the matter of
marriage, and imagines acting out a heroism beyond the confines of
her estate.

If Brontë embodies a gendered active/passive dichotomy in the
two heroines through their split relation to free speech, she again splits
the conflict by representing that division within Shirley herself. Like
the typical Brontë heroine, Shirley confesses her taste for submission
to a more powerful figure: "it is glorious to look up" (104). To satisfy
that desire, Brontë introduces a late entry into the narrative, an almost
literal deus ex machina, Louis Moore, Robert's long lost brother and
Shirley's true but hitherto secret object of desire. A sensitive tutor
rather than a ruthless businessman, Louis is brought in as a male
supplement to relieve the rivalrous tension between the two women.
Once Louis enters, each heroine has a proper mate; nothing of desire
or rage remains. While he seems at first a more palatable hero, more
vulnerable in his poverty, more sympathetic, indeed, more woman-
like, very quickly, in spite of his poverty and lack of social power, Louis
becomes a familiar Brontëan figure of male dominance, the Teacher to
whom Shirley as student humbly bows, to whom she relinquishes the
power of the voice.

Indeed, in the final chapters of *Shirley,* the narrative voice itself gets humble, shifting from Brontë's third-person voice to the first-person notebooks of Louis Moore, and thus yielding narrative authority to the male voice. It is as if the narrative voice, having repressed its desire to speak as a male subject with all the assumed mastery of that position, is finally gratified, revealing a major source of the text's symptomatic fragmentations. On the one hand, Brontë plays with and indulges in role reversals that unveil sexual difference as a kind of social masquerade, so that both male and female characters can be powerfully masculine or submissively feminine; on the other, she represents sexual desire as essentially dependent upon the heroine's submissive relation to a powerful male figure. Recurrently making her heroines bondswomen to romance, Brontë repeatedly undercuts her criticism of women's social oppression. Earlier in the novel, when Shirley, the figure who is invested with the power of the voice, uses it, it is Caroline, not her male auditors, who tells her: "Shirley, you chatter so, I can't fasten you: be still" (20). By the end of the novel, Brontë has not only inhibited Shirley's political speech, but has turned it into romantic chatter. If the novel begins with the question of the legitimacy of women's discursive authority, Brontë's implicit answer ultimately defeats the third-person female voice of *Shirley.*

VILLETTE, BRONTË'S LAST novel, returns to these issues but avoids the pitfalls of *Shirley* by containing its conflict in the first-person female narrative voice of Lucy Snowe, a voice that emphatically does not chatter. Quite the contrary, Lucy withholds information, displaces her own desires onto other characters, even directly lies to both the reader and characters within the text, and generally evades her conventional narrative task of disclosure while seducing the reader into the interstices of allusion and innuendo. Lucy employs various strategies of dissemblance that bear an affinity to the strategies of the hysteric. She continually displaces herself as the subject of her story, switching narrative tracks a number of times to the stories of other characters— Paulina, Miss Marchmont, Ginevra—who are all represented as potential splits of the female subject of narrative action. Lucy hides her actions by narrative omissions of important details and her motivations by shifting at key moments of expected revelation to the more indirect modes of allegory and allusion, requiring the reader's interpretation to fill in the gaps. She promotes confusion by manipulating the ambiguities and duplicities of language itself, using terms that function like Freudian switchwords to suggest alternative paths of meaning.

Yet by these devices, Lucy also suggests the overdetermined nature of her desire and the difficulties of representing it through the conventions of Victorian narrative. Indeed, by alluding at various points to the problematics of women's writing and self-exposure, Lucy becomes a stand-in for the author behind the text, the narrative voice confusing the issues of authorship and inhibition confronting Brontë as a writer with the cultural limitations imposed on Lucy. Thus, both Brontë and Lucy hide in the shadows of a duplicitous discourse in order to exercise its power without revealing their own. At the same time, as in hysterical narrative, their very silences often result in a tortured syntax that itself divulges secrets they would withhold.[28] Within the context of my discussion, I want to focus on one untold secret: Lucy's passionate rage and its effects on her narrative voice.

Like *Shirley*, *Villette* is concerned with the silencing of the woman's voice; unlike *Jane Eyre*, it gives vent only indirectly to rage at being silenced, and then, lays blame on the woman's body. Take, for example, a key moment when Lucy wants to indulge her secret passion for Dr. John by an exchange of letters which, in displacing the corporeal presence of the voice, allows her to feel less inhibited in her expression. Brontë constructs Lucy's internal conflict as an allegorical dialogue with Reason, described as a cold and venomous stepmother: "Talk for you is good discipline," Reason tells her:

> "You converse imperfectly. While you speak there can be no oblivion of inferiority."
> "But," I again broke in, "where the bodily presence is weak and the speech contemptible, surely there cannot be error in making written language the medium of better utterance than faltering lips can achieve?" (1979, 306)

The passage introduces a difference between speech and writing that is essential to any interrogation of sexual difference, the difference the presence of the body makes in the articulation of the female subject. Although at this point in the novel, Lucy is refused the approval of Reason for desiring to disguise her weak "bodily presence" and its unwelcome revelations by writing rather than speaking, the question is not mute and recurs several times in the course of the novel. It is given another turn when Lucy undergoes an oral examination by "the professors" on the basis of their having seen an essay of hers. Confronted with their presence and their questions, she can only answer, "Je n'en sais rien" (493). As Brontë writes through Lucy, "Though answers to the questions surged up fast, my mind filling like a rising well, ideas were there, but not words. I either *could* not, or *would* not speak—I am not sure which: partly, I think my nerves had got wrong, and partly my humour was crossed" (493).

Recalling Alice James' intellectual constrictions, here Brontë's text makes clear the link between rage and the hysterical inhibition of the voice, especially as the passage continues:

> I wish I could have spoken with calm and dignity, or I wish my sense had sufficed to make me hold my tongue; that traitor tongue tripped, faltered. Beholding the judges cast . . . a hard look of triumph, and hearing the distressed tremor of my own voice, out I burst in a fit of choking tears. The emotion was far more of anger than grief; had I been a man and strong, I could have challenged that pair on the spot. (494)

In Brontë's text, the female voice is itself an ambivalent object, at once devalued as weak when tied to the limitations of its origin in the female body—the faltering lips—and made inarticulate by a rage that fractures language; but once projected into the disembodied voice of writing, and thus anonymous, that voice is empowered and empowering. Writing in this context becomes a phallic mask for the woman's voice; the disembodied voice of representation allows Brontë to lay claim to an equality that the female body as situated in a phallocentric order disallows. Without being physically subject to the gaze, one can "oubliez les professeurs" and speak through the disguise of language. That this remains a performance, however, with all the ambivalence implicit in speaking only through an other, remains a central insight of *Villette.*

Perhaps the most revealing passage that allows us to see the need for the mask as well as what it hides is Lucy's impassioned digression on the actress Vashti, in some sense that most potent but invisible presence in the novel. A foil to the fleshly Cleopatra, which the novel proffers as an image of the repulsive female body, Vashti is represented as transcending the limits of that body by the force of her articulated rage. Of course, as an actress, Vashti is performing a rage dissociated from her own existential being; indeed, the play she performs makes her passions the result of "evil forces" that inhabit her, "devils which cried sore and rent the tenement they haunted, but still refused to be exorcized" (339). Yet Brontë makes clear that the power of Vashti comes from her mastery of the passions she articulates rather than her being captured by them.

Indeed, while women's rage is conventionally allowed social expression by being contained as and in theatrical spectacle, in Brontë's representation of that spectacle, the actual body falls away, revealing the phenomenal power of rage to explode all limits. While we as readers are not given a direct description of Vashti's performance, we are given its reflection in Lucy's response, for once, without disguise. Lucy's articulated identification with Vashti allows her to break out of the mode of suppression and evasion that has characterized her own voice and actions. In a moment of extraordinary liberation and revelation, Lucy breaks open her carapace and with it the romance of Victorian fiction:

> I thought it was only a woman, though an unique woman, who moved in might and grace before this multitude. By-and-by I recognized my mistake. Behold! I found upon her something neither of woman nor of man: in each of her eyes sat a devil. These evil forces bore her through the tragedy, kept up her feeble strength—for she was but a frail creature; and as the action rose . . . how wildly they shook her with their passions of the pit! They wrote HELL on her straight, haughty brow. They turned her voice to the note of torment. They writhed her regal face to a demoniac mask. Hate and Murder and Madness incarnate she stood.
>
> It was a marvelous sight: a mighty revelation.
> It was a spectacle low, horrible, immoral. (339)

In Vashti as spectacle is exposed the rage that *Jane Eyre* keeps locked in the attic in the figure of Bertha. Moreover, unlike the masochistic hysteric, Vashti does not embrace her pain but attacks it; her rage is not turned inward but transgressively directed against the other. "To her, what hurts becomes immediately embodied; she looks on it as a thing that can be attacked, worried down, torn in shreds. . . . Before calamity she is a tigress; she rends her woes, shivers them in convulsed abhorrence. . . . Wicked perhaps she is, but also she is strong; and her strength has conquered Beauty, has overcome Grace, and bound both at her side, captives peerlessly fair, and docile as fair" (340). Paying tribute to a female figure freed by the license of poetic discourse from the corporeal limitations of both femininity and the body that represents it, *Villette* puts on stage a mighty paean to hatred, murder, and madness, whose meaning only Lucy consciously recognizes and approves, her own rhetoric liberated by this identification with rage. In contrast, Dr. John, the handsome hero of conventional romance and the keeper of the bourgeois flame, is made instinctively uncomfortable by Vashti. When Lucy asks his opinion, "He judged her as a woman, not an artist: it was a branding judgment" (342).

The appearance of Vashti in Lucy's narrative is a turning point in a novel that repeatedly turns from one narrative line to another. This turn, however, allows Lucy, and Brontë's narrative, to turn away from Dr. John, to bury his letter and the conventional romance plot it signifies. Thus, after Vashti's passions are released, a fire breaks out in the theater—one recalls Dora's dream-rescue by her father from her burning house—an event that brings back the Victorian angel in the house as the proper heroine of the Victorian domestic plot and compels Lucy to move into a new story. Thus, Lucy buries the letters of Dr. John. With that burial, M. Paul, until this point an emphatically little albeit comically ferocious figure, suddenly assumes the primary male place in a new plot of fraternal rather than romantic union. Or at least that is ostensibly what Lucy wants from him.

Yet if Brontë's narrative seemingly dispenses with romance, sexuality, and the problematic body, the turns are too quick and too many in this final section of the novel. Mme. Beck, Lucy's ambivalent model of female independence, whose faults have heretofore been indulged by Lucy, is abruptly and arbitrarily unmasked as a hateful rival, the bad mother as well as evil sister, Lucy's primary antagonist and the object of her rage. Dreamlike antagonists to Lucy's desire suddenly multiply: Mme. Walravens, Père Silas, and even the ghostly nun seem more dream visions than characters on the same plane as Lucy. The line between fantasy and reality becomes increasingly tenuous for the reader as Brontë through Lucy reaches for a new vision and a new destiny for the Victorian heroine.

The climax of this quest for a new vision is Lucy's fantasmatic midnight tour of the park, in which a drugged, cloaked, and seemingly disembodied Lucy floats around overhearing and overseeing the figures in her story. Interestingly, the only friendly figure in this dream space, the only one to recognize Lucy as Lucy in spite of her cloak, is the bookseller, who, telling her she "is not well placed" in her situation, secures Lucy a better place at the main event. Like a dream conversation, his diction resonates with alternative meanings that apply even more to Brontë as writer than to Lucy; neither can be "well placed" at the main event without the friendly bookseller, who disseminates the woman's voice as writing.

In Lucy's case, however, it is ultimately M. Paul who gives her a better place, by setting her up in her own school and thereby allowing her to live out her independence from the old school, Mme. Beck's school. Yet Brontë's old conflict still remains: if Paul is meant to be a brother spirit, another version of Hirsch's "the man who understands," he nevertheless also is the familiar dominant teacher-figure of Brontë's romances. This double view of the male hero, as fraternal and paternal, as equal and as superior, again returns us to Brontë's problematic configuration of desire as requiring two scenes: one of equality and one of dominance and submission. The narrative ultimately evades this dilemma by a sudden turn—Paul's ambiguous disappearance and presumed death, and Lucy's withdrawal from the social contest and the marriage plot which conventionally resolved it.

Although this ending, which allows Lucy to have her own place while not giving up the fantasy of romantic union in some beyond, is an advance over the contrived romantic ending of *Shirley*, it is not a resolution. Brontë permits Lucy her autonomy only by retaining the suspect trope of tragic thwarted passion, of an incomplete story, a story suspended rather than concluded. Indeed, if the final chapter is entitled "Finis," the narrative voice ironically refuses to put final closure to romantic desire. Instead, symptomatically marking this refusal by giving us a series of torturous sentence fragments that promote verbal ambiguity, by shifting back and forth from the past to a present tense that preserves a hovering stasis, the narrative voice projects a fissuring of meaning that resists closure or climax.[29] Moreover, the very page is fissured, as the syntax leaves large white spaces on the page that also presumably "let sunny imaginations hope" (596), spaces that also call the reader to imagine an unrepresented ending projected into the future. This is truly an hysterical strategy, for both reader and heroine remain locked in a state of ambivalent suspense, in that border territory that characterizes hysterical conflict: "Peace, be still! Oh! a thousand weepers, praying in agony on waiting shores, listened for that voice, but it was not uttered—not uttered till, when the hush came, some could not feel it: till, when the sun returned, his light was night to some!" (596).

Yet if *Villette* ends with fragments of a case of hysteria, it is also a powerful narrative exploration of various facets of hysterical subjectivity to the very end.[30] Indeed, *Villette* is Brontë's most complex and mature work precisely because rather than projecting the confusions of its utterance into a third-person voice, Brontë contains it within the voice of a discrete hysterical character, who reveals through the duplicities of her narration the problematics of the woman's speaking voice. This strategy makes *Villette* one of the great modern novels of the nineteenth century and precursor to such first-person modern tales of self-conscious self-revelation and repression as Ford Madox Ford's *The Good Soldier*. What becomes increasingly clear is that first-person narration is an effective way to contain and yet represent those splits in the voice of the subject that come to characterize modernist fiction, splits that are intricately bound up with gender ambivalence.

Chapter Four

Medusa's Voice

Male Hysteria in *The Bostonians*

A voice, a human voice is what we want.
—Olive Chancellor, in *The Bostonians*

IN HIS ARTICLE "Medusa's Head: Male Hysteria under Political Pressure," Neil Hertz discusses what he calls "a recurrent turn of mind: the representation of what would seem to be a political threat as if it were a sexual threat" (1983, 27). Hertz introduces his discussion with reference to a dramatic scene of Freud's in which Freud simulates the terror of the little boy discovering that his mother has no penis, and then adds, "In later life grown men may experience a similar panic, perhaps when the cry goes up that throne and altar are in danger" (27). *The Bostonians* is Henry James' representation of that panic, both sexual and political. Such panic is not confined within the borders of the tale, however, for like his conservative hero Basil Ransom, James' narrator also evinces alarm at the feminist challenge to male privilege, an alarm especially provoked by the figure of the feminist orator.

The tradition of oratory, classically a male tradition, had been revived on the nineteenth-century American political scene, in great part through the expansive rhetoric of Jacksonian discourse—optimistic, hyperbolic, and incredibly egoistic in its taking of the measure of the world by the self. Not surprisingly, the appropriation of that ego by a woman speaking with a female voice of political rights and equality was experienced as a particularly radical gesture. It is no accident that in the histories of the American feminist movement, the item always mentioned first to illustrate its revolutionary impact is the appearance of the woman speaker before a mixed audience.[1] The 1867 New York Constitutional Convention rejected suffrage as an innovation "so revolutionary and sweeping, so openly at war with a distribution of duties and functions between the sexes as venerable and pervading as government itself, and involving transformations so radical in social and domestic life" that it demanded vigilant defeat.[2] Moreover, as I suggested in chapter 1, in speaking from the platform—the height of immodesty—and calling for women's political rights, the woman orator not only appropriated a male political province, but in her very self-exhibition challenged the sexual pieties of her audience.

The Bostonians is an exemplary representation of that double-barreled challenge; it is exemplary also in its representation of narrative ambivalence, manifesting in its symptomatic discourse an anxiety about the boundaries of desire and identification that it cannot speak directly.[3] Alfred Habegger's (1990) observations on the narrator of *The Bostonians* provide strong support for a reading of James' hysterical voice. Not only does James' narrator speak out far more often in *The Bostonians* than in James' other narratives, but "the contradiction between [the narrator's] calm overview and his brittle, nervous, punctuated sneers" (189) as well as the narrator's frequent use of parentheses that "function as intrusive markers of another voice speaking through an already intrusive first person narrator" (182–83)—all indicate an essential splitting of the voice of the text. As Habegger succinctly points out, the contradictions and inconsistencies of the narrator "warn us that in some way the authorial identity is gravely at risk" (189). That risk, I argue, is provoked by authorial ambivalence about feminism and the figure of the speaking woman.

The textual ambivalence of *The Bostonians* is externally reflected in the critical debate it has elicited about James' representation of the women's movement. Sara de Saussure Davis (1978), for example, argues that James was extremely well informed about the feminist issues of the period; on the other hand, Habegger (1990) demonstrates with equal fervor that the novel is full of historical inaccuracies.[4] Critics also have been at odds in their judgment of James' feminist sympathies, some seeing in the sexist male protagonist a critique of masculine ruthlessness and a vindication of feminism (Habegger 1990, 26),

others judging the hero as inevitably but sensitively bringing the heroine into a heterosexuality far more preferable than her feminist
relationships (Brodhead 1986, 153). What these contrasting positions
again suggest is an equivocal narrative voice that implicates the reader
as well as the author in its ambivalent point of view.

James described *The Bostonians* as "an episode connected with the
so called 'woman's movement' " (italics mine), a subject that profoundly engaged him by 1883, when he wrote these words to his
publisher. Having returned to America in 1881 to settle his late father's
estate, James had taken up temporary residence with his sister Alice in
Boston while she recovered from a severe hysterical attack. Thus, he
observed at close quarters both the political controversy over wom-
en's suffrage that dominated the Boston social scene of the 1880s and,
through Alice's friendship with Katherine Loring, the evolving patterns of female intimacy in American culture, "those friendships between women that are so common in New England" and which apparently fascinated him.[5] Inspired by his observations to write "a very
American tale . . . characteristic of our social conditions," in a revealing early comment about his prospective novel, James described its
most salient features as "the situation of women, the decline of the
sentiment of sex, the agitation on their behalf" (*Notebooks* 1947, 46).
The bracketing of "the decline in the sentiment of sex" by feminist
"agitation" and "the situation of women" syntactically conveys precisely the unspoken nature of James' concern, for his very sentence
structure envisions a kind of impending doom of aphanisis, a loss of
desire, of the sentiment of sex itself.

The ostensible plot concerns the struggle between two blatantly
antithetical figures—Olive Chancellor, a New England feminist tormented by her inability to speak in public, and her Southern cousin,
the conservative masculinist Basil Ransom, an aspiring political writer
—for the love and possession of Verena Tarrant, a young ingenue
gifted with a politically seductive speaking voice. Significantly, Verena
assumes no agency for her speech; rather, she is a vessel, a medium
inspired by her father's laying on of hands to speak a text that passes
through her in a voice that captivates her audience. Yet if James
constitutes her entrance into the novel as an object rather than a
subject of speech, he accords her voice a fetishistic power that everyone
desires. Marveling at Verena's voice—"What a power"[6]—Olive would
appropriate it for the public cause of women's rights to which she is

passionately committed; Basil, described as "a representative of his sex" (4), desires it for his private pleasure. James represents their conflict as the ultimate civil war, the battle between male chauvinist and female avenger for the power of the voice with all its accrued cultural privileges.

Yet while their clash of difference to determine cultural authority is the novel's primary structuring trope, at the same time James refuses the victory to either side. North and South, freedom and slavery, speech and writing, the tongue and the touch, public and private— the novel repeatedly sets up these cultural oppositions, binds them to the difference between masculine and feminine, and then provocatively flirts with their collapse. In its oscillating movement, *The Bostonians* would seem to support the precocious vision of Margaret Fuller that while "male and female represented two sides of a great radical dualism . . . in fact they are perpetually passing into one another. Fluid hardens into solid, solid rushes to fluid, there is no wholly masculine man, no purely feminine woman."[7] Similarly, James' text both institutes a radically dualistic structure and insistently shows the boundaries of difference to be permeable.

What is most notable in this regard, however, is that at those moments when difference does seem to collapse, the narrative flow is suddenly disrupted by a digression, an eruption of rage, a bizarrely inappropriate commentary. Listen for a moment to the sound of this passage in which Basil reveals his desire "to save" his sex, and when asked by Verena, "To save it from what?" replies:

> From the most damnable feminization! I am so far from thinking, as you set forth the other night, that there is not enough woman in our general life, that it has long been pressed home to me that there is a great deal too much. The whole generation is womanized; the masculine tone is passing out of the world; it's a feminine, a nervous, hysterical, chattering, canting age, an age of hollow phrases and false delicacy and exaggerated solicitudes and coddled sensibilities, which if we don't soon look out, will usher in the reign of mediocrity of the feeblest and flattest and the most pretentious that has ever been. The masculine character, the ability to dare and endure, to know and yet not fear reality, to look the world in the face and take it for what it is—a very queer and partly very base mixture—that is what I want to preserve, or rather as I may say, to recover; and I must tell you that I don't the least care what becomes of you ladies while I make the attempt! (318)

The exclamation points, the syntax of accumulation and release, the breathless, pauseless sentences that amass signifiers of rage—this is a frenzied, hysterical utterance not inappropriate in a character who is so avowedly disgusted by feminism as Basil Ransom. Yet James' narrator tells us that "the poor fellow delivered himself of these narrow notions with low, soft earnestness . . . that it was articulated in (a) calm, severe way, in which no allowance was to be made for hyperbole" (318). This disjunction between the textual effect of Ransom's voice and the narrative commentary on it, a commentary that seems without irony, marks the narrator's ambivalent investment in his hero.

In "The Relation of the Poet to Daydreaming," Freud had remarked of romantic fantasies: "They all have a hero who is the center of interest, for whom the author tries to win our sympathy by every possible means, and whom he places under the protection of a special providence" (1908, *SE* 9:50); this hero represents "His Majesty the Ego, the hero of all daydreams and all novels" (51). Ransom is surprisingly close to that figure in *The Bostonians*. As the principal deictic center of the novel and one whose utterances often echo those of Henry James Sr., Ransom is set apart from the more consistently ridiculed characters, his elitist pronouncements rendered with more sympathy than irony.[8] Like Freud with Herr K., James seems to think Ransom extremely prepossessing, for only Olive Chancellor actively dislikes him, and that dislike is depicted as hysterical, a consequence of her fear of men and her rivalrous desire to possess Verena. Thus, although at various points in the novel James' narrator intervenes to dissociate his opinions from Ransom's, as when he alludes to the brutal impulses underlying Ransom's male code of chivalry and his sadistically toned relation to women, those very interventions indicate a textual confusion between Ransom and the narrator, and by implication, between Ransom and James.

The most blatant coincidence between Ransom and the narrator is their use of ridicule. Just as Ransom in the novel is made to laugh whenever he is confronted with a feminist challenge to his masculinist assumptions, so the narrator ridicules and satirizes the feminists, primarily by representing female authority as absurd or self-serving. It is perhaps significant that the figure subject to the greatest ridicule, Miss Birdseye, the pathetically ineffectual feminist of the transcendentalist generation, is also the figure who elicits the only other blatantly hysterical outburst in the text, uttered by the narrator himself rather than by his ambivalently depicted surrogate. In fact, the portrait of Miss Birdseye, who resembled Elizabeth Peabody in certain habits of being, is drawn with so much overt ridicule that after reading the manuscript, William James cautioned his brother about causing her public embarrassment.[9]

The narrator first deprecates Miss Birdseye by constructing an allusive analogy between her and her "common residence":

> Number 756 was the common residence of several persons among whom there prevailed much vagueness of boundary. . . . Many of them went about with satchels and reticules, for which they were always looking for places of deposit. What completed the character of this interior was Miss Birdseye's own apartment, in which her guests presently made their way, and where they were joined by various other members of the good lady's circle. Indeed, it completed Miss Birdseye herself, if anything could be said to render that office to this essentially formless old woman, who had no more outline than a bundle of hay. But the barrenness of her long, loose, empty parlor (it was shaped exactly like Miss Chancellor's) told that she had never had any needs but moral needs. (27–28)

The house with its vague boundaries, the satchels and reticules that cannot find their proper place, the "long, loose, empty parlor, shaped exactly like Miss Chancellor's"—this description figures a disordered body, sexless and barren. It is followed by an interpolation comparable in its rage only to Basil Ransom's outburst. Having remarked on her belonging to the Short Skirts League, in a disparaging comparison that familiarly analogizes feminism to sexual exhibitionism, the narrator suddenly erupts venomously:

> This did not prevent her being a confused, entangled, inconsequent, discursive old woman whose charity began at home and ended nowhere, whose credulity kept pace with it, and who knew less about her fellow-creatures, if possible, after fifty years of humanitary zeal, than on the day she had gone into the field to testify against the iniquity of most arrangements. (26)

Why this surprising narrative intrusion of rage? Described as totally lacking in knowledge of the real, Miss Birdseye seems a representation of transcendental excess:[10] she opens her house to everyone, gives succor indiscriminately to Negroes and refugees—and James fumes, as in this shrill and at times incoherent passage that begins, significantly, with a reference to her ineffectual talk,

> She talked continually, in a voice of which the spring seemed broken, like that of an over-worked bell-wire; and when Miss Chancellor explained that she had brought Mr. Ransom because he was so anxious to meet Mrs. Farrinder, she gave the young man a delicate, dirty, democratic little hand, looking at him kindly, as she could not help doing, but without the smallest discrimination as against others who might not have the good fortune (which involved, possibly, an injustice) to be present on such an interesting occasion. (26)

The narrator's irritation with her impotent talk is joined to an insidious little trio of signifiers—delicate, dirty, democratic—to give us James' moral sensibility at its crudest. A precursor to the xenophobia of such modernist writers as Eliot and Pound, who seemed especially to fear contamination by the immigrant hordes, it marks again the novel's concern with boundaries, with a violation that comes from being too "open" and identified as feminine. Through such images as the short skirt and the delicate, dirty, democratic hand, James transforms a political threat into a physical and sexual one in the kind of hysterical slippage that pervades the narrative voice.

While the text is saturated with images of fetishized hands—the hands of the feminists are "cold and limp"; their judgment is "like a soft hand"—the primary fetish object of the novel is not the hand but the voice. Each of the characters is in some essential way defined by a relation to the speaking voice, a relation that also marks their sexual positionality as phallic or castrated. Mrs. Tarrant, Verena's mother, descended from a line of public speakers, is humiliated by her husband's inability to speak, and although he has proved his "eloquence of the hand," her family "had never set much store on manual activity; they believed in the influence of the lips" (70). The speech of the unctuous journalist Matthew Pardon is replete with sentences "imperfectly formed" and punctuated by such effete exclamations such as "Goodness gracious" and "Mercy on us" (116). Drawing a broad picture of the effeminacy of Pardon, James conjures up conventionally stereotypical features attributed to the male hysteric through the markers of speech:

He talked very quickly and softly, with words, and even sentences, imperfectly formed; there was a certain amiable flatness in his tone, and he abounded in exclamations—"Goodness gracious!" and "Mercy on us!"—not much in use among the sex whose profanity is apt to be coarse. He had small fair features, remarkably neat, and pretty eyes, and a moustache that he caressed. . . . His friends knew that in spite of his delicacy and his prattle he was what they called a live man. (116)

Like Ransom, who characterizes the age as "too talkative"—"talk" being an emptying out of the power of speech—James constructs the novel as full of chatter, of women's talk. Mrs. Luna, her name evoking the symbolic link between femaleness and lunacy, is represented as "a woman of many words," guilty of a verbal incontinence that is in stark contrast to the controlled and balanced speech of Basil, who "could hold his tongue" and not be "drawn into an undue expenditure of speech" (182). Interestingly, in an age described as "too talkative" by Carlyle, Ransom's favorite writer, and by Ransom himself, holding one's tongue becomes a masculine attribute. Olive's voice recurrently performs a breathlessness that the text subtly caricatures: "I can't talk to those people, I can't" (34); "I want to give myself up to others; I want to know everything that lies beneath and out of sight, don't you know? I want to enter into lives of women who are lonely, who are piteous. I want to be near them to help them. I want to do something—oh, I should so like to speak!" (34–35).

Marking potency or its lack through the voice of his characters, James implicitly criticizes the increasing flatulence of American discourse and explicitly associates it with a feminization of culture. At the same time, it seems clear that he is concerned with his own potency as a writer, a concern that might have been exacerbated by the fact that his own style could be characterized as feminine. If we recall that in hysteria what is repudiated is femininity, James' narrator reveals himself as increasingly hysterical in his shrill caricatures of female influence on cultural productions and especially on writing.

In this context it is not surprising that Basil, the writer—nominated even by his enemy Olive Chancellor as the "real man" and by the narrator as "the most important personage in my narrative" as well as "a representative of his sex" (4)—is brought in to do battle with this effete company. Ransom is described at his entrance in flagrantly phallic terms:

he was very long . . . and even looked a little hard and discourag-
ing, like a column of figures . . . a head to be seen above the level of
a crowd on some judicial bench or political platform. . . . His fore-
head was high and broad, and his thick black hair perfectly straight
and glossy, and *without any division,* rolled back from it in a leonine
manner. (4)

Yet after presenting this accumulation of unmistakably masculine signifiers, so that Ransom—grim and hard—is an image of the Law, the
One "without any division," James remarks that "if we are readers
who like a complete image, who read with the senses as well as with
the reason" (5)—and senses and reason are gender-coded—then we
are entreated not to forget the feminine components of this phallic
being, which James locates in his speaking voice. Ransom "prolonged
his consonants and swallowed his vowels, . . . he was *guilty* of elisions
and interpolations which were equally unexpected, and . . . his discourse was pervaded by something sultry and vast, something almost
African in its rich, basking tone, something that suggested the teeming expanse of the cotton field" (5). Playing on the same geopsy-
chological dichotomy that Tocqueville first introduced and Henry
Adams exploits in the *Education*—the warm, earthly, sensual South
represents the "feminine" principle, while the North, judicial and
cold, is "masculine"—James shows the integrity of his judicial erect-
ness riven by a suspiciously sensual voice that is identified with the
feminine.

Indeed, Ransom's Southern drawl reveals itself guilty through the
voice, its guilt signified by the interpolations and elisions that are the
textual signs of repression. What is it guilty of? James remarks on
the "African" warmth that has infused the voice of the South, insin-
uating a guilty intercourse, a hidden history that has resulted in the
"curious feminine softness with which Southern gentlemen enunci-
ate" (5). In this passage of allusive innuendo James suggests a history
of sexual transgression in the "teeming cotton fields," a miscegenation embodied in the voice. Although James had originally thought to
make his hero a Westerner, by writing him as a Southerner he could
use the drawl—the voice of an already violated South—not only to
identify an erotic component of the male hero that makes Ransom
attractively vulnerable, but to allude to a past history of sexual violation in both North and South that will continue to resonate in the

text. Through a number of such sexual allusions to a past transgression, the narrator points to an inaccessible scene of origin for each character's relation to the voice and makes it suspect.

Olive Chancellor, the feminist reformer who is Ransom's antagonist is given the most neurotic relation to speech.[11] Articulate in private but voiceless in public, Olive is described as morbidly obsessed with the unhappiness of women on the one hand, and enraged at men on the other:

> The voice of their silent suffering was always in her ears, the ocean of tears that they had shed from the beginning of time seemed to pour through her own eyes. . . . Uncounted millions had lived only to be tortured, to be crucified. . . . The just revolution . . . must triumph, it must sweep everything before it; it must exact from the other, the brutal, bloodstained, ravening race, the last particle of expiation. (35–36)

In this double identification with both victim and avenger, Olive desires to be a martyr-savior in the tradition of Christ, one who, like Nightingale's Cassandra, would save through the power of her complaint: "I want to give myself up to others; I want to know everything that lies beneath and out of sight. . . . I want to enter into the lives of women who are lonely, who are piteous. I want to be near to them— to help them" (34).

Not only does this sentimentalizing diction undermine Olive's relation to feminism, but her morbid longing for martyrdom, for an erotic merger with women victims, her flirtation with the romance of suffering, and above all, her inability to give voice to her desire, which defines her as a hysteric, are made the suspect source of feminist agitation more generally: "It proved nothing of any importance with regard to Miss Chancellor, to say that she was morbid; any sufficient account of her would lie very much to the rear of that. Why was she morbid, and why was her morbidness typical? Ransom might have exulted if he had gone back far enough to explain that mystery" (11). In a sense the novel is James' representation of that mystery, constructed through the indirect modes of insinuation and allusion. Why might Ransom have exulted? And how far back would Ransom have to go to explain that mystery? How far back does James go? In this remark, the narrator implies a psychohistory to Olive's morbidity, which he coyly supplies through the textual innuendo of an erotically tendentious discourse.

James' image of morbidity is a woman crying, a recurrent figure in the text that is attached to each of the three central characters; the image connects each to a scene of suffering and a relation to the voice. It appears not only in Olive's obsessive vision of an ocean of women's tears to which she would give voice, but also in "the desire of Ransom's heart" to protect the South, figured as a violated woman, by holding his tongue. It most strikingly occurs in Verena's perception of Olive herself on their first meeting: "she looked as if she had been crying (Verena recognized that look quickly, she had seen it so much)" (73). What does this parenthesis signify? Where has she seen it so much? Again, while the text tells us nothing directly, it leads us to speculate on this parenthesis, indeed, within the context of the novel, leads us to imagine, as Olive has, a commonality of women's experience as victims of male abuse. And if Verena so quickly recognizes that look, it also insinuates a scene of a woman crying into her own family history, casting suspicion on her father as well.

James' narrator links Selah to the Oneida community of free love, "a community of long-haired men and short-haired women" (68) who have confused the forms of gender and have broken the laws of marriage and the family on which they depend, by giving the Father free access to all the women, by therefore symbolically instituting incest. Although Verena herself touts "free union," thus identifying with her father's beliefs, the narrator continually insinuates that Selah's sexual behavior has caused his wife suffering, that "the poor woman had a great deal, matrimonially, to put up with" (69). Past scenes of female suffering as a result of male sexual transgression are thus implied by the narrator as well as imagined by Olive. Dr. Prance, remarking that if Selah were a little more dry, it might be better for him, doesn't "want him to be laying his hands on any of her folk; it was all done with the hands, what wasn't done with the tongue" (42). The sycophantic Matthew Pardon, who has Selah's permission to "handle" his daughter, wants Verena "to 'shed' her father altogether; she didn't want him pawing round her that way before she began" (121).

Perhaps the most outrageously eroticized description of Tarrant is his relation to the newspaper offices and vestibules of hotels, the centers of worldly power to which he desires access. Although the passage satirizes Selah's avid desire for publicity,[12] his social pandering is made more repulsive by its erotic overtones:

> he . . . had a general sense that such places were national nerve-centres, and that the more one looked in, the more one was "on the spot." The *penetralia* of the daily press were, however, still more fascinating, and the fact that they were less accessible, that here he found barriers in his path, only added to the zest of forcing an entrance. . . . He was always trying to find out what was "going in"; he would have liked to go in himself, bodily, and failing in this, he hoped to get advertisements inserted gratis. (99)

Casting suspicion on the father through a familiar trope—"forcing an entrance"—which in the Dora case signified rape, James also introduces a level of suspicion into Verena's vocal transports that continues to function when Olive assumes Selah's role as the kindling agent of Verena's impassioned speech.[13] In short, through a rhetoric of sexual innuendo, Selah is depicted not only as a suspect father and husband, but also as an interloper who threatens the boundaries of family and class, if not of sexual positionality itself.

Olive wants the power of the voice to unveil the father's guilt and the daughter's suffering; Basil wants to keep the secret, to hold his tongue; James' narrator positions himself in between. As James tells us, Basil's "heart's desire" is "to be quiet about the Southern land, not to touch her with vulgar hands, to leave her alone with her sounds and her memories, not prating in the market-place either of her troubles or her hopes" (48). To be quiet and not to touch—these prohibitions on the voice and the hand are also narrative prohibitions on revealing the sadomasochistic ground of sexual relations that James' narrator both uncovers and covers over in a recurrent and classically hysterical act of playing secrets through textual allusion.

Perhaps the most revealing secret moment of the text, however, concerns a different aspect of Basil's desire: he is aroused not by Verena's image—"her exhibition is not exciting" (57)—but by her voice. At the same time, Basil is particularly disturbed that her voice is elicited by her father's touch; he resents "Tarrant's grotesque manipulations . . . as much as if he himself had felt their touch. . . . They made him nervous, they made him angry" (57). In this surprising textual revelation of Basil's nervousness, James points to Basil's own hysterical identification with Verena, his own fear of being handled, being manipulated, being objectified by the carpetbagging Selah, his apprehension intensified by being a conquered and violated Southerner. Although the narrator quickly covers over this moment of anxiety, Basil as listener remains vulnerable to and therefore defensively derisive of Verena's speech, which, as we are given it, is certainly seductive: Verena "pours into the ears of those who still hold out, who stiffen their necks and repeat hard, empty formulas, which are as dry as a broken gourd," a feminist vision of enlightened self-interest, of relations based on "generosity, tenderness, sympathy where there is now only brute force and sordid rivalry" (255).

In this gendered contrast of social relations, Verena's speech again accuses the father/man and idealizes the mother/woman of a past scene. Obliterating the words as signifiers, Basil persistently hears only the music of her voice, the erotics of the voice, the voice of the nightingale. She can sing but not signify; she can give pleasure but not "mean." Thinking that "she speechifies as a bird sings" (216), "I don't listen to your ideas," he tells her. "I listen to your voice" (316). Like Philomela, Verena also will be silenced in the presence of Basil, will be abducted by him in a climax that resonates both etymologically and psychologically as a rape, and which turns her, too, literally into a crying woman. For it is this prophetic image of a woman crying that reappears at the novel's conclusion, an image of Verena's future as a wife that reiterates the image from the past: "It is to be feared that with the union, so far from brilliant into which she was about to enter, these [tears] were not the last she was destined to shed" (426).

At the same time that the text suggests that marriage itself as a patriarchal institution produces tears, as if Nature herself demands only this brutal patriarchal plot, requires the ransom of heterosexuality to maintain human culture, the narrative moves inexorably to take Verena from the woman and give her to the man by reversing in a series of confrontations the place and proprietorship of the speaking voice. Thus, the narrator portrays the inexplicable effects of Basil's voice on Verena even though she would reject what it says: "Strange I call the nature of her reflections, for they softly battled with each other as she listened . . . to his deep, sweet, distinct voice, expressing monstrous opinions with exotic cadences and mild, familiar laughs" (313).

The voice of Nature itself enters the text as Basil's agent when Olive wanders around Washington Square contemplating Verena's future:

> The trees and grass-plats had begun to bud and sprout, the fountains splashed in the sunshine, the children of the quarter, both the dingier types from the south side, who played games that required much chalking of the paved walks, and much sprawling and crouching there, under the feet of passers, and the little curled and feathered people who drove their hoops under the eyes of French nursemaids—all the infant population filled the vernal air with small sounds which had a crude, tender quality, like the leaves and the thin herbage. (300)

This representation of the sounds of the air—crude, tender—made by the infant population signifies a Nature that requires Verena's complicity in her abduction. And it is presented as a sharp contrast to the topography of the southern cape, the feminist enclave to which Olive takes Verena in an effort to elude Basil:

> The ripeness of summer lay upon the land, and yet there was nothing in the country Basil Ransom traversed that seemed susceptible of maturity; nothing but the apples in the little tough, dense orchards, which gave a suggestion of sour fruition here and there, and the tall, bright goldenrod at the bottom of the bare stone dykes. (329)

In the midst of this highly allusive suggestion of "sour fruition" and "bare stone dykes" at Marmion, Basil—finally authorized to be legitimate hero by having had a piece of *writing* accepted for publication—converts Verena's desire to his own. Although he tells her, "It's not to make you suffer. . . . I don't want to say anything that will hurt you," as she entreats him "to spare her," the text emphasizes his rhetoric of attack and conquer: "a quick sense of elation and success began to throb in his heart, for it told him . . . that she was afraid of him, that she had ceased to trust herself, that the way he had read her nature was the right way (she was tremendously open to attack, she was meant for love, she was meant for him)" (349). Basil's words of masculine attack and feminine suffering confirm Olive's earlier prophetic but impotent admonitions:

the words he had spoken to her . . . about her genuine vocation, as distinguished from the hollow and factitious ideal with which her family and her association with Olive Chancellor had saddled her— these words the most effective and penetrating he had uttered, had sunk into her soul and worked and fermented there. . . . The truth had changed sides; the radiant image began to look at her from Basil Ransom's expressive eyes: it was always passion, but now the object was other. (365)

From this point to the climax of the novel, Basil's actual abduction of Verena, his words are supported by the narrator's own violent discursive manipulations, which move the plot to its "natural" oedipal conclusion: Verena's voice will be made to "lubricate" her private life rather than "gush out at a fixed hour" (370–71). In a muddled sequence of internal contradictions, the narrative voice redefines her relation to Olive and feminism as "a desire to please others," her relation to Basil as "a push to please herself" (367); at the same time, it insists that this reconstitution of her desire is precisely not what her fate is to be. Rather, yielding her desire to Basil's, unable to resist the languor of objectification, Verena becomes Basil's possession, her recognition of this capitulation described as "a kind of shame" (392). Although there is one final attempt at rescue by Olive, who keeps Verena isolated until she can speak in a climactic moment of feminist oratory at the Music Hall, Basil ultimately wins what Olive has called their "war to the knife" (364) for Verena. In a concluding scene almost surreal in its representation of tensions and contradictions, and an increasingly libidinized diction, the howling and thumping of the mob waiting in the auditorium to hear Verena (but in the novel's wings)—that fearsome mob anxiously reproduced in countless fictional scenes of revolution—sound as a counterpoint to the offstage scene, "behind the scenes of the world" where the novel's climax is enacted. Verena shrieks for Olive as Basil wrenches her away "by muscular force" but is also glad to be taken. As Basil leads the weeping girl away, the narrator remarks in perhaps the most subversive ending to a heterosexual marriage plot a sentence worth repeating, "It is to be feared that with the union, so far from brilliant into which she was about to enter, these were not the last [tears] she was destined to shed" (426).

This final turn of the screw both returns the wandering heroine to the marriage plot and sustains the ubiquitous figure of the crying woman as a figure of closure. This closure is also undermined, however, for there is another final scene, one that we can only hear, since it takes place on stage while the reader is behind the scenes. At the same time that Verena is abducted into private service, Olive enters the public arena; she goes on stage in Verena's place, expecting to be hooted and insulted, "seeing fierce expiation in exposure to the mob" (425). James likens Olive to "a feminine firebrand of Paris revolutions, erect on a barricade, or even the sacrificial figure of Hypatia, whirled through the furious mob of Alexandria . . . offering herself to be trampled to death and torn to pieces" (425). Although this discourse points again to Olive's "morbid" desire for martyrdom, James does not gratify this desire in the text. At the climax of the novel, the crowd falls silent, leaving open the possibility of an alternative ending to the story of feminine desire, an open ending through which James' own hysterico-political ambivalence could be given play. Olive as a potential "feminine firebrand" becomes a potential virile feminist like Hertz's revolutionary woman on the barricades, and we are left wondering if Olive will be able to speak, if she can voice herself and the women she would rescue into the circle of privilege and power.

Finally, then, it is Olive who emerges as the figure of tragic and heroic loss, the real interest of the novel, the enigmatic subject to be explored. The character who will never marry, whose most passionate relations are with her own sex, Olive not only recalls Alice James but also ultimately figures James' own problematic desire. Like Freud with Dora, James had to identify with his subject to investigate the sources of her morbidity and constitute this subject in language.[14] Judging from the lability of his narrative voice, that identification led him to his own hysterical drama, constituted by a fantasy of violation that equates speaking with potency and silence with being raped or castrated.

Chapter Five

From Dream
to Night-Mère

The Poetics of Hysteria and Masochism
in *The Story of an African Farm*

The old is dying and the new cannot be born;
in this interregnum there arises
a great diversity of morbid symptoms.
—Antonio Gramsci, *Prison Notebooks*

IT SEEMS AN uncanny irony of literary history that Henry James' idea
for *The Bostonians* and his narrative exploration of the morbid and
hysterically muted Olive Chancellor was articulated in the same
year that an actual feminist named Olive—Olive Schreiner, a self-
acknowledged hysteric but reputedly a charismatic speaker—was being acclaimed in England for her first novel, *The Story of an African
Farm*.[1] Published in 1883 under the suggestive pseudonym Ralph
Iron,[2] Schreiner's novel has come down to us primarily because of the
scandalous voice of Lyndall, its androgynously named New Woman,[3]
who argues passionately as did Schreiner for women's political and
economic liberation. While Lyndall's rhetoric would continue to inform feminist politics and women's writing well into the twentieth
century, within the text, Lyndall dies young, totally thwarted in her
ambitions, her feminist voice silenced in the conventionally feminine
fictional triad of seduction, childbirth, and death. Certainly this plot

was not uncommon in women's fiction of the late nineteenth century, but its political implications in this avowedly feminist fiction has troubled many readers.[4]

Schreiner herself recorded a number of significant intersections between her life and the novel that illuminate its problematic politics.[5] Born in South Africa of a minister father whom she depicted as tender, sensitive, and childlike—the model for the naive Otto in *The Story of an African Farm*—and a mother she described as pragmatic, well-educated, and beautiful, but "cold and unloving," Olive Schreiner seems by her report to have valued her mother's strength as a hardy antidote to her father's dreaminess. It was her mother who confirmed her intellectual and literary precocity, praised her talents, and encouraged her ambition. That Schreiner gave her strongest character her mother's maiden name, Lyndall, suggests that Rebecca Schreiner remained a potent presence in her daughter's memory.

If Rebecca Lyndall was the psychic ground for her daughter's feminist voice, she seems also to have been a primary determinant of its hysterical subversion. Schreiner records her childhood hatred of her mother's tyrannous severity in describing the whippings Rebecca Schreiner meted out for even minor infractions of propriety. Such punishments as fifty blows with a small cane for disobediently loitering in the rain, or for exclaiming in Dutch, "Ach, how nice it is outside!" when the use of that language was forbidden within the Schreiner family—the Boers were seen as an ignorant and vulgar people—were indelibly inscribed in Schreiner's memory: " 'Ach' was Dutch and so I got my first great whipping. . . . I was taken up the little passage in the bedroom where I was born, and my clothes were raised and I was laid out on my mother's knees, and got about fifty strokes with a bunch of quince rods tied together" (quoted in Berkman 1989, 16). Left in what she called a state of "unutterable anger," unable to express or direct her rage against its true object, Schreiner describes getting under her bed and banging her head against the wall. While this performance of rage is not uncommon in childhood, it foreshadowed a habit of masochistic resolution that illuminates the more problematic aspects of Schreiner's life and fiction.[6]

The Story of an African Farm implicitly asks this question: What happens to a story if you take the typical features of the hero of the nineteenth-century bildungsroman—intelligence, ambition, a desire for action—and bestow them on a female character, and the features of the idealized Victorian heroine—a religious sensibility and a desire to submit self to other—and assign these to a male character? Exploiting this strategy of gender reversal, Schreiner splits these aspects of her own life story into two protagonists—the perceptive orphan Lyndall and her companion, the dreamy shepherd boy Waldo—and introduces them as children living on a Boer farm. Ambitious, articulate, and acutely resentful of her powerless and dependent situation, Lyndall identifies herself with Napoleon and anticipates doing heroic battle with the social order when she grows up; in contrast, her inarticulate companion Waldo is absorbed by religious desire and longs to submit himself to a deserving god. Neither Lyndall nor Waldo, however, is able to move the story forward, or even to approach their desires. If we define the subject of a narrative as the one whose desire drives the action, the split subject of this story projects a contradiction in desire that blocks the story's development in a mimesis of hysterical paralysis.

This initially simple splitting and reversal breaks down into further splits of both subject and story. Thus, for example, Lyndall is, like Brontë's Shirley, represented as a split figure. Given a power of intellect and voice far outstripping the other characters, she is insistently feminized by diminutives—her "little feet," "her little teeth." Taking not only Napoleon but also the portrait of a fashionable woman as an icon of identity, Lyndall is made to embody a gender-defined split between doing and seeming that she recurrently decries.

Schreiner's narrator comments on this problematic of narration: "It is not until the past has receded many steps that before the clearest eyes it falls into co-ordinate pictures. It is not till the 'I' we tell of has ceased to exist that it takes its place among other objective realities, and finds its true niche in the picture."[7] The "I" she is telling of, however, has not ceased to exist, has not become an object in the past. The contradictory desires and demands of childhood still torment the narrative consciousness. Just as the narrative voice describes Waldo's broken attempt to narrate within the novel as "a confused disordered story" (170), so the narrative voice itself is increasingly torn between tensions that it can neither control nor resolve: between action and stasis, between speaking and silence, between those culturally gendered polarities that constitute the tensions of hysterical discourse.

This tension is also a structural principle of the text, which is formally split into two sections. Part 1 presents a fairly conventional linear comic plot with a primarily omniscient narrative voice presenting a central action: the disruption of the network of familiar relations on the farm by an intruder, the comic con man Bonaparte Blenkins. A frontier-type teller of tall tales, Blenkins attempts to take over as a figure of paternal authority. Before he can complete his plot to marry Tant Sannie, the grotesque stepmother of Lyndall's cousin Em, to whom the farm legitimately belongs, and become master, he is hilariously unmasked as a lecherous villain, drenched in dirty brine-water by the outraged Tant Sannie, and exiled. Domestic harmony is thus restored. Yet there is a double rupture of the comic surface of part 1 that cannot be recuperated: the death of Waldo's father Otto, who (like Schreiner's own father) is a maternal figure of loss that haunts the narrative voice;[8] and the eruption of a gratuitous sadism, manifest most blatantly in Blenkins' bizarre beating of Waldo, a scene that uncannily recalls Freud's essay on masochism, "A Child Is Being Beaten" (1919, *SE* 17). Both events disturb the otherwise essentially comic fabrication of part 1; both impel the movement from illusion, as represented by Lyndall's heroic identification with Napoleon and her confident use of the first-person singular, to a disillusion articulated when Lyndall shifts to the first-person plural to voice her impotence: "we will not be children always; we shall have the power too, someday" (127), she says to Waldo, deferring her dream. Like Nightingale's use of the first-person plural to identify with the commonality of victimized women, Schreiner uses the "we" to mark a loss of individual agency and a compensatory identification with oppressed subjects.

Part 2 also opens with a "we" but it is a very different first-person plural, a privileged and neuter "we" used by a transcendent narrative voice narrating an allegory of human development that generalizes the particularities of the realist fiction it shadows. Although part 2 soon shifts back to the realist mode, to the farm three years later, it introduces new characters and different modes of narration that fracture both voice and plot. If in part 1 the farm is the bounded space of the action, in part 2 the farm is a narrative matrix to which actions occurring elsewhere are brought back in the form of letters, stories, and parables. The philosophical parable of the hunter told by a character called only "Waldo's stranger," the story of Lyndall's death narrated by her patient but persistent suitor Gregory Rose, and Waldo's letter to Lyndall telling his tale of recurrent victimization—all disperse the narrative voice into a multiplicitous subjectivity precariously held together by the unity of a maternally inflected place, the farm. Moreover, this fragmentation of the subject voice blurs the lines that constitute various differences not only between male and female, but also between human and animal, so that even the pet dog is given a point of view and the dumb chickens a wisdom.

It is precisely this hysterical structure of fragmentation, however, that is the most innovative feature of Schreiner's text. Through its reversals of gender and its manipulations of multiple internal genre, *The Story of an African Farm* went beyond the constraints of conventional linear narrative form and opened up new possibilities for representing the subject.[9] In this sense Schreiner's narrative voice is a precursor to present-day representations of a subject-in-process, representations privileging hysteria as a subversive mode of discourse that articulates a dis-ease with the cultural ordering of desire.[10] Yet it does not sustain its radical potential; rather, it illustrates the debilitating effects of hysteria that continue to situate it as a pathology. For in spite of the experimentation with splitting and reversal, with multiple genres and different voices, the novel about the New Woman ultimately takes refuge in an old story: Lyndall's quest for self-liberation ends in pregnancy and death; Waldo's quest for a figure of truth is so totally thwarted that at the end he longs only for an escape from consciousness and dies in a welcome submersion into sleep. The salutary hysterical tension of part 1 yields to a masochistic resolution in part 2 that privileges stasis, silence, and death.

In this context, Schreiner's patterns of narrative identification are suggestive. Lyndall, bearing the maiden name of Schreiner's "cold and unloving" mother, is given the power of the voice and speaks the feminist rhetoric of the historical, politically active Schreiner. Lyndall also speaks with the voice of the hysterical Schreiner, tormented by her often debilitating dread of heterosexual relations: Lyndall's remark to Waldo, "When I am with you I never know that I am a woman and you are a man" (210), reveals a desire to eradicate difference that recurs in Schreiner's own letters.[11] Although Lyndall's voice is thus doubly identified with Olive Schreiner's, it is the verbally inhibited and effectively sexless *male* protagonist Waldo to whom Schreiner

gives her most intimate and painful childhood experiences, the beat-
ings by her mother, the death of her father—experiences of misery
and loss that Schreiner called "unutterable" but to which her text
persistently returns in a masochistic compulsion to repeat.

Thus, for example, Waldo's climactic scene in part 1, the beating at
the hands of the sadistic Blenkins, is repeated in displaced form in part
2, when the emphatic Waldo narrates the beating to death of an ox,
the last straw in the burden of his experience driving him back to the
farm. In giving the masochistic passion to Waldo rather than Lyndall,
in clearly identifying him rather than Lyndall as the child being beaten
in the novel's fantasmatic subtext of suffering humanity, Schreiner
confirms Kaja Silverman's incisive claim that because the feminine
subject is normatively defined as masochistic, masochism per se is best
represented through a male subject:[12]

> The basic dilemma of female masochism is that a woman's position
> within the symbolic order is already so subordinated that the female
> masochist's wish can be realized only at the site of male subjectivity;
> for her passive desire to be represented, the female masochist makes
> herself into a homosexual man, who desires to be castrated, and
> thereby gains access to what Freud calls femininity. (1992, 62)

Masochism can be read not only as a desire to be castrated within an
oedipal economy but also as a desire to return to the preoedipal
fullness of a fantasmatic maternal body. Gilles Deleuze defines masochism as a desire for that "dual unity and the complete symbiosis
between child and mother" (1991, 58), a desire that Deleuze locates in
the fantasy of a cold and powerful preoedipal mother.[13] In Deleuze's
formulation, the masochist longs for death but defers that final gratification, obsessively returning to the moment of separation from the
oral mother, reenacting a repetition of loss in a masochistic *fort/da*
game that sustains desire. It is that preoedipal register of masochistic
desire that convincingly drives Waldo's story; unfortunately, it comes
to define Lyndall's as well. While Lyndall's story of feminist protest in
the name of self-liberation initially engages in a contestation with
Waldo's story of suffering, Waldo's desire increasingly exceeds the
boundaries of his character and comes to dominate the desire of the
narrative voice.[14]

One can already hear this desire in Lyndall's dialogue early in part 2 when Waldo, marveling at Lyndall's powers of speech, wonders why she will not use those powers to help change the condition of women, why she does not speak publicly rather than only to him. Although Lyndall interrupts him with the force of her indignation—"Speak . . . the difficulty is to keep silence" (195)—she follows this exclamation with a remark that effectively foretells her silencing as the voice of protest: "I will do nothing good for myself, nothing for the world, till someone wakes me. I am asleep, swathed, shut up in self; till I have been delivered I will deliver no one" (196). This metaphor of feminine repression recalls the repressive metaphorics of feminine passivity at the origin of romance narrative, most evidently in *The Romance of the Rose* and in its fairy tale complement, *The Sleeping Beauty*. It speaks a wish for external deliverance that may be appropriate to Waldo's religious yearnings, but should be anathema to Lyndall's—and Schreiner's—feminist project. While, as Ann Ardis rightly points out, the passage reveals "Lyndall's inability to believe in herself as a speaker, as someone whose words might have the power to bring about that longed-for future" (1990, 67), it reveals even more: the very word *deliver* functions here like a Freudian switchword, its multiple meanings taking us in contradictory directions. Shifting in meaning from a heroic trope of rescue to a domesticated metaphor of maternity, the word foreshadows Lyndall's doomed delivery of the sickly infant. If Lyndall herself remains the undelivered infant within the mother-infant dyad, in conflict over being herself delivered, she can become neither mother nor "virile" feminist, the two terms of female identity allowed in the text, but must continually negotiate between these two polarities.

It is when Lyndall actually becomes a mother that this hysterical negotiation is curtailed and her story is brought to a crisis. Already pregnant when she enters part 2, she has become herself the ambivalent embodiment of the mother-infant dyad as well as the seduced romantic heroine even as she continues to articulate a powerful social critique of those positions. When she agrees to elope with that shadowy gothic hero named only "Lyndall's stranger," an unrealized melodramatic figment of Schreiner's imagination, her words "take me away with you" (239)—words that are echoed in her cousin Em's dreamy folk song, "Blue Water" ("And take me away" [244])—signal a turn in the narrative trajectory: from a struggling feminist resistant to oedipal seduction, Lyndall becomes a tired, compliant girl-child seeking a nonsexual, maternal comfort. Even the stranger's "low and melodious" (235) voice—a recurrent trope of seductive power—becomes at this juncture maternal and sexless: "'Poor little thing . . . you are only a child.' She looked into his eyes as a little child might whom a long day's play had saddened. He lifted her gently up, and sat her on his knee. 'Poor little thing!' he said" (240).

Lyndall's subsequent confession confirms a narrative exhaustion that inevitably ends in silence:

> "I am so tired. . . . Why am I alone, so hard, so cold? I am so weary of myself. It is eating my soul to its core—self, self! I cannot bear this life! I cannot breathe! I cannot live! Will nothing free me from myself? . . . I want to love! I want something great and pure to lift me to itself! . . . I am so cold, so hard, so hard; will no one help me?" (241)

Her words "so cold, so hard," evoking Schreiner's references to her cold and unloving mother as well as her own pseudonym, Ralph Iron—a trope of identity uncannily similar to Alice James' "hard core" and Lucy Snowe's cold name—provoke a splitting of herself that mimes the novel's splitting of the subject into the first-person plural. Thus, before Lyndall leaves with her stranger, Schreiner again presents her engaged in a mirror dialogue, this time literally with her own image:

> "We are all alone, you and I," she whispered; "no one helps us, no one understands us; but we will help ourselves." The eyes looked back at her. There was a world of assurance in their still depths. So they had looked at her ever since she could remember when it was but a small child's face. . . . "We shall never be quite alone, you and I," she said; "we shall always be together, as we were when we were little. . . . Dear eyes! we will never be quite alone till they part us; till then." (242)

This symbiotic image recalls the "we" near the end of part 1—"we will not be children always" (127)—in which Lyndall and Waldo had become linguistically one subject. Here Schreiner shows Lyndall still captive to the mirror stage, having given up her claim to the first-person singular voice of the feminist hero. Thus, in spite of her astute feminist anatomy of the power politics of heterosexual romance, Lyndall disappears with her stranger into the bush, and when next we see her, through the narrative voice of Gregory Rose, she has become the dying mother of a dead infant.

In a passage that sentimentalizes the mother-infant relation as the ideal "we," as the literal first person that is plural, the text exploits the pathos of loss:

> "Its feet were so cold; I took them in my hand to make them warm, and my hand closed right over them they were so little." There was an uneven trembling in the voice. "It crept close to me; it wanted to drink, it wanted to be warm." She hardened herself—"I did not love it; its father was not my prince; I did not care for it but it was so little." (278)

The reference to the infant's "little" feet echoes the numerous references to Lyndall's own fetishized little feet and verbally identifies the infant as a cold reembodiment of a cold and hardened mother. Here, Lyndall's maternal rejection of the child not only ties her to Schreiner's own "cold and unloving mother," but also indicates the daughter's more general rejection of a maternal identity and of the infant as emblem of her desire. There is, however, a psychic cost to this rejection that the novel continually demonstrates. Indeed, the passage suggests that a double identification is being negotiated for both Lyndall and the reader—with the mother in a fantasy of loss and with the child in a fantasy of abandonment, the two I's of a divided consciousness. In this melancholy logic, death becomes for Lyndall an illusory rapprochement with the dead child, confirmed by a narrative voice that indulgently sentimentalizes, even eroticizes, suffering, that represents death as a route back to the mother-child dyad.

None of this do we know directly, for once Lyndall elopes she virtually disappears as a voice in the text. We learn of her destiny through a mediated discourse, her story told by Gregory Rose, the rejected suitor whom Lyndall had contemptuously identified as the "true woman." Ironically, he comes to represent the text's ideal "true woman"—the elusive good mother. Gregory selflessly tracks Lyndall into the bush, "only to see her, only to stand . . . where she has stood" (248), and when he finds her ill and abandoned, he literally metamorphoses from lover to nurse:

> Gregory sprang down into its red bed. It was a safe place and quiet. . . . The high red bank before him was covered by a network

of roots and fibres washed bare by the rains. Above his head rose the clear blue African sky; at his side were the saddle-bags full of woman's clothing.

"Am I, am I Gregory Nazianzen Rose?" he said.

It was all so strange, as the fantastic, changing shapes in a summer cloud. (270)

Dressed in women's clothes—clothes identified as similar to those of his own mother—the disguised Gregory Rose is reborn as a maternal figure of pure service and the narrator of the final part of Lyndall's story. In this final transference of the woman's voice from Lyndall to Gregory, from desiring to self-abnegating subject, from feminist daughter to transsexual mother, the voice of protest has been extinguished. Although Gregory displaces Lyndall as the female subject, his is not the feminist quest. On the contrary, as the religious allusion in his name suggests, his progress as a character—from foolishness and self-interest to quasi-religious self-abnegation, from eros to agape—sustains the familiar self-denying form of the feminine lure that maternity has come to signify.[15] At the end, only the masochistic Gregory and the self-sacrificing Em remain on the farm to perpetuate a *mise-en-abyme* of pain and loss.

IN TRACING THROUGH Lyndall a movement from hysterical desire to masochistic gratification in the narrative, I have been suggesting that *The Story of an African Farm* is torn between being a novel of feminist protest and a novel of masochistic surrender to a pervasive melancholia. Indeed, it is the narrative desire to recuperate a lost maternal object that undermines its political quest and perpetuates its masochistic desire. In a sense, an important function of all narrative is to recuperate lost objects, to reincarnate past experience by remembering the fragments of memory as discourse. As Freud noted in describing the structures of mourning and melancholia, however, the lost object is inevitably regarded with ambivalence, and in Schreiner's case, as she herself pointed out, excessively so.[16] In mourning, "the shadow of the lost object is cast on the ego; one part of the ego is set against the other so that reproaches belonging to an internalized loved object that has been lost are turned against the self as self-reproaches": "if the object love . . . takes refuge in narcissistic identification, while the object is abandoned, then hate is expanded upon this new substitute object, railing at it, abusing it, debasing it, making it suffer and deriving sadistic satisfaction from its suffering" (1917 [1915], *SE* 14:251).[17] Through this splitting of, and internal assault on, the ego, mourning turns into masochistic melancholia.

This dynamic ultimately controls the plot sequence of Schreiner's text which, haunted by its own ambivalence, obsessively returns to scenes of loss. While the loss of a father and of a child are literally represented as events in the plot, the loss of a mother is not (although in a sense Lyndall's death enacts such a loss). An absence in the plot, maternal loss has nevertheless already occurred three times before the story begins—Em, Waldo, and Lyndall have no mothers. I want to suggest that this already-lost maternal object is nevertheless the most persistent presence in the novel, dispersed into, and reembodied in, the very language of the narrative voice.

Language as a symbolic embodiment of absence is, of course, a central tenet of psychoanalysis. As Lacan remarked, "language is not immaterial. It is a subtle body, but body it is. Words are trapped in all the corporeal images which captivate the subject" (1977, 87). Kristeva (1993) also suggests that to the extent that language produces sensations and affect through words, phonemes, rhythm, to the extent that metaphor and metonymy join thought to sense, part to part, a sentence, a book can function as the embodiment of a lost object.[18] Especially for the hysteric, who confuses the body and language, words, even phonemes, the equivalent of part-objects, can function as embodied memorials of the lost object.

In this sense, language itself can be the ambivalent object of hysterical conflict, duplicitous, untrustworthy, the voice hiding secret meanings in its very syllables. For example, in "The Watch," itself an ambiguous signifier that opens the novel, Lyndall having awakened in the night calls for a response but gets no answer: "she opened her eyes and looked at the moonlight that was bathing her. 'Em' she called to the sleeper in the other bed, but received no answer" (36). Literally voicing the maternal letter, "Em," Lyndall's unanswered call initiates the text's underlying call to a nonresponsive, silent maternal object. In what follows I want to read more closely the melancholic voice of the text at key moments for the ways it ambivalently embodies and attempts to recuperate the lost maternal object as language.

The opening chapter, "Shadows of Child Life," is split into three short fragments, "The Watch," "The Sacrifice," and "The Confession." "The Watch" introduces an eerie African night scene, in which a "full African moon" "pours" its white light onto a desiccated landscape, transfiguring and animating the objects it illuminates:

> The full African moon poured down its light from the blue sky into the wide, lonely plain. The dry, sandy earth, with its coating of stunted karroo bushes a few inches high, the low hills that skirted the plain, the milkbushes with their long fingerlike leaves, all were touched by a weird and an almost oppressive beauty as they lay in the white light. (35)

These opening lines present at the very beginning a familiar childhood trope of the moon as a benevolent maternal presence looking over a landscape that has also been anthropomorphized by references to body parts: the "fingerlike leaves" of the milkbushes; the "thorny arms" of the prickly pears (35). This sensual evocation is augmented by the auditory register of the language: the succession of stressed long open vowels ("wide, lonely plain"; "they lay in the white light") and the haunting croon audible in the oo's ("moon, blue, karroo") phonetically sustain the illusion of lullaby, of sleep.

Both the succession of open vowels and the uninterrupted line of the visual plain, however, is ruptured by a protrusion—the "kopje":

> In one spot only was the solemn monotony of the plain broken. Near the centre a small solitary "kopje" rose. Alone it lay there, a heap of *round iron-stones* piled one upon another, as over some giant's grave. Here and there a few tufts of grass or small succulent plants had sprung up among its stones, and on the very summit a clump of prickly pears lifted their thorny arms, and reflected, as from mirrors, the moonlight on their broad fleshy leaves. (35, italics mine)

The "kopje"—a word always in quotes to signify its alien importation—not only breaks the *mono*-tony/monotone of the plain, but as the first Boer word in the English language text, it also disrupts the book's linguistic homogeneity. Moreover, the reference to this heap of "iron-stones" protruding from the flat earth injects Schreiner's pseudonym, her cover-up, as a material signifier into the text; it thus asks us to read Schreiner's language for its allusive disclosures. Like the "kopje" that seems to mark and cover over a "giant's grave," the narrative voice will also paradoxically reveal itself as a burial site of the lost mother, a figure split into an idealized, benevolent, and dispersed dream-presence and a disgustingly corporeal nightmare mother.

From this opening night scene Schreiner shifts to several sleeping characters within the homestead, the first being the grossly fat Tant Sannie, dreaming of "sheep's trotters she had eaten. . . . She dreamed that one stuck fast in her throat, and she rolled her huge form from side to side, and snorted horribly" (36). A terrifying figure even in sleep, she is described as at risk from her own voracious orality. The trotter stuck in her throat is an image of retaliation that also recalls Charcot's taxonomy of hysteria and the *globus hystericus,* the lump rising to the throat, as well as Nightingale's representation of being force-fed in *Cassandra.* In contrast, the sensitive Waldo huddles awake in another house, as if himself devoured by darkness: "Nothing was visible, not even the outline of one worm-eaten rafter, nor of the deal table, on which lay the Bible from which his father had read before they went to bed. No one could tell where the tool box was, and where the fireplace. There was something very impressive to the child in the complete darkness" (36). This obliteration of perceptual boundaries between self and object produces in Waldo not only terror but also a titillation conveyed by the narrative voice through an incremental repetition of negation—"nothing, not even, nor, no one."[19]

That repetition of negation becomes the dominant trope of "The Watch," the very title shifting its meaning from the protective surveillance of the opening scene to the relentless temporality of a timepiece that Waldo hears: "It never waited; it went on inexorably; and every time it ticked a man died! He raised himself. . . . How many times had it ticked since he came to lie down? . . . 'dying, dying, dying!' said the watch" (37). In a paradoxical textual moment, the narrative voice initiates a pattern of triadic repetition that will recur in the text—a repetition that ritually functions in childhood to signify temporal extension and thus to prevent time from passing,[20] but used here to mime the clockwork insistence of time passing ("dying, dying, dying"). Through the recurrent use of such triadic repetition, the text persistently reveals its desire to stop the temporal movement that is narrative, and repeatedly links this desire with a maternally inflected image of death. Thus, for example, late in the novel, Lyndall's cousin Em sings "an old childish song she had often heard her mother sing long ago"; its refrain is "Dead, Dead, Dead!" (250). Significantly, the final triad of the novel, Waldo's "muttering, muttering, muttering" before he falls into his final sleep—a triad that homonymically puns on the German word *Mutter* (mother)—ironically injects a maternal signifier into the representation of Waldo's last sleep.

In contrast to the opening night scenes, the fiercely sunlit Africa that opens "The Sacrifice" is meant to delineate sharply a multitudinous object world, its light ostensibly stripping away the illusion associated with a maternal fantasm and instead disclosing the real. Yet here again, the narrative voice anthropomorphizes and subjectivizes the object world so that it becomes a projection of some imaginary interiority:

> The farm by daylight was not as the farm by moonlight. The plain was a weary flat of loose red sand sparsely covered by dry karroo bushes, that cracked beneath the tread like tinder, and showed the red earth everywhere. Here and there a mill-bush lifted its pale-colored rods, and in every direction the ants and beetles ran about in the blazing sand. . . . The two sunflowers that stood before the door, outstared by the sun, drooped their brazen faces to the sand; and the little cicada-like insects cried aloud among the stones of the "kopje." (38)

Unlike the earlier gaze of "the loving moonlight . . . that hid defects" (36), here the sun's gaze is represented as brutal and pitiless, as intrusively phallic: "At midday, the sun's rays were poured down vertically; the earth throbbed before the eye" (39). The trope of the sun tyrannizing the "sunflowers" through the power of the gaze suggests a familiar oedipal economy in which the "flowers" bearing the sun's name but gendered feminine through the word *brazen* are inevitably "outstared" by the more potent and victorious sun, the harsh antithesis of the beneficent moon.

Although this imagery would suggest a conventional oedipal exchange between father and daughter, sun and sunflower, the pervasive textual dynamic of gender reversal and masochistic desire creates gender ambiguities. Certainly in the hysterical masochism of the text, it is Waldo, the son, and not the brazen daughter who bows down to the sun's rays in order to receive and become one with the Word.

> The fierce sun poured down its heat upon his head and upon his altar. . . . Then at last he raised himself. . . . There were the clumps of silent ewes and his altar—that was all. He looked up—nothing

broke the intense stillness of the blue overhead. He looked round in astonishment, then he bowed again, and this time longer than before. When he raised himself the second time all was unaltered. (40)

Here the phonemic echoes—*altar, all, unaltered*—invoke the sound of the "All" that Waldo calls upon, an All which, in spite of Waldo's address to a Father-god, seems beyond mother or father, an All by its very meaning without boundaries.

The opening narrative movement from the one to the many, from illusion to disillusion, foreshadows the oedipal advent of a number of strangers who act as figures of disruption. Yet part 1 is essentially anti-oedipal, its comedy subversive of paternal authority. Bonaparte Blenkins' most striking feature, his pendulous red nose, mocks the paternal phallus just as his name parodies the heroic Napoleon. These ironies are also sustained formally in the chapter titles: Blenkins arrives in a chapter entitled "I was a stranger and ye took me in," a pun on his taking them in that is echoed when Tant Sannie cries twice in response to Blenkins' request for shelter, "I'm not a child . . . and I wasn't born yesterday. No, by the Lord, no! You can't take me in! My mother didn't wean me on Monday" (51).

In referring to weaning, the infant's oral experience of separation and disillusion, Tant Sannie gives comic voice to the text's more somber concerns. Her phrase "take me in" (recall Lyndall's "take me out of this world") shifts and divides to signify not only shelter, but also deception and incorporation. If, as Tant Sannie boasts, "the man isn't born that can take me in," the narrative confirms that boast: one can choke on trying to take in this mother, as Blenkins discovers. In part 1, it is Tant Sannie, the powerful, comic, but untrustworthy maternal surrogate, who has the last word, who indeed becomes emblematic of a fundamental duplicity embodied in the text's ironies and puns. Through such linguistic shifters the narrative voice sadistically performs the duplicity of language and the inaccessibility of a truth associated with the maternal body that is in great part Schreiner's subject.

The subversive ironies of voice also extend to the descriptions of the characters' voices. The fuller and more appealing the voice of a character is, the more potentially treacherous that character is. Blenkins has a "full sonorous voice" (58); Waldo's stranger and Lyndall's stranger also have notably musical and seductive voices. Insofar as the semiotic materiality of the voice is associated with maternal presence, these representations of the voice cast suspicion on that presence. Even the sweet voice that sings rather than speaks, Em's voice nostalgically singing "Blue Water" and reconstituting an idealized mother and child, is under the shadow of betrayal in its naive evocation of an impossible desire.

In this context of equivocations and suspicion, the cry is the only signifier one can trust: the cry is at one with its signified; the cry is real; pain is real. In part 1 it is the sadist Bonaparte who wants to elicit the cry from Waldo: "'You don't seem to have found your tongue yet. Forgotten how to cry?' said Bonaparte, patting him on the cheek" (125). Bonaparte functions not only as a sadistic father, but as the displacement of a desire for truth that is itself sadistic, a probing hunger to know that Melanie Klein theorizes as the epistemophilic drive.[21] For Klein, that drive is first attached to an imaginary maternal body that contains all objects of desire, all truth, and is subsequently displaced to the entire field of knowledge. Thus, after having savagely beaten Waldo, Bonaparte returns the next day and "carefully scratched open the cuts with the nail of his forefinger, examining with much interest his last night's work" (126). This image of sadistic disclosure resurfaces as a trope of the allegorical voice in part 2: "If you will take the trouble to scratch the surface anywhere, you will see under the skin a sentient being writhing in impotent anguish" (149). Divided between a sentimental tear-jerking of the reader that indulges a masochistic release and the cold irony that asserts a sadistic mastery, Schreiner's narrative voice repeatedly scratches the surface of loss and then indulges the pain that results.

This sadomasochistic structure is linked to maternal loss in the philosophical allegory "Times and Seasons" that opens part 2, a narrative of the seven stages of the human subject that shadows the particular events of part 1 and remarkably foreshadows Freud's narrative of psychosexual development. Moving from the mother-child dyad through infantile curiosity about origins to the awakening of desire, it glaringly omits any reference to sexual difference or sexual desire. Closely identified with Waldo's story, the narrative voice is the asexual, or transsexual "we," terrified of the body and what it signifies:

> Now the pictures become continuous and connected . . . the line
> of a life is traced. . . . One day we sit there and look up at the blue
> sky, and down at our fat little knees; and suddenly it strikes us, Who
> are we? This I, what is it? We try to look in upon ourself, and ourself
> beats back upon oneself. Then we get up in great fear and run home
> as hard as we can. We can't tell anyone what frightened us. We never
> quite lose that feeling of *self* again. (139)

By the time "we" reaches the seventh stage of "Times and Seasons,"
having passed through the indeterminacy of meaning in language and
identity, the subject gives voice to a satanic despair recalling Carlyle's
"Everlasting No" and imaged in the familiar tropes of coldness associated with the cruelty of maternal absence. Desperate to recuperate
both the maternal figure and meaning through some transcendental
affirmation beyond the body, in a sudden turn, Schreiner constructs it
by a device of language: analogy.

> A gander drowns itself in our dam. We take it out, and open it on the
> bank, and kneel, looking at it. Above are the organs divided by
> delicate tissues; below are the intestines artistically curved in a spiral
> form, and each tier covered by a delicate network of blood vessels
> standing out red against the faint blue background. Each branch of
> the blood vessels is comprised of a trunk, bifurcating and rebifur-
> cating into the most delicate, hairlike threads, symmetrically ar-
> ranged. . . . This also we remark: of that same exact shape and
> outline is our thorn-tree seen against the sky in mid-winter; of that
> shape also is delicate metallic tracery between our rocks; in that
> exact path does our water flow when without a furrow we lead it
> from the dam; so shaped are the antlers of the horned beetle. How
> are these things related that such deep union should exist between
> them all? Is it chance? or, are they not all the fine branches of one
> trunk, whose sap flows through us all? (153)

Here are the accents of a romantic organicism that speaks Schreiner's
desire for the One;[22] here the narrative voice forges a vision of the
world as one body with which it can identify through analogy: "This
thing we call existence; is it not a something which has its roots far
down below in the dark, and its branches stretching out into the
immensity above, which we among the branches cannot see? Not a
chance jumble; a living thing, a One. The thought gives us intense
satisfaction, we cannot tell why?" (153).

This optimism of the voice is not sustained: for when this same metaphysical quest for meaning is articulated within the diegesis, it is Waldo's stranger, a "man who believes nothing, hopes nothing, fears nothing, feels nothing" (159), who gives voice to the novel's final vision. Speaking in the same cadences as the privileged allegorical voice, "an uncommonly melodious voice" (156), a "voice, rich with a sweetness that never showed itself in the clouded eyes, for sweetness will linger on in the voice long after it has died out in the eyes" (158), Waldo's stranger predicts Waldo's failed quest through the parable of the hunter: "He saw there was no use in striving, he would never hold Truth, never see her, never find her. So he lay down, for he was very tired. He went to sleep for ever. He put himself to sleep. Sleep is very tranquil. You are not lonely when you are asleep, neither do your hands ache, nor your heart" (167).

Similarly, at the end of the novel, in the chapter entitled "Waldo goes out to sit in the sunshine," the omniscient narrative voice welcomes death as a reunion with an idealized maternal body that is not cold:

> there comes a pause, a blank in your life . . .when the old hope is dead, when the old desire is crushed, the Divine compensation of Nature is made manifest. She shows herself to you. So near she draws you, that the blood seems to flow from her to you, through a still uncut cord: you feel the throb of her life. . . . Then, oh with a beneficent tenderness, Nature enfolds you. . . . Well to die then, for if you live, so surely as the years come, so surely will passions arise. They will creep back, one by one, into the bosom that has cast them forth. . . . Desire, ambition and the fierce agonizing flood of love for the living—they will spring again. Then Nature will draw down her veil; with all your longing you shall not be able to raise one corner. . . . Well to die then! (298–99)

In this passage, the dominant trope is parturition, a fantasy of primal separation that reactively gives rise to the most regressive moment of the novel, the novel's conclusion.[23]

As Waldo "muttering, muttering, muttering," falls asleep, the narrative voice denies parturition and restores him to a Mother Nature, bathetically redeemed in the image of a mother-hen.

> The mother-hen was at work still among the stones, but the chickens had climbed about him, and were perching on him. One stood

upon his shoulder and rubbed its little head softly against his black curls; another tried to balance itself on the very edge of the old felt hat. One tiny fellow stood upon his hand, and tried to crow; another had nestled itself down comfortable on the old coat-sleeve, and gone to sleep there. (300)

The novel's final words ("the chickens were wiser"), which indirectly inform us that Waldo is dead, ironically communicate this knowledge not by direct articulation but through the nonhuman apperception of the chickens—who will in turn get eaten, as the text repeatedly has indicated. At the end, there is no meaningful human voice that can sustain desire. Schreiner's novel thus joins in what Nancy Miller rightly terms the "dysphoric" ending of so many nineteenth-century novels by women or about women as speaking subjects.[24]

In short, split between hysteria and masochism, the narrative voice presents a double register of conflict about female identity and difference: through Lyndall's dialogues the voice of the text engages in a vigorous social critique of the cultural constitution of sexual difference and its promotion of feminine masochism; through Waldo, it yields to it, revealing an anxiety about separation from an untrustworthy maternal presence that paralyzes the narrative subject. Masochism resolves that conflict in both registers, the subject escaping sexual difference, separation, and loss by becoming an object of and for an other, and in particular, of and for the Mother, now figured as Death. At the level of narrative voice, hysterical aphasia has turned into masochistic silence, a trajectory that ultimately stifled Schreiner's own political and creative voice.

Chapter Six

The Great Refusal

The Voyage Out

If we follow the successive readings of the Dora case, do we not
end up saying that the essence of hysteria is played out in the
traumatic relation to the maternal, a relation affecting every
demand that, addressed to a man, derives from that relation
its absolute character and that, for that reason too,
takes the form of a violent refusal?
—Monique David-Ménard, *Hysteria from Freud to Lacan*

IN THE LAST chapter of *Mill on the Floss*—"The Final Rescue"—
Maggie is swept away in a flood; later she is found drowned, locked in
the arms of her brother. Eliot's narrator notes the "wondrous happiness that is one with Pain" (1966, 456) in this ending, a happiness
inscribed in both the novel's epigraph and last line, its literal first and
last words, "In their death they were not divided." This representation of absolute closure, which literally turns the inscription of temporality that is narrative into a timeless epitaph, could have easily served
as a final commentary on Schreiner's narrative as well. In both texts,
closure is represented through a fantasmatic reunion signifying that
the gendered division of the subject is finally healed in some beyond.

The ending of *The Voyage Out*, Woolf's first and not entirely suc-
cessful novel, bears a strong resemblance to these two fictions of
impossible desire: at its conclusion its young heroine, Rachel Vinrace,
having become engaged to be married, dies of an illness unexpectedly
contracted on a voyage into the interior of a mythical South America.
Instead of approaching through death some utopian reunion with the

other, Rachel withdraws into a state of narcissistic singularity, in a submission to her body that at the same time frees her from the cultural legislation of its destiny. If Maggie is rescued from alienation by a final fraternal embrace, and Waldo is rescued from disillusion by an imagined dissolution through sleep into some maternally inflected Nature, Rachel is rescued from division by her own solitary oneness, rescued by her body from the marriage plot and its demands for the couple, for coupling.

In *The Voyage Out*, marriage and the woman's body do not converge, but continue a familiar tension between the demands of the symbolic order and the body that resists them that I have been tracing in narrative voice, a tension that generates hysterical representation and its unresolved questions. What is a man? What is a woman? Can there be a (sexual) relation between men and women that allows both to know and speak their desire? And most important for these texts, how does the body figure, and figure in, sexual identity and desire? While these familiar questions continue to resonate in Woolf's later fiction, *The Voyage Out* is her first fictional elaboration of the problematics of gender identity and its relation to the speaking subject. Just as in hysteria the subject poses the question of sexual difference to an other who knows, so Rachel will force a number of seemingly knowing figures—Richard and Clarissa Dalloway, Helen Ambrose, Terence Hewet—to answer the question, "What does, and even more, what should, a woman want?"

The novel poses this question most overtly through the dialogues of its central heterosexual couple, Terence the writer and Rachel the musician, their respective relation to words and music signifying a gendered split that a new kind of marriage might heal. Woolf would later conclude *A Room of One's Own* with this androgynous ideal in the image of a man and a woman coming together and taking a cab, but *The Voyage Out* is far less sanguine about the possibilities of togetherness. If heterosexual marriage, in bringing together two sexual bodies that figure sexual difference, implies an acceptance of the terms of difference, the terms are effectively refused by Rachel. Rachel's voyage out into the world becomes first an extended interrogation of woman's place in the marriage plot, and then, after discovering her options, a kind of reverse birth—a voyage in, down, and ultimately out of the world.

The plot in brief in this: Helen and Ridley Ambrose (a Victorian couple loosely based on Woolf's own parents) embark for a vacation in South America on the *Euphrosyne,* a ship captained by their widower brother-in-law, Willoughby Vinrace. Although Helen, introduced as grieving at her separation from her children, seems at first to be the protagonist whose desire the narrative voice will track, once they board the ship, the story shifts its deictic center to her young niece, Rachel. At Willoughby's request, Rachel becomes Helen's ward, to be educated in what it means to be a woman in late Victorian culture. Once they arrive at the British resort that is their destination, the father as figure of eros and authority virtually drops out of the plot, and Helen and Rachel become sisterly intimates in a narrative that interrogates love, marriage, and the nature of sexual identity. Meeting a number of characters at a nearby hotel, a virtual microcosm of middle-class English society, Rachel becomes romantically involved with a young writer, Terence Hewet; Helen strikes up an ambiguous friendship with his friend St. John Hirst. A dance and two group expeditions into the interior of the country comprise the major events that promote this coupling, but after the second expedition, Rachel, having just become affianced to Terence, abruptly succumbs to a fever and unexpectedly dies. The novel ends with various characters attempting to incorporate this death into some larger world design.

Critics have explained the abrupt curtailment of the feminine bildungsroman as a narrative realization of the heroine's anxious evasion of sexual initiation.[1] From this perspective, Rachel is virtually acting out an extreme form of conversion hysteria, her sexual anxiety converted into a killing fever that removes her from the oedipal drama and allows her to retain her virginal integrity. Certainly the novel is replete with references to the dangers of feminine sexuality: literary allusions to "Bluebeard," to "The Rape of Lucrece," to *Comus,* repeatedly summon the brutal oedipal father into the text as a figure threatening an innocent woman with assault and even rape.[2] Resurfacings of the word *brute* linguistically circulate a thematics of male brute force throughout this text, as when Terence reads lines from *Comus* that specifically call up "father Brute."[3] Woolf's text moves beyond the heroine's ambivalent relation to the paterfamilias to her more ambiguous attachment to a maternal figure, a figure ultimately more seductive than the father, but one who threatens identity itself.

The Dora case provides an illuminating analogy to Rachel's situation. Like Dora, Rachel is initially captivated by both paternal and maternal figures who present her with various potential shapes of desire and identity. As the novel progresses, the figure of the father virtually disappears and, like Dora, Rachel is increasingly drawn to a maternal figure as the origin of an eroticism beyond the law. Even the male suitor, Terence, is represented as more womanly than masculine, heroinized to make him palatable to the narrative voice as well as to Rachel. Like Dora who, caught between her feelings for Frau and Herr K., refuses the man and longs for the woman, Rachel ultimately enacts a hysterical refusal of difference, revealing a narrative desire for the same that can neither be articulated nor satisfied.[4]

What is most striking in Woolf's first novel is that this hysterical enactment is represented more through the semiotic resonances of the voice—its disjunctions, its evocations of affect through rhythm and sounds—than through the plot. If the order of language rests on maternal loss, on a gap covered over by symbolization as representation, Woolf's text seeks to represent the gap itself, the unsayable, privileging it as the site of a maternally inflected presence where meaning resides.[5] Thus, Rachel is made an inarticulate heroine who distrusts speech: "It appeared that nobody ever said a thing they meant or even talked of a feeling they felt, but that was what music was for. Reality dwelling in what one saw and felt, but did not talk about" (37). "Everyone I most honor is silent" (*Letters* 4, 422), Woolf writes, and like her figure of the writer, Terence, who wants to write a novel of silence, herself attempts to convey a nonspoken reality by promoting what Patricia Ondek Laurence (1991) calls "unconscious body-mind states," through a narrative voice that constitutes meaning in the resonant space between, or beyond, words.[6] Thus, in contrast to Schreiner's feminist valorization of the active subject of speech, which makes Lyndall's death in childbirth a defeat, Woolf refuses to privilege the figure of the speaking woman, favoring instead, like Schreiner's Waldo, a truth beyond speech.

To this end, metaphor has a privileged place in Woolf's text, a place that becomes increasingly prominent in her later, more modernist works. Metaphor is a constant way of promoting the idea of an unspeakable original elsewhere. At the same time metaphor, materializing symbolic discourse by keeping sentience and sense in the idea, keeps the body in language and thus performs what Kristeva calls "a feat of transubstantiation."[7] Just as hysterical symptoms represent past events as a body language that restores "the original meaning of the words" (*Studies on Hysteria*, 1893–95, *SE* 2:181) so Woolf's narrative voice, foregrounding the dynamics of metaphor, moves to take language back to its fantasmatic origin as thing.

In this context, names themselves can function as metaphor, bringing past narratives to bear on the present. The names Helen, Rachel, and the *Euphrosyne* resonate in counterpoint to the action of the present story and extend its meaning, evoking *sub rosa* prior cultural inscriptions of women—Helen as the sexually desirable Greek woman abducted and raped, Rachel as the biblical mother weeping for her children, Euphrosyne as both Greek grace and Christian ascetic—classic figures of the feminine that shadow Rachel as a female protagonist.[8] Moreover, the very sounds and syllables in names can excite the imaginary, summoning the reader's projective associations into the text as part of its meaning. The "Hel" in Helen, the "terror" in Terence, even the "hearst" in Hirst, are not beyond the strategies of a narrative voice that would make the common reader complicit in reconfiguring a multivalent maternal presence both in and beyond the text. Indeed, in Woolf's quest for a truth beyond language, she not only encourages but at times requires the reader to fill in the gaps, to make sense as well as experience the sense of a voice that uncannily evokes meaning in the material resonances of its narration.

Woolf's labile voice sounds its instability from the very beginning: *The Voyage Out* seems at first to open like a typical Victorian novel, with a London street scene, but whereas the Victorian reader would expect a stable ground of exposition that would locate the time, place, and protagonists, this narrative voice gives the reader an ambiguous warning in the very first sentence that will continue to echo throughout the narrative:

> As the streets that lead from the Strand to the Embankment are very narrow, it is better not to walk down them arm-in-arm. If you persist, lawyers' clerks will have to make flying leaps into the mud; young lady typists will have to fidget behind you. In the streets of London where beauty goes unregarded, eccentricity must pay the penalty, and it is better not to be very tall, to wear a long blue cloak, or to beat the air with your left hand. (9)

Inscribing anxiety in the syntax itself, this sentence makes the reader, "you," the tentative subject of a prohibition about walking arm-in-arm, the very goal of domestic fiction's marriage plot. While the novel will ultimately obey that warning, it takes a long detour, playing out the possible variations on walking hand-in-hand, and its antithesis, walking single file. Thus, the very next paragraph introduces a Victorian couple who ignore the prohibition while "angry glances struck upon their backs" (9).

Moreover, if an initial exposition demands an introduction to the protagonists, here neither woman nor man, allegorized first as beauty and eccentricity, later as sorrow and thought, is named or contextualized. Repeatedly the narrative voice defers exposition, suspends the meaning of an action it describes, and thus creates an uneasy space of potential meaning evoked by the resonance of words without context that draws the reader into the space of interpretation. This disorientation is furthered by the narrative's apparent refusal to locate a stable point of focalization. At times the voice assumes a transcendent distance from the object; at times, it is in such proximity that the object cannot be seen. For example, in the opening chapter, a disembodied and transcendent voice suddenly shifts its point of focalization, from looking *at* the as-yet unnamed Mrs. Ambrose to looking *out from* her interiority:

> this lady looked neither up nor down; the only thing she had seen, since she stood there, was a circular iridescent patch slowly floating past with a straw in the middle of it. The straw and the patch swam again and again behind the tremulous medium of a great welling tear, and the tear rose and fell and dropped into the river. (10)

The reader, placed literally behind the eyes of "the lady," sees through her tear "a circular iridescent patch slowly floating past with a straw in the middle of it." Seeing through tears is a familiar trope of the distortion of perception by sorrow; here that trope is literalized, but what is seen—the floating patch—remains ambiguous. Perhaps an external object, like an oil patch floating on the river, or perhaps a literal "floater" in the eye of the viewer such as Edvard Munch supposedly included in his paintings;[9] in either case, the perceived object remains irritatingly unclear, one of the text's little mysteries that appear and disappear as the narrative voice jolts the reader from one scene to the next, from one sense to the next.

Significantly, the mystery of vision is almost immediately supplanted by another, as the reader is moved from the lady's vision to her confused audition of fragments of a poem entering the text from an unknown source:

> There struck close upon her ears
>> Lars Porsena of Clusium
>> By the nine Gods he swore—
>
> and then more faintly, as if the speaker had passed her on his walk—
>> That the Great House of Tarquin
>> Should suffer wrong no more. (11)

Only after these fragments "struck upon her ears"—verbal echo of the angry glances that "struck upon" her back earlier—do we get enough context to understand the event as her husband declaiming "The Rape of Lucrece" as he walks past her, an allusion to rape that will continue to resonate in the text. Although Mr. Ambrose is especially ironized here by his linguistic association to St. Ambrose—who was noted for being the first man of antiquity to practice *silent* reading—Mr. Ambrose's vocal recitativo is in some measure disturbingly analogous to the action of the poem he recites, an assault on the ear at the level of language that adds to the intimations of disruption, separation, tearing that rapidly accumulate in the opening chapter.

Indeed, as it describes this couple making their way through London to an as-yet unspecified site, the text is increasingly marked by violent verbal fragments that are scattered like shot upon the pages. Cabs "plunge"; streets "shrink"; boats "shoot past." "The beauty that clothed things" is suddenly unveiled to reveal "the skeleton beneath" (12). Mrs. Ambrose's mind is "like a wound exposed to dry in the air," a simile of anxiety quickly reified as a real external danger: "At this point the cab stopped, for it was in danger of being crushed like an egg shell" (13). Sudden shifts from wish to act without transition, extravagant verbs, and animated objects construct a kind of Alice-in-Wonderland world of perpetual and uneasy metamorphosis.

Once the story shifts from the streets of London to the ship, the deictic center shifts from grieving mother to motherless daughter, from Helen Ambrose to her niece, Rachel Vinrace, but the same kind of uneasy voice continues to resound:

> Down in the saloon of her father's ship, Miss Rachel Vinrace, aged twenty-four stood waiting for her uncle and aunt nervously. . . . As

she occupied herself in laying forks severely straight by the side of knives, she heard a man's voice saying gloomily:

"On a dark night one would fall down these stairs head foremost," to which a woman's voice added, "And be killed." (14)

This disembodied dialogue about sudden death heard by Rachel is soon followed by a series of social exchanges between the irascible Mr. Pepper—"a little man who was bent as some trees are by a gale on one side of them" (15)—and the Ambroses, all of which play bizarre variations on the same gloomy theme:

"Once rheumatic, always rheumatic, I fear," he replied. "To some extent it depends on the weather, though not so much as people are apt to think."

"One does not die of it, at any rate," said Helen.

"As a general rule—no," said Mr. Pepper. . . .

"You knew Jenkinson, didn't you Ambrose?" asked Mr. Pepper across the table.

"Jenkinson of Peterhouse?"

"He's dead," said Mr. Pepper. (15)

Both the staccato rhythm of this dialogue and the large white gaps on the page are continued in the next exchange on death, in which another Jenkinson, whose wife has died, has a daughter who, like Rachel, keeps house for her widower-father.

Such doublings of name and situation without context fold back on themselves, so that the affective resonance of words and the ironic juxtaposition of phrases rather than the development of plot carry the narrative implications. Just as the narrative voice later notes "the strange way in which some words detach themselves from the rest" (101), so gratuitously violent phrases echoing with a weird wit separate themselves, or are separated by white spaces on the page, from the normal flow of linear sequence. Rachel remembers buying a piano: "my aunts said the piano would come through the floor, but at their age one wouldn't mind being killed in the night" (20). Rachel goes out on deck: "'It blows—it blows!' gasped Rachel, the words rammed down her throat" (18). Helen and Rachel look into a room: "they saw Mr. Ambrose throw himself violently against the back of his chair" (18). Even the description of a tapestry seems sinister, not only in its images, but in its explosive p's and b's: "twisted shells with red lips like unicorn's horns ornamented the mantlepiece, which was draped by a pall of purple plush from which depended a certain number of balls" (18). Out of such orts and fragments of sound and rhythm, the voice constructs a narrative in which nothing "happens" on the level of action but in which a portentous discourse suggests something happening elsewhere.

The very basis of representation is at times threatened by a sudden materialization of metaphor. Mr. Pepper's remark, "A screw loose somewhere, no doubt of it," is followed by a passage that reifies the metaphor: "a tremor ran through the table, and a light outside swerved" (16). Similarly, Rachel characterizes Mr. Pepper by a materialized simile: "'He's like this,' said Rachel, lighting on a fossilized fish in a basin, and displaying it." A few lines later, similitude seemingly drops out; word and thing become one: "'His heart's a piece of old shoe leather,' Rachel declared, dropping the fish" (19). What fish is dropped? the real one or the simile? "Dropping the fish," the narrative voice blurs the differential space between metaphor and material referent, between representation and reality, as it attempts to suggest a discourse impossibly at one with its origins.

The instability of boundaries at the level of discourse that draws the reader into the text's precarious world functions also to support the novel's thematic interrogation of difference by continually blurring the lines that constitute it. As in hysteria, all ego boundaries that should hold are vulnerable—from the primary boundary between self and other, the body, to the kinship boundaries that constitute family relations, between mother and daughter, father and daughter, to the boundaries that define sexual difference. Not only are these relations all called into question, but so is the oedipal law that presumably regulates them. The father's plotting of the daughter's destiny, a plot to violate the daughter's integrity that enters the English novel with *Clarissa* and culminates in rape, remains a thematic undercurrent as the novel unfolds.[10]

The particular place of the father in *The Voyage Out* is problematic from the very beginning. Of the two fathers initially represented, Ridley, literally named Bluebeard by some children on the London streets, is made eccentric to the family concerns of the plot by his absorption in his scholarly texts. Willoughby, on the other hand, is immediately made suspect as the true Bluebeard: Helen "suspected him of nameless atrocities with regard to his daughter, as indeed, she had always suspected him of bullying his wife" (24). The narrative voice furthers this suspicion when, after Rachel and Willoughby welcome Helen aboard, it foregrounds a disturbing ambiguity in the father-daughter relation through an ambiguous syntax: "Still holding Helen's hand he drew his arm round Rachel's shoulder, thus making them come uncomfortably close, but Helen forbore to look" (21). Who comes too close to whom? Helen and Rachel? Rachel and Willoughby? Helen and Willoughby? "Them" is an indeterminate reference that raises the question of proper distance in family relations, between father and daughter, between mother and daughter.

That question of distance returns in the climactic paternal transgression of the first section, Richard Dalloway's traumatic embrace of Rachel.

> You have beauty," he said. The ship lurched. Rachel fell slightly forward. Richard took her in his arms and kissed her. Holding her tight, he kissed her passionately so that she felt the hardness of his body and the roughness of his cheek *printed* upon hers. She fell back in her chair, with tremendous beats of the heart, each of which sent black waves across her eyes. . . . "You tempt me," he said. The tone of his voice was terrifying. He seemed choked in fight. They were both trembling. (76, italics mine)

Violating the proper boundaries of the paternal relation, Dalloway's embrace of Rachel is strikingly similar to Herr K.'s embrace of Dora. Terrified by Dalloway, Rachel, like Dora, is also excited and disgusted. Her subsequent dream of a damp and oozing tunnel-vault inhabited by a little deformed man projects into the text a disgust with her interior space and a terror of its being inhabited by a repulsive phallus that is also a terror of and disgust with the sexual body she will reject.[11]

Terror and disgust, the primary affects of hysteria, recur at significant moments during Rachel's initiation into sexual knowledge. When Helen tells Rachel about prostitution, " 'It is terrifying—it is disgusting' Rachel asserted, as if she included Helen in her hatred." Indeed, Helen complicitously justifies Dalloway's assault as an inevitability Rachel must accept: "You oughtn't to be frightened. . . . It's the most natural thing in the world. Men will want to kiss you, just as they want to marry you. The pity is to get things out of proportion.

It's like noticing the noises people make when they eat, or men spitting; or, in short, any small thing that gets on one's nerves" (81). Yet in comparing kissing and marriage to noises of eating and men spitting, Helen herself repeats the logic of hysterical disgust that she would disavow in an upward displacement characteristic of hysteria.[12]

Significantly, it is Helen who, like Frau K. with Dora, reveals to Rachel the secrets of sexuality: "Helen's words hewed down great blocks which had stood there always" (81). The very word *hewed* phonetically links Helen to Hewet, the writer, who with Helen will constitute the two objects of Rachel's ambivalent desire. That it is Helen—bearing the name of Leda's daughter who was abducted because of her beauty, herself the daughter of a raped mother—who counsels Rachel to accept the risks of heterosexual relations is especially ironic. Indeed, the name *Helen* and the prior narrative that it silently inscribes open a space for questioning Helen's desire as well as Rachel's, questioning whether female desire is itself complicitous in the scene of rape.

In *Melymbrosia*, an earlier version of *The Voyage Out*, for example, Helen, jealous of Rachel's encounter with Dalloway, is described as wanting herself to be the object of Dalloway's dalliance; that motive is missing from *The Voyage Out*, as is any reference to Helen's sexual desire. These absences serve to distance Helen from the narrative conflict and thus to give her a more disinterested, privileged voice. Nevertheless, Helen remains the most ambiguous and ambivalently regarded character in the novel, her motives continually made suspect. If rape is a central trope of heterosexual relations in *The Voyage Out*, the daughter's text implicitly questions the mother about her complicity in fostering this plot. What was she feeling? Did she like it? Did she put on his knowledge with his power? These disturbing questions, more overt in the text of *Melymbrosia*, recur subtextually in the interstices of the voice, in a silent interrogation of woman's desire.

In this context, the overdetermined name of the ship *Euphrosyne* becomes itself a signifier of woman's desire, the ship a screen on which the narrative voice projects different representations of the feminine. Described as powerfully phallic in her virginal integrity at the beginning of the voyage, "a bride going forth to her husband, a virgin unknown of men; in her vigour and purity she might be likened to all beautiful things, worshipped and felt as a symbol" (32),[13] after the text's revelation of oedipal desire, she is seen as demeaned and vulnerable, now "open" to violation: "From a distance she was pronounced a tramp. . . one of those wretched little passenger steamers where people rolled about among the cattle on deck. . . a ship passing in the night" (87). By the time the ship arrives at its destination, Woolf's description carries the weight of previous allusions to sexual assault on the female body: "immediately, as if she were a recumbent giant requiring examination, small boats came swarming about her. She rang with cries; men jumped on to her; her deck was thumped by feet. The lonely little island was invaded from all quarters at once, and after four weeks of silence it was bewildering to hear human speech" (87–88).

Yet if this image of a recumbent female giant invaded by little men extends the rape trope, it also suggests a more benign "incursion" of a maternal body "invaded" by children, figured by those "small boats" that "came swarming around her." As in a field-ground oscillation, the initial representation of sexual violation looks from another angle of vision to be a representation of the child's innocent exploration of the maternal body.

It is the maternal terrain that gets explored in the South America of the novel, in Santa Marina, a place of otherness where male figures of oedipal power like Richard Dalloway and Willoughby Vinrace are irrelevant. In this fluid "new world" in the lower hemisphere, the risks of heterosexual romance, construed as an external assault on the integrity of the woman's body by an intrusively phallic figure, are more than matched by the risks of too intimate a relation with the maternal body, which threatens singularity itself. Of this aspect of the hysterical problematic, Kristeva remarks: "the hysterical woman suffers because she sets the affect that is her mother's prisoner within an unspeakable homosexual erotics. . . . She aims at and succeeds in consolidating her primal border between the not-yet-self and the Other; it is the verge of narcissism, of the emptiness that laps against the ideal, the promised land of primary idealizations" (1987b, 311). In moving into this promised land, Woolf's narrative crosses the verge.[14]

IN THE FIRST section of the novel, Helen is principally a maternal surrogate, but in Santa Marina she becomes more a sisterly companion, joining Rachel in a romance plot in which the sexual possibilities

of couples and coupling proliferate. In a series of interchanges constructed as a kind of dance, two homosocial couples—Rachel and
Helen, Hewet and Hirst—form and reform as two heterosexual
couples, Hewet and Rachel, Helen and Hirst. The couple is doubled
yet again in the minor characters Susan Warrington and Arthur Venning, whose conventional courtship is contrasted with the confused
romance quest of Evelyn Murgatroyd, who acts the part of the hysteric within the plot—unable to know her desire, vacillating between
suitors, seeking an intimacy that at the same time she would avoid.

This structure of splitting and switching turns into a literal dance at
the novel's center. A typical event in nineteenth-century novels to
further the marriage plot, the dance of *The Voyage Out* is the site of a
seduction into coupling that results in chaos. Here, for example, is
Woolf's description of the dance as a family of musicians begins to
play, a family in which the mother is significantly absent, seemingly
displaced into the music itself:

> After a few minutes' pause, the father, the daughter, and the son-in-
> law who played the horn flourished with one accord. Like the rats
> who followed the piper, heads instantly appeared in the doorway.
> There was another flourish; and then the trio dashed spontaneously
> into the triumphant swing of the waltz. It was as though the room
> were instantly flowed with water. After a moment's hesitation first
> one couple, then another, leapt into mid-stream, and went round
> and round in the eddies. The rhythmic swish of the dancers sounded
> like a swirling pool. . . . The eddies seemed to circle faster and
> faster, until the music wrought itself into a crash, ceased, and the
> circles were smashed into little separate bits. (152)

If the dance promotes coupling, here the coupling is deadly. Like rats
seduced by the music of the Pied Piper to their own suicide, the
couples leap into the water to be ultimately "smashed into little separate bits" in a "plunge" that recalls the cab's "plunge" into London at
the novel's opening. Both images suggest a fall into preobjectal chaos,
a recurrent Woolfian representation of fragmentation that imperils the
subject.

In *Powers of Horror*, Kristeva develops the concept of abjection, her
term for the primal disavowal of the archaic maternal body necessary
for the subject to emerge. A concept that speaks to Woolf's concern
with fragmentation, the abject derives from a narcissistic crisis pro-

voked by separation of one body from another, specifically a separation of a not-yet subject from the maternal chaos before it becomes an object. Abjection as Kristeva defines it is also an affect as well as an act:

> an extremely strong feeling which is at once somatic and symbolic, and which is above all a revolt of the person against an external menace from which one wants to keep oneself at a distance, but of which one has the impression that it is not only an external menace but that it may menace us from inside. So it is a desire for separation, for becoming autonomous and also the feeling of an impossibility of doing so. (1982, 135–36)

The abject is thus what threatens both identity and distinctions; in *The Voyage Out*, the most prominent of such threats is maternity itself. The novel is liberally sprinkled with references to death in childbirth as well as to the gross distortions of the body induced by pregnancy. Indeed, the abject is that which evokes terror and disgust with the body. As we have seen already, the text repeatedly evokes such affects through images that ambiguously threaten to invade bodily boundaries: "Is it true, Terence, that women die with bugs crawling across their faces?" (301), Rachel asks in a seemingly gratuitous abjection of the body. Similar references keep appearing for no apparent reason: bugs, rats, black beetles, spiders, snakes, a host of such images of abjection arbitrarily crop up to promote disgust at, and terror of, the vulnerable body.

Yet since women share an identification with the maternal body, this abjection is always ambivalent, always presupposing a loss for women, always in some sense suicidal. To refuse abjection, however, is to fuse with the maternal chaos in an ecstatic but terrifying union. Terror and disgust on the one hand, and rapture and ecstasy on the other, this splitting of affects increasingly defines Rachel's and the text's relation to the maternal body, and seems to occur whenever the text evokes a desirable female body. Thus, for example, Helen's beauty, heightened by the flush of dancing, is said to arouse the transgressive desire of the ladies "to touch her" (159). Almost immediately, however, the text shifts to another totally gratuitous description of a grotesque female body, which negates that desire:

> a lady. . . waddling rather than walking and leaning on the arm of a stout man with globular green eyes set in a fat white face. . . . She

was very stout, and so compressed that the upper part of her body hung considerably in advance of her feet. . . . On the summit of a frothy castle of hair a purple plume stood erect, while her short neck was encircled by a black velvet ribbon knobbed with gems, and golden braceleters were tightly wedged into the flesh of her fat gloved arms. She had the face of an impertinent but jolly little pig mottled red under a dusting of powder.

St. John could not join in Helen's laughter.

"It makes me sick," he declared. "The whole thing makes me sick." (160)

St. John's "sickness," his disgust, is confirmed by the grotesque description of the fat woman that issues from the narrative voice; St. John, the misogynist who is repulsed by women's breasts, is thus made a spokesperson for a corporeal aversion that belongs also to the narrative voice.

Nevertheless, Woolf's voice does not rest in terror and disgust; it is also seduced by the pleasures of fluid boundaries and the ambiguities of the subject, by the possibility of a relation with a man who resembles a woman, a woman who acts like a man. This fluidity of positions is what is at issue in the primal scene of hysteria and what is questioned in *The Voyage Out*. If we probe the sequence of events in the novel within this context, we can discover a series of scenes of ambiguous erotic exchanges viewed by a subject attempting to determine or deny the meaning of this scene and her or his relation to it.

Early in the novel, Rachel inadvertently sees Mr. and Mrs. Ambrose kiss and, disquieted at the sight of their marital intimacy, immediately displaces her look to the sea:[15] "They went a few paces and Rachel saw them kiss. Down she looked into the depth of the sea" (27). Not only is there a clear displacement downward in the move from one sentence to the other, but the abrupt juxtaposition, the trochaic stress on the last word of the first sentence and the first word of the next, creates a silent but emphatic space between sentences ("saw them kiss./ Down she looked") that signals repression. At the same time, the phonetic play between "sea" and "saw" mimes the narrative preoccupation with vision, with forbidden sights/sites:

While it was slightly disturbed on the surface by the passage of the Euphrosyne, beneath it was green and dim, and it grew dimmer and dimmer until the sand at the bottom was only a pale blur. One could scarcely see the black ribs of wrecked ships, or the spiral towers made by the burrowings of great eels, or the smooth green-sided monsters who came by flickering this way and that.

"—And, Rachel, if any one wants me, I'm busy till one," said her father, enforcing his words as he often did, when he spoke to his daughter, by a smart blow upon the shoulder. (27–28)

In this displacement of the look, Rachel's own murky interiority is reflected in the dim depths of the sea, its mysterious wrecked ships and "smooth green-sided monsters" visual projections of a netherworld of disturbed affect.

This underwater world recalls the nearly contiguous passage in which Mr. Pepper discourses on "the white, *hairless*, blind monsters lying curled on the ridges of sand at the bottom of the sea, which would explode if you brought them to the surface, their sides bursting asunder and scattering entrails to the winds when released from pressure" (23, italics mine). Unlike Pepper's gory description, which suggests both the consequences of undoing repression and a birth that shatters the body, and narrated "with considerable detail and with such show of knowledge that Ridley was disgusted and begged him to stop" (23), Rachel's sea-vision is comfortably murky. The contiguity of passages and the similar subject matter, however, suggest that a displaced anxiety about childbirth and body fragmentation informs her look and what she sees. Although Rachel's absorption by the sea is interrupted by her father's blow (here Willoughby takes his place as the first of those many Woolfian paternal figures of interruption—Mr. Ramsay's beak of brass in *To the Lighthouse*, Peter's pocket knife in *Mrs. Dalloway*), she will find herself repeatedly confronting an enigmatic scene that demands interpretation: Who is doing what to whom? What are the consequences? If here Rachel, like the true hysteric, turns away from the sight, in Santa Marina, Rachel will attempt to discover something about sexual difference and the body by making sense of her place in this ambiguous scene.

There are four such scenes in Santa Marina, scenes that confuse the distinctions between voyeur-subject and the object of its look, which shift their point of focalization between male and female, seer and seen, subject and object of the gaze, playing out variations on the primal scene and its structuring sexual identifications. In each scene the reader, like the voyeur within the plot, is compelled by the textual ambiguities to ask "What is happening?" and in essence to construct a sexual body from the answer.

In the first scene, the voyeurs are two women, Helen and Rachel; described as "eavesdroppers" in peeping through the uncurtained windows of the brilliantly lit hotel, they are unwittingly discovered by St. John Hirst:

> Helen and Rachel started to think that some one had been sitting near to them unobserved all the time. There were legs in the shadow. A melancholy voice issued from above them.
> "Two women," it said.
> A scuffling was heard on the gravel. The women had fled. (102)

Shifting focus from the two women outside looking in to the disembodied voice inside looking out, the narrative turns the two women subjects into objects of an unknown gaze and voice.

In the second scene, the voyeur is a heterosexual couple and vision rather than voice is primary as Terence and Rachel discover Susan and Arthur in an embrace. "They lay in each other's arms and had no notion that they were observed. Yet two figures suddenly appeared among the trees above them. . . . They saw a man and woman lying on the ground beneath them, rolling slightly this way and that as the embrace tightened and slackened. . . . Nor could you tell from her expression whether she was happy or had suffered something" (141). Here Susan and Arthur, first represented as the subjects ("they lay") become the objects of the gaze of Terence and Rachel ("they saw a man and woman"). As the text shifts its focus from one couple to the other, there is no sound, no voices as in the first scene, no words to interpret the scene, and the woman's place in it, "whether she was happy or had suffered something." The silent image offering no access to its meaning, "the intensity of the vision remained with them" (141).

The third scene returns to the primacy of audition but in a reversal of gender gives us a man eavesdropping on two women. As Terence listens in the darkness outside the house occupied by Rachel and Helen, he hears a voice "reading aloud": "The voice quickened, and the tone became conclusive, rising slightly in pitch, as if these words were at the ends of the chapter. Hewet drew back again into the shadow. . . . He had almost decided to go back, when suddenly two figures appeared at the window, not six feet from him" (186). This description of the rising rhythm of Helen's narrating voice as it comes to its climax, itself an allusive commentary on the linear form of narrative, is then contrasted with the conversational voices of Helen and Rachel speaking fragments of an unknown but intimate discourse: "The broken sentences had an extraordinary beauty and detachment in Hewet's ears, and a kind of mystery too, as if they were spoken by people in their sleep" (187). Terence's detached listening turns into a classic pornographic response, however, when he hears "a certain amount of scuffling, entreating, resisting, and laughter" between the two women and is himself physically excited.

Why does this scene excite him? For the male voyeur of an erotic scene between two women, the pleasures typically come from the elimination of oedipal rivalry and castration anxiety; the women are completely his; the father's oedipal law has been eliminated.[16] It is this last point that speaks most loudly to the concerns of *The Voyage Out*, for this scene presents an eroticism that erases sexual difference. While the typical primal scene fantasy constructs sexual difference for the voyeur through imaginary identifications with the different gendered positions observed or heard, this scene offers the voyeur only the play between two women as the site of identification and desire, offers an all-female primal scene for voyeuristic identification.[17] Disguised through Terence's point of view, a lesbian erotic economy surfaces here that operates throughout the novel. Indeed, described as being like a woman, Terence is effectively a woman in male masquerade, a textual strategy for masking the representation of lesbian desire. Not surprisingly, this transgressive play is interrupted by a paternal prohibition—"a man's form appeared" (presumably Ridley)—and punctuated by an overdetermined sentence that ends the illicit performance: "there was dead silence, and all the lights went out" (187).

Nevertheless, Terence experiences a rapturous dispersal of his social identity as the narrative voice plunges with him into an experience of heterogeneity that leads this time not to abjection but to the raw material of poetry:[18]

> He shouted out a line of poetry but the words escaped him, and he stumbled among lines and fragments of lines which had no meaning at all except for the beauty of the words. . . . "Here am I," he cried rhythmically, as his feet pounded to the left and to the right, "plunging along, like an elephant in the jungle, stripping the branches as I

go (He snatched at the twigs of a bush at the roadside), roaring innumerable words, lovely words about innumerable things." (188)

Terence's singular dance of rhythmic pounding is very different from the coupling of the social dance; analogously, this scene is narrated in a very different voice, one that foreshadows Woolf's experimental and elastic voice in *The Waves*.

The climactic primal scene of this temporal sequence that takes us toward the center of the novel's desire occurs during the voyage into the interior that provides the immediate cause for Rachel's death. Occupying the fluid subject position that Woolf privileges, both Terence and Rachel take a walk that is a journey into a watery world in which only silence speaks: "the noises of the ordinary world were replaced by those creaking and sighing sounds which suggest to the traveler in a forest that he is walking at the bottom of the sea" (270). Speech becomes "little meaningless words floating high in air" (276).

> "We are happy together." He did not seem to be speaking, or she to be hearing.
> "Very happy," she answered.
> "We love each other," Terence said. . . .
> "We love each other," she repeated.
> The silence was then broken by their voices which joined in tones of strange unfamiliar sound which formed no words. Faster and faster they walked; simultaneously they stopped, clasped each other in their arms, then, releasing themselves dropped to the earth. (271)

Speaking ritual words emptied of content in a hollow parody of romantic courtship, Rachel and Terence here become themselves the primal couple they had previously observed, in a nonphallic representation of sexual intimacy displaced into, and performed by, syntactic rhythms.

As in the previous scenes, however, this new world coupling is interrupted, this time not by the father but by the maternal figure:

> Voices crying behind them never reached through the waters in which they were now sunk. The repetition of Hewet's name in short, dissevered syllables was to them the crack of a dry branch or the laughter of a bird. The grasses and breezes sounding and mur-

muring all round them, they never noticed that the swishing of the grasses grew louder and louder, and did not cease with the lapse of the breeze. A hand dropped abrupt as iron on Rachel's shoulder; it might have been a bolt from heaven. She fell beneath it, and the grass whipped across her eyes and filled her mouth and ears. Through the waving stems she saw a figure, large and shapeless against the sky. Helen was upon her. Rolled this way and that, now seeing only forests of green, and now the high blue heaven, she was speechless and almost without sense. At last she lay still, all the grasses shaken round her and before her by her panting. Over her loomed two great heads, the heads of a man and woman, of Terence and Helen. (283)

Shifting to Rachel's disordered vision, the text abruptly reconstitutes the primal couple as Terence and Helen, with Rachel again on the outside, looking in: "Both were flushed, both laughing, and the lips were moving; they came together and kissed in the air above her. Broken fragments of speech came down to her on the ground. She thought she heard them speak of love and then of marriage" (284). What sort of revelation is this? What is happening? The text demands that the reader, like Rachel, put things back into normal perspective, compose these fragments: Rachel and Terence are interrupted by Helen who, from Rachel's perspective on the ground, appears to be a deity, her hand a bolt from heaven. Helen tumbles Rachel around on the grass in a suggestive image of sexual play. Terence and Helen speak not of their love and marriage, but of Rachel's and Terence's.

Yet even before our reordering of the confusion, one thing is certain for both reader and Rachel: "Helen was upon her." The sentence, suggesting an assault both violent and sexual, indeed, a maternal rape, is disturbing in its ambiguous resonance. Significantly, in *Melymbrosia* it is Helen and Rachel, not Terence and Rachel, who take a walk; and it is Helen who, tumbling Rachel to ground in an act of sexual play, asks her to say she loves her, Helen, better than Terence. In *The Voyage Out*, however, this homoerotic scene between two women is literally displaced, first as the "scuffle"—a word also used in the first voyeuristic scene between Helen and Rachel that Terence hears/witnesses—and later, as an explicit competition between Terence and Helen for Rachel's company, which Terence, not Helen, wins.[19]

Nevertheless, heterosexual romance is not the ultimate victor in

The Voyage Out. If Rachel in her disorientation feels again excluded from the primal couple—here, Terence and Helen—she is allowed to "realize" the rapture of the maternal embrace: "Raising herself and sitting up, she too realized Helen's soft body, the strong and hospitable arms, and happiness swelling and breaking in one vast wave" (284). In the "she too," the narrative voice, speaking from Rachel's consciousness and of her desire, extends the couple into the desired triad. Yet the original sight, like the originary site, remains powerful: the intensity of the vision of Helen as a *magna mater* who, filling Rachel's horizon, was "upon her."

Thus, when the characters move to the farthest verge of their voyage in—and significantly, this is the only point at which "the natives" (289) are represented—what is revealed is the archaic power of the mother, embodied in the native women who, "squatting on the ground in triangular shapes" (one recalls the triangular wedge of darkness that Mrs. Ramsay becomes in *To the Lighthouse*), unabashedly and silently stare at the intruders, "their long narrow eyes slid round and fixed upon them with the motionless inexpressive gaze of those removed from each other far, far beyond the plunge of speech" (284). Here linked to speech, the "plunge" that is Woolf's recurrent trope of action is superseded by an uncanny stasis beyond language: here, a maternal gaze "followed them, passing over their legs, their bodies, their heads . . . like the crawl of a winter fly" (285). Recalling Rachel's earlier remark about bugs crawling over a dead woman, this mortifying gaze culminates in the stare of an anonymous mother-woman: "As she drew apart her shawl and uncovered her breast to the lips of her baby, the eyes of a woman never left their faces, although they moved uneasily under her stare, and finally turned away, rather than stand there looking at her any longer" (285).

In this representation of an alien scopic potency, Woolf not only colonizes the natives as symbols of otherness, but also problematically evokes the patriarchal cliché of a natural, primitive, maternal power in a contorted syntax that desubjectivizes and depersonalizes the woman, reconstituting her as a series of totemic body parts—eyes, lips, breast—a nonsexual, nongenital maternal triangle constructed by the hysterical wish. Indeed, it is "the *eyes* of a woman" that is the subject-agent of the sentence, her stare, not her, which engages with the intruders in a contestation of the look. The signifier *woman* is, like *her breast,* slipped into the sentence between the *lips* of the infant and the look of the Europeans. At the presumed site of Rachel's contraction of the disease that kills her, the voice unveils not the Freudian primal drama in which masculine and feminine positions are constructed by a gaze controlled by the law of the father but an indifferent and annihilating maternal stare.[20]

This inscription of maternal power at the heart of the voyage out links Woolf's narrative to a number of anthropological inquiries that appeared simultaneously with the writing of *The Voyage Out.* As Elizabeth Abel points out, such texts as J. J. Atkinson's *Primal Law* (1903), and Frazer's *The Golden Bough* (1907–15) and *Totemism and Exogamy* (1910), with their investigations of mother goddess cults, provided material for Woolf's own fantasmatic representations of an archaic mother.[21] In this context, Conrad's *Heart of Darkness* with its own voyage to a cannibalistic core of desire is analogous to Woolf's exploration of a maternal terrain. In fact, Conrad's text is literally inscribed into *The Voyage Out* when after Rachel's death, Arthur reiterates, "Miss Vinrace. . . She's dead" (361), miming Conrad's "Mr. Kurtz, he dead." The difference in the gender of the subject, however, has altered the story and its meaning. While Kurtz dies after he kicks the earth to pieces as a consequence of his murderous aggressivity against the maternal body, Rachel dies in a withdrawal from, which is also a withdrawal into, that body.

In the text's most perverse primal scene, a seemingly gratuitous depiction of the decapitation of a terrified chicken by a knife-wielding old woman, the maternal gaze is not merely indifferent but actively malevolent.[22] The scene is foreshadowed by a dialogue between Rachel and Evelyn Murgatroyd, who, coded as a classic hysteric, looks out the window of her hotel room and remarks, "They kill hens down there. . . . They cut their heads off with a knife—disgusting!" (251). Her reference to hens is fulsomely elaborated when Rachel, disturbed by Evelyn's excessive proximity, escapes the room and, having confusedly wandered down "the wrong side of hotel life," stumbles upon a scene that demands interpretation: "Two large women. . . were sitting on a bench with bloodsmeared tin trays in front of them and yellow bodies across their knees" (252).

Before we are given access to its meaning, the sentence provokes questions and raises anxiety: Who are these two women? What are they doing? What follows tells us; the passage is worth quoting in full:

> They were plucking the birds and talked as they plucked. Suddenly a chicken came floundering, half flying, half running into the space, pursued by a third woman whose age could hardly be under eighty. Although wizened and unsteady on her legs she kept up the chase, egged on by the laughter of the others; her face was expressive of furious rage, and as she ran she swore in Spanish. Frightened by handclapping here, a napkin there, the bird ran this way and that in sharp angles, and finally fluttered straight at the old woman, who opened her scanty grey skirts to enclose it, dropped upon it in a bundle, and then, holding it out, cut its head off with an expression of vindictive energy and triumph combined. The blood and the ugly wriggling fascinated Rachel, so that although she knew that some-one had come up behind and was standing beside her, she did not turn round until the old woman had settled down on the bench beside the others. Then she looked up sharply, because of the ugli-ness of what she had seen. It was Miss Allan who stood beside her. (252)

The details of the old woman's action—opening her skirts, enclosing the chicken, holding it out, and cutting off its head—insinuate the familiar trope of castration into the scene. Evoked by the textually pervasive oedipal apprehension about female identity and desire, that trope is linguistically foregrounded when Rachel is described as "fasci-nated"; the word—derived etymologically from the Latin *fascinum*, a phallic amulet that freezes the viewer—literally links Rachel to a pri-mal scene of castration. The "blood and ugly wriggling" also evoke a repugnant scene of childbirth and recall the earlier image of white monsters at the bottom of the sea that explode when brought to the surface, both fantasms of an abjected body that paralyzes Rachel.

Indeed, from this scene onward, Woolf's text moves quickly to associate the trapped chicken with Rachel as she attempts to know and to represent her own desire, to emerge as a separate subject. When Rachel turns away from the killing space, she is taken in hand by two other women who embody onerous destinies, first by Miss Allan, the archetypal British spinster, who has been described as resembling more an elderly man than a woman (178), and then by the invalided Mrs. Paley, who blocks Rachel's passage with her wheelchair, forcing her into an "intolerable cul de sac" (257). Repeating the phrase "block in the passage," the text represents Rachel as "wriggling" in the midst of a crisis of identity that is figured by the text as a thwarted birth. "For the time her own body was the source of all the life in the world, which tried to burst forth here—there—and was repressed now by Mr. Bax, now by Evelyn, now by the imposition of ponderous stupidity—the weight of the entire world" (258).

Insofar as the maternal body is the source of being and birth, the image of maternal blockage in *The Voyage Out* turns the universe itself into an unbearable cul-de-sac that does not allow the articulation of a female subject. Trapped like the chicken in the maternal skirts, oppressed by the weight of the world—another trope of the suffocating maternal body that is "upon her"—Rachel experiences an intense rage against Miss Allan: "An uncomfortable sensation kept Rachel silent; she wished to whirl high and strike a spark out of the cool pink flesh" (255). As I have suggested, such a rage directed at the maternal body menaces the daughter as well; immediately suppressed, it is converted into a "melancholy lethargy" (258), that familiar symptom that surfaced in the texts of Nightingale and Schreiner.[23] From rage to melancholy, hostile affect is swallowed, dissociated, repressed, in a kind of self-castration that leaves loss and emptiness at the novel's very center.

Indeed, while *The Voyage Out* raises the specter of the castrating old woman with a knife—she appears again in Rachel's fevered hallucination—in effect, Rachel cuts off her own head, silencing her rage and her desire by totally submitting to the corporeality of the body. As in illness, when the critical faculties are relaxed and meaning comes through the senses, in the final three chapters of the novel the narrative voice speaks from a site only flirted with before, in a hallucinatory distance from the ordinary that Rachel's illness sanctions, that privileges sensation over sense.[24] Thus, as Rachel listens to Terence read, words take on a material "substance and shape, so that it was not necessary to understand what he was saying; one could merely listen to his words; one could almost handle them."

> There is a gentle nymph not far from hence,
>
> he read,
>
> That with moist curb sways the smooth Severn stream.
> Sabrina is her name, a virgin pure;

> Whilom she was the daughter of Locrine,
> That had the sceptre from his father Brute.

> The words. . . seemed to be laden with meaning. . . . They
> sounded strange; they meant different things from what they usu-
> ally meant. Rachel. . . went off upon curious trains of thought sug-
> gested by words such as "curb" and "Locrine" and "Brute," which
> brought unpleasant sights before her eyes, independently of their
> meaning. (326–27)

Curious trains of thought are suggested to the reader as well by
these now familiar words, which inscribe a chain of associations
through reversal, condensation, displacement, the curious mechanisms of dream language: locrine / lucrece, father Brute / brutal father,
moist curb / moist curve; these suggestive verbal variations evoke
"unpleasant sights" / sites associated with oedipal violation and
sexuality.

Yet once Rachel succumbs to her illness, the oedipal plot becomes
irrelevant, merely a disconnected sequence of empty signifiers: "some
plot, some adversary, some escape" (341). Thus, while Helen and
Hewet, ironically now a couple "on an expedition together" (337) to
recuperate Rachel, engage in a silent argument about her condition,
Rachel herself, "isolated alone with her body" (330), withdraws from
all contention, all desire. As Kristeva writes of another hysteric, "it is as
though Dora was freezing up and attempting to enclose within her
own body as a totality. . . everything having to do with her own
jouissance. Such enclosure ensures that nothing has to be represented
as lost" (1987b, 103). Attempting the same kind of enclosure in her
narrative, Woolf does not conclude the novel with Rachel's death but
rather encircles it with a new discourse on beginnings, in a new voice
that speaks from elsewhere. The penultimate chapter opens with the
genesis of being from emptiness, of sound from silence, representing
the birth of human consciousness out of a maternal body that is,
however, only audible in the silence:

> For two or three hours longer the moon poured its light through
> the empty air. Unbroken by cloud it fell straightly, and lay almost
> like a chill white frost over the sea and the earth. During these hours
> the silence was not broken, and the only movement was caused by
> the movement of trees and branches which stirred slightly, and the

shadows that lay across the white spaces of the land moved too. In this profound silence one sound only was audible, the sound of a slight but continuous breathing which never ceased, although it never rose and never fell. It continued after the birds had begun to flutter from branch to branch, and could be heard behind the first thin notes of their voices. It continued all through the hours when the east whitened, and grew red, and a faint blue tinged the sky, but when the sun rose it ceased, and gave place to other sounds.

The first sounds that were heard were little inarticulate cries, it seemed, of children or of the very poor, of people who were very weak or in pain. (355)

Circling back to origins, to cries, to the *sounds* of pain, *The Voyage Out* tries to recuperate pain by recuperating the maternal body. Paradoxically, the pain of loss becomes everything; beginnings and endings are drowned in the same grief which, having been submerged for the course of the novel, erupts after Rachel's death in Terence's anguished cry near the novel's end. Terence's cry, "Rachel, Rachel"—an ironic reversal that alludes to the biblical Rachel weeping for her lost children—gives voice to the child's part in the grieving scene at the novel's beginning, the other side of Helen's maternal tears. While Helen's loss was recuperated by the entrance of Rachel, Rachel's death reinstitutes pain and loss as the principal truth, grounding Woolf's novel, like Schreiner's, in an aesthetics that links mourning and melancholia to hysterical representation.

Like Schreiner's *Story*, Woolf's text suggests that the thematics of rage and loss inevitably subtend the female bildungsroman, which typically tells the story of the woman who must give up the bond to the mother in order to enter heterosexual culture and the marriage plot. As we noted above (see chap. 3), this maternal loss is made more intolerable by a woman's lack of a cultural signifier to represent her desire. Like a depressed person in the process of mourning when the signifiers that are meant to recuperate loss fail, the hysterical female subject, battling an insupportable rage at this lack, takes refuge in inaction and withdrawal, the symptoms of a hysterical melancholia. Thus, *The Voyage Out* begins with references to loss—Rachel's loss of her mother, Helen's loss of her children, both constituting a specifically female loss—and after a detour that awkwardly ventures into new erotic possibilities for representation, returns at the end to loss—

Terence's loss, Helen's loss. Finally, the passions of the voice yield to a general melancholy that envelops even the minor characters, all of whom function at the conclusion as disembodied voices in a chorus of loss.

In the final turn of the novel, Woolf's narrative voice, after extending the personal trauma of Rachel's death to the trauma of a generation about to lose its innocence, moves to rescue the world as body through the prophetic vision of two unexpected characters who suddenly become figured as mother and child: the misogynistic St. John Hirst, depicted at the end as a sleepy child whose hypnagogic vision of a unifying pattern is the novel's last word, and the suddenly inflated matriarchal Mrs. Flushing, who, opening the door, pronounces a judgment of natural harmony: "The driving air, the drone of the trees, and the flashing light which now and again spread a broad illumination over the earth filled Mrs. Flushing with exultation. Her breasts rose and fell. Splendid! Splendid! she muttered to herself" (374).

If earlier St. John, repulsed by the woman's breasts, voiced the novel's disgust with the female body, here the breasts of Mrs. Flushing, rising and falling with the rhythms of nature, become part of an ecstatic vision of the splendor of being-in-the-mother. This seems Woolf's wishful answer to Conrad's "the horror, the horror!" that for the moment gives the victory to the maternal breast over the little man, the deflated phallus. "'It was the move with your Queen that gave it away, Pepper'. . . . 'What? Pepper beaten at last? I congratulate you!' said Arthur Venning, who was wheeling old Mrs. Paley to bed. All these voices sounded gratefully in St. John's ears as he lay half-asleep, and yet vividly conscious of everything around him" (375). Through St. John's ears, we hear voices announce the defeat of the old Victorian order imaged in the game of chess. Yet that it is Pepper's Queen that is the most potent agent of that order, the Queen that must be "beaten at last," suggests again the narrative ambivalence about maternal power. If *The Voyage Out* seems to move away from oedipal rivalry and difference to a vision of a beneficent maternal body, the maternal figure remains at the end a locus of anxiety. The recuperative vision of the final chapter cannot obliterate the disturbing sights and sounds that preceded it.

The Voyage Out is clearly a text pointing toward modernism, questioning past constructions of desire and straining for a visionary new moment. It stands as a fascinating experiment with a new narrative voice that attempts to break up the conventional boundaries between subject and object, between masculine and feminine, boundaries that proved so inhibiting to the woman as writer.[25] In the service of that experiment, Woolf attempted to excavate the figure of the maternal body to represent a truth beyond culture, a presence beyond language. Yet, as we have seen, in *The Voyage Out* the maternal body remained too much a figure of ambivalence, maternity itself too much a Victorian demand, for it to sustain the more radical moments of her narrative voice. In those scattered moments in which she does break through the syntax of social realism, however, Woolf opens up that speaking silence, that resonance of language she and other modernist writers would so successfully plumb.

Chapter Seven

Male Modernists and the Ear of the Other in *Heart of Darkness* and *The Good Soldier*

For the subject to confront his truth,
there has to be an ear.
—Jacques Derrida

To TURN FROM *The Voyage Out* to the early modernist fiction of Conrad and Ford is to return to the field of male hysteria, to a specifically male narrative voice in conflict with its own sexual positionality. This return through modernism is, however, marked by a significant difference. While the narrative voices of Freud in the Dora case and James in *The Bostonians* were hystericized by their own imaginative constructions of the figure of the speaking woman, the hysterical voice in the texts of Conrad and Ford seems more an intentional strategy of the authors than an unconscious effect.[1] Using a first-person narrator, these texts seem to flaunt hysterical anxiety as the very condition of the modern subject. In asserting this intentionality I am raising some critical questions. Are these authors somehow beyond hysteria? Are they masters of its unconscious discourse? What does it mean even to speak of hysteria in texts whose very poetics deliberately mime the symptoms of hysteria—splitting, fragmentation, digression, dissociation?

An instructive preface with which to begin an answer to these questions is T. S. Eliot's hybrid prose poem, "Hysteria," which appeared in his first book, *Prufrock and Other Observations* (1917). For "Hysteria" announces in its very title its intention to appropriate a pathological dislocation as a poetic subject. Erasing the line that distinguishes poetic form from prose, "Hysteria" technically performs the obliteration of boundaries that threatens its speaker; at the same time it exposes the issues of male hysteria that I want to address as I move toward a conclusion in this chapter:

> As she laughed I was aware of becoming involved in her laughter and being part of it, until her teeth were only accidental stars with a talent for squad-drill. I was drawn in by short gasps, inhaled at each momentary recovery, lost finally in the dark caverns of her throat, bruised by the ripple of unseen muscles. An elderly waiter with trembling hands was hurriedly spreading a pink and white checked cloth over the rusty green iron table, saying: "If the lady and gentleman wish to take their tea in the garden. . . ." I decided that if the shaking of her breasts could be stopped, some of the fragments of the afternoon might be collected, and I concentrated my attention with careful subtlety to this end. ([1917] 1952, 19)

It could be Dowell in Ford's *The Good Soldier,* or the would-be misogynist St. John Hirst in *The Voyage Out,* turning anxiously away from women's breasts, or, of course, Prufrock himself who speaks these lines. The sheer terror induced by the presence of the woman's body, the defensive calm with which he articulates the imaginary experience of being dispersed by her laughter, inhaled with her breath, swallowed and digested into her cavities, marks the speaker as a hysteric even before the waiter confirms it. Moreover, the sequence of oral dangers that he literally faces in the embodied laughter—being "drawn in by short gasps, inhaled at each momentary recovery, lost in the dark caverns. . . bruised by the ripple of unseen muscles"— suggests through an upward displacement a kind of reverse birth as well as an oral incorporation, a return trip through a dangerous canal more feared than desired. Although this voyage in is not unlike Rachel's in *The Voyage Out,* the speaker's panic and projected disintegration before the body's unknown interior marks an affective difference in their imaginary relation to that body.

Indeed, there is an intensely paranoid element to the speaker's hysteria. As André Green points out, "the paranoiac is caught in the same dilemma as the hysteric: 'Who am I, man or woman?' However, whereas the hysteric asks the question in terms of secondary identification. . . the paranoiac does so in terms of primary identification" (1986a, 105). That is to say, the speaker's hysteria can be read as itself a defense against a more profound panic of being that is provoked by the woman's laughing mouth.[2] In the final sentence, the speaker's shift in focus from "the unseen muscles" to the breasts, from the invisible interiority of the female body to its visible exteriority, is an attempt to halt his disintegration through visual control of an object. As a visible object subject to the gaze, the shaking breasts can be "stopped" by a focused act of attention; similarly, the shards of the afternoon, a reflected projection of the speaker's own fragmentation, can be collected and ultimately composed as contained object—the very objective correlative that is the poem.

If the speaker moves to contain through his focus on the visible female form his inchoate apprehensions of self-dispersion, one can argue that Eliot as poet makes the same move, containing dispersion by formally embodying it in the poem's mimesis of hysteria, in its purposeful undoing of the old poetic line. In presenting a discursive embodiment of hysteria as poetic object, Eliot distances his voice as controlling author from that of the hysterical speaking subject. "Hysteria" is, of course, not a narrative but a kind of interior dramatic monologue; the relation of reader to text is unmediated; we are given neither commentary nor context for the devastating effects of the woman's body on the speaker. If Eliot as dramatic poet thus places himself outside the hysterical economy, this strategic distance does not free the implicit authorial subject, Eliot, from being implicated in the linguistic structure that is the poem and its performance of voice.

In her discussion of the filmic authorial subject, Kaja Silverman pointedly asks, "What are the conditions under which the authorial subject is sustained as a discursive category" even though he or she is absent from the scene? (1988, 187–88). The question can be raised even more incisively in relation to written dramatic monologues. In the case of Eliot's "Hysteria," the answer, I submit, begins with a recognition that although Eliot's authorial voice is absent as itself from the scene, "he" is nevertheless present as the mental agency responsible for the reader's relation to the text, as the presumed point of origin for the cluster of desire in language that is the text. This authorial subject is inscripted in the reader by means of the text's materiality—its rhythms, sounds, images, character, point of view—and thus realized through its effects on the reader. When those effects are repeated in a body of work, the authorial subject becomes linked to the historical subject. Indeed, in the readings that follow, I will argue that it is precisely the obsessive mimicry of hysteria that uncovers in modernist texts an existential anxiety pointing beyond the narrator to the textual unconscious of the authorial subject.

Joseph Conrad and Ford Madox Ford also deliberately create narrators whose voices are disordered by the implications of the tales they tell, narrators who function in part to distance the implied authorial subject from that disorder. Unlike the speaker in Eliot's dramatic monologue, however, these narrators present themselves in turn as distanced from the action of their stories; instead, they are narrating frames for an interior story whose ambiguous meanings they only dimly apprehend. Their distance turns out to be an illusion, however, for their voices become acutely distressed in the course of their narration, uncovering their own subjective involvement in the problematic tales they unfold. At the same time, the texts are structured to entangle the reader in their narrative distress. Thus, the frame that initially serves to separate narrator from story ultimately becomes a linguistic bridge that connects narrator to story, author to narrator, and reader to each.

In an analogous reading of *The Turn of the Screw*, Shoshana Felman describes the way in which the prologue frames the inner story of the governess through a chain of narrative voices: the reader hears the story from a narrator who has heard the story from his friend Douglas, who reads the manuscript of his former governess to a circle of listeners seated around a fire. James thus draws the reader and the narrator into the story as members of that circle, "enclosing [in the story] what is usually outside it: its own readers." As Felman notes, the frame at the same time does the very opposite, pulling the inside outside: for "in passing through the echoing chain of the multiple, narrative voices. . . the interior of the story. . . becomes somehow exterior to itself, reported. . . by a voice inherently alien to it" (1977, 123). Although I would question how "inherently" alien the voice is, certainly this inclusion of the imaginary reader inside the narrative frame by a narrative voice functionally estranged from the story it tells points to a structural technique congenial to both modernist fiction and hysteria. Just as the frame of James' tale does not allow readers direct access to the story's meaning, in the broadest sense, the narrative voice of modernist fiction programmatically estranges itself from its own story, anxiously asserting its alienation from a center of meaning or knowledge. Yet at the same time that the center fades, the frame of narration, circumscribing that absence, draws the reader into a circle of listeners who function as the listening ear to an echo of a prior voice. The reader is thus made the necessary interlocutor of the narrative voice, an assumedly privileged site for the apprehension of narrative meaning or its lack.

This is the structural principle in Conrad's *Heart of Darkness* as well as Ford's *The Good Soldier.* Conrad and Ford each make use of framed narratives to incorporate the listener into the discourse of the speaker, who tells someone else's story. Each locates the reader as listener within a circle of oral storytelling, and as in the psychoanalytic dialogue, each posits the ear of the listener as necessary to the speaker's articulation, evoking the ur-scene of psychoanalysis in a seductively disturbing discourse. Just as in *The Turn of the Screw* the narrator hears in Douglas's voiced reading "a rendering to the ear of the beauty of his author's hand" (1966, 6), so in the works of Conrad and Ford the auditory power of discourse is foregrounded as both theme and technique.

What is perhaps most striking in this regard is that also within the inner story of both *Heart of Darkness* and *The Good Soldier,* a "rendering to the ear" appears regularly to provide a critical complication in the plot. It is, however, specifically a scene of overhearing, of hearing something that should not be heard. If *The Voyage Out* raised its specters through primal scenes of forbidden looking, the texts of Conrad and Ford rely on scenes of transgressive audition. In *Heart of Darkness,* Marlow overhears a private conversation about Kurtz that inflames his interest in the man whose rescue becomes his obsession. In *The Good Soldier,* Maisie's heart attack and Florence's suicide as well as Edward's own suicide are consequences of an intimate conversation each has unwittingly overheard. In both novels, listening proves to be a risky activity so that the reader drawn into the diegesis also becomes vulnerable, open to the aggressive and libidinal permutations of the voice and its provocative mode of revelation.

Neil Hertz has pointed out that Freud in his autobiographical essay has given us the classic scene of overhearing "secrets": Freud overhears the elders of his profession narrating a sexual joke, which turns on women's sexual frustration as the source of their hysteria. In this scene, as Hertz remarks, Freud plays the ingenue: overhearing the joke, he occupies the feminine position as he himself defined it in his theory of jokes:

> Freud's distinctly marginal relation to this scene of professional knowingness, almost out of earshot, listening to two men talking— in French, of course—about suggestive matters, secrets d'alcove, locates him close to the position of the woman in his analysis of obscene jokes, just as his being paralyzed with amazement aligns him with the (mostly female) victims of hysterical paralysis. In his innocence, in his capacity to receive impressions, he is feminized. (1990, 239)

Not surprisingly, within these male modernist texts, the very act of listening is rendered a gendered problematic, the listener represented as a passive recipient of an often destructive knowledge. As with Freud's Dora case, these texts in representing the dynamics of talking and listening both meditate on and enact the effects of that exchange.

"*Heart of Darkness* is a tale told *viva voce* by a ship's captain on the deck of a cruising yawl," Ford Madox Ford writes, stressing Conrad's aural technique.[3] The *viva voce* is a key element, but it is Marlow, not the ship's captain, who speaks most *viva voce*, Marlow who mimes the present tense of live conversation, with its breaks, confusions, retractions, digressions. Before we shift into Marlow's voice, however, *Heart of Darkness* first places us as listeners to the anonymous ship's captain, whose meditative voice conveys a mood of melancholic retrospection. Through a play on sound, especially the wail of vowels, long "oo's" and lulling l's, as in the excessive textual reiteration of "gloom brooding" and "brooding gloom," this primary frame narrator sets a mood for the tale to which he in turn will listen as darkness falls on the becalmed ship (7–9).[4] In a series of concentric frames that enclose the heart of the tale—an outer frame narrative into which the anonymous narrator draws the reader-as-listener and an inner frame narrative in which Marlow in turn captivates his listeners—Conrad encloses a core tale, in which Kurtz fascinates Marlow by the power of his voice and the implications of his story.

If the heart of the story is thus enclosed by a double-voiced frame, paradoxically, as the outer frame narrator tells us, Marlow believes "the meaning of an episode was not inside like a kernel but outside,[5] enveloping the tale which brought it out only as a glow brings out a haze in the likeness of one of these misty halos that sometimes are made visible by the spectral illumination of moonshine" (5). In this characteristically Conradian discourse of aural insinuation, the narrator both describes and performs Marlow's belief in the resonance of the voice, what Barthes, in an uncannily similar trope, calls the "immense halo" of implications provoked by language. While in his famous dictum on writing Conrad insists that the purpose of his fiction is to "make you see" (Preface, *Nigger of the Narcissus*), vision is purposefully obscured in *Heart of Darkness*. Instead, evincing a radical distrust of Enlightenment discourse and the illusion of clarity it fosters, the voice of the text insistently makes the reader hear, substituting voice for vision as a more effective conduit toward truth. Yet the only truth of the voice that *Heart of Darkness* ultimately offers is Kurtz's echoing whisper of the ultimate ambiguity, "the horror, the horror" (250).

The voice is recurrently shown to exert an uncanny power; Marlow repeatedly recalls the memory of Kurtz as "a voice, a voice" (69), and is seduced by that voice even before he meets him:

> I had travelled all this way for the sole purpose of talking with Mr. Kurtz. Talking with . . . I . . . became aware that this was exactly what I had been looking forward to—a talk with Kurtz. I made the strange discovery that I had never imagined him as doing, you know, but as discoursing. . . . The man presented himself as a voice. . . . The point was in his being a gifted creature, and that of all his gifts the one that stood out preeminently, *that carried with it a sense of real presence* was his ability to talk, his words—the gift of expression. (48, italics mine)

The gift of presence in expression: this is the shape of Marlow's desire, what he as a narrator would dispense, what the writer behind his fictional alter ego also desires, fantasmatically projected onto the enigmatic object of fascination, Kurtz. Yet although Marlow characterizes Kurtz's gift as a figure of presence, Kurtz's eloquence is pointedly an absence in the text, a ghostly attribute beyond the narration. Except for the reiterated phrase, "the horror, the horror," there is no transmission of a potent voice. Indeed, it is not Kurtz's voice but Marlow's that we hear as readers. Ironically, the more it attempts to convey the presence of Kurtz, the murmuring voice of the wilderness, of the very origin of desire that Africa ultimately signifies to Marlow, the more Marlow's voice becomes disembodied.

Paradoxically, the only word that continues to resonate with a sense of presence after the end of Marlow's tale is precisely "the horror," a word on the edge of the unspeakable, as close as one can get to a "primal cry," Peter Brooks points out (1984, 250) in his canny reading of this affective ejaculation that effectively stops discourse. Yet within the metaphoric structure of *Heart of Darkness,* this cry is also a demand and comes to signify a particular horror to which the text repeatedly alludes, a voraciousness that has no limits, no restraints, an oral desire embodied in a repeated image that obviously fascinates Marlow: "I saw him open his mouth wide—it gave him a weirdly voracious aspect as though he had wanted to swallow all the air, all the earth, all the men before him" (59). Or again, "I had a vision of him on the stretcher, opening his mouth voraciously, as if to devour all the earth with all its mankind" (72).

This vision of Kurtz's mouth, a gendered inversion of the image in Eliot's "Hysteria," is foreshadowed in Marlow's earlier self-representation when, standing before the map of Africa and the Congo River, he describes himself as a bird fascinated by a snake. The image depends for its effectiveness on its evocation of a snake's mouth, which unlocks its jaws to swallow its prey whole.[6] *Heart of Darkness* is saturated with such images of insatiable hunger, not only Kurtz's, but the hunger of the wilderness itself, which had "taken him, loved him, embraced him, got into his veins, consumed his flesh, and sealed his soul to its own" (49).[7] Indeed, the "as if" clause—"as if to devour all the earth with all its mankind"—in the above excerpt is no mere simile; the row of human skulls adorning Kurtz's jungle house suggestively images a literal ravenous incorporation of the other, a gratification of the fantasmatic desire to take it all in. Uncannily recapitulating infantile fantasies of omnipotence and oral aggression, Conrad's text presents an eat-or-be-eaten world, with Marlow attempting to avoid both fates.

In *Totem and Taboo* Freud also imagines a primal cannibalism through the totem meal but gives it an antithetical valence: through "the act of devouring [the father, the sons] acquired a portion of his strength. The totem meal, which is perhaps mankind's earliest festival, would thus be a repetition and a commemoration of this memorable and criminal deed, which was the beginning of. . . social organization, or moral restrictions, and of religion" (1913 [1912–13], *SE* 13:142). If for Freud the totem meal thus signifies the beginning of European social organization through the restraint on desire imposed by symbolic and social institutions, *Heart of Darkness* allegorizes cannibalism to signify its antithesis: a voracious European imperialism that enacts a regressive return to preoedipal omnipotence, that knows no law, that is indeed the other side of an idealism enraged at its own impossibility. Both idealism and omnipotence, condensed in the figure of Kurtz as a representative of nineteenth-century Europe, function to dissolve the underpinnings of patriarchal limits. At the same time, Conrad portrays among the African cannibals a restraint that comes from their own social taboos, their own version of the law. Marlow's story thus uncovers the horror of a primal orality at the dark heart not of "savage" Africa but of nineteenth-century European civilization.

Yet even though he has marveled at the natives' restraint of their hunger, Marlow contradicts his own perception in order to justify Kurtz. "No fear can stand up to hunger, no patience can wear it out, disgust simply does not exist where hunger is" (3). It is not Kurtz who is blamed for his transgression and regression, but the object that has aroused his desire, which has seduced him. Kurtz, we are told, falls prey to "the heavy mute spell of the wilderness—that seemed to draw him to its pitiless breast by the awakening of forgotten and brutal instincts, by the memory of gratified and monstrous passions" (65). In Woolf's novel, the wilderness is also a site of maternal power, figured by the native women nursing infants at the breast. *Heart of Darkness*, in contrast, figures the maternal breast as pitiless in its cruel evocation of unsatisfiable desire and embodies its power in the "savage and superb" phallic woman warrior who gestures to the European intruders in formidable silence. It is she who "awakens" repugnant instincts, a "memory" of passions from another age that are acted out by the adult Kurtz, who "lacked restraint in the gratification of his various lusts" (57).

In attempting to conjure up the powers of horror and desire evoked by the wilderness, Marlow's voice becomes itself hystericized by its own lack, by its very inability to communicate the horror or even to give it shape. His repeated angry interruptions of his own narrative, his frustration at not being able to transmit the presence behind the words, mark those moments of his own desire for the voice as imaginary phallus, for the "gift of expression" that was Kurtz's. This desire for the power of the voice is also a desire for an idealized communion, a desire to incorporate and be incorporated by a community of male listeners in a homosocial bond that defends against "the horror." This is the desire that underlies Marlow's attempts to tell the story and be understood; thus, the story must be told and retold, Conrad seems to imply, as a defense against the wilderness, against that unutterable potentiality lurking in silence and identified with a deadly maternal embrace.

In *Heart of Darkness* the circulation of the voice becomes an ambivalent means of sustaining the fraternal bond that is civilization, the symbolic order, while at the same time recognizing that it covers over a radical abyss. Indeed, language itself assumes the burden of presence while it indicates absence, serving as a bridge bearing the speech of the Other to a community of the same—of specifically male listeners. This is the reason Marlow's lie, demanded of him by the Intended, that shadowy ideal constructed by the symbolic order as the perfect woman, is devastating, why he associates lying with death. Lying undermines identity through shared language, and thus undermines fraternal interconnection. Yet lying seems an inevitability, Conrad suggests, language itself being ultimately a lie.

In this context, that it is the Intended, the woman as a figure of the ideal that cannot be realized, who is responsible for weakening that bond, is both a critique of idealism as well as of the woman that represents it. The Intended first appears to Marlow as the Madonna, the lady of sorrows, the antithesis of the "pitiless breast" of the wilderness:

> This fair hair, this pale visage, this pure brow, seemed surrounded by an ashy halo from which the dark eyes looked out at me. . . . She carried her sorrowful head as if she were proud of that sorrow. . . . For her he had died only yesterday. . . . I saw her and him in the same instant of time—his death and her sorrow—I saw her sorrow

in the very moment of his death. Do you understand? I saw them together—I heard them together. (73)

Marlow's insistence on converting her into a figure of the Pietà, on seeing "his death and her sorrow" together, and even more, on hearing them together, fixes the Intended in a culturally idealized mother-son dyad that is beyond time and history; it also speaks to his own desire for an ideal union, which is the other side of Kurtz's voracious hunger for the All. As Marlow listens to the Intended speak of Kurtz's great gift, her voice takes on for him the features of his own desire:

> the sound of her low voice seemed to have the accompaniment of all the other sounds, full of mystery, desolation, and sorrow, I had ever heard—the ripple of the river, the soughing of the trees swayed by the wind, the murmurs of the crowds, the faint ring of incomprehensible words cried from afar, the whisper of a voice speaking from beyond the threshold of an eternal darkness. (74)

In a diction that returns us to the melancholy cadences of the frame narrator, Marlow describes her seductive plea to hear Kurtz's last words that, uttered in a low and sensuous voice, compels him to lie: "The last word he pronounced was—your name" (75).

Marlow's lie is meant to keep "the horror" unvoiced, to sustain her illusion. One can read this line for what it literally keeps unvoiced— the word *horror* itself. For Marlow's lie and its very syntactical construction, which substitutes "your name" for "the horror," give textual voice to an unvoiced "truth," Conrad's implicit equation of the woman's name, absent from the story except as "the Intended," with the horror. Woman *is* for Conrad the horror, the figure of illusion that inevitably leads to bad faith, the Intended that conceals the unspeakable. More profoundly, she is the unspeakable itself. For to turn the screw once more, insofar as the word *horror* is voiced, one can hear it as one of those Freudian switchwords that homonymically switches the tracks of association, that voices a familiar patriarchal judgment on "woman": *horror* as voiced is *whore*, a word embedded as the repressed in Conrad's text.[8]

Even though it is Kurtz who has the dangerous mouth, in a projective reversal, the textual unconscious condemns woman for provoking that desire for the All that can never be gratified, for leading to the lie and disillusion. Just as Marlow overtly blames Kurtz's descent (or ascent, for "he had kicked the very earth to pieces" [65]—the ultimate fantasy of destructive rage against the maternal figure) on the savage maternal wilderness, so his narrative covertly blames the female figure of ideality for the fall of man. Thus, the Intended and the Wild Woman, literally illuminated in the text as twin points of light, become by the end twin points of darkness.

In the end, *Heart of Darkness* in returning to the frame converts the extremity of an undiminished and self-annihilating oral desire into a desire for an omnipotent language, the desire to speak to a listener, and specifically a male listener, who will totally understand. Conrad's text unveils the drive to talk as the passion that drives Marlow's hysterical narrative, a desire for communication with another in a fullness that eradicates difference, including gender difference. That eradication is also dangerously aggressive, simultaneously destroying what is desired—the otherness of a validating listener, the otherness of a text. Thus, paradoxically, this desire for full communication leads to silence. As Peter Brooks astutely remarks, what Conrad's fictions insist is that the quest of life is full utterance to the perfect ear at the same time that neither full utterance nor the perfect ear is attainable (1984, 253). "Are not our lives too short for that full utterance which through all our stammerings is of course our only and abiding intention?" Conrad writes in *Lord Jim*.[9] We can also formulate this intention as a desire to be one with a primal figure of utterance, a spectral mother who can transform our childlike stammerings, the cry for an other that is also the self, into a communion that does not destroy its object. It remained in Conrad's texts a consummation devoutly to be wished.

IT IS NOT surprising that Conrad and Ford became close companions and collaborators in fictional experimentation, nor that they co-authored a novel, for there are powerful links between the two, not only in their experiments with narrative voice but in the desires that drive their protagonists.[10] In Ford Madox Ford's *The Good Soldier*, subtitled "A Tale of Passion," the narrator Dowell muses that the essence of love is to be one with the object of passion: "The real fierceness of desire, the real heat of a passion long continued and withering up the soul of a man is the craving for identity with the woman he loves."[11]

Dowell's desire is analogous to Conrad's desire for full utterance, although it is formulated here within the context of heterosexual passion. The context itself complicates the dangers of a desire for identity with the other, for identity with the loved woman is precisely the hysterical problematic; it places Dowell in that feminine position that unmans him and keeps his desire in a permanent state of repression. Invoking as its narrative paradigm the psychoanalytic dialogue, *The Good Soldier* probes and deconstructs the surfaces and depths of heterosexual romance and its homosexual implications as constructed in the European cultural imagination through a narrator who veers between a passionless description of seduction and death on the one hand and the frenzied eruption of panic in the face of seemingly trivial events on the other.

The Good Soldier is at least a thrice retold tale. Most evidently, it is a retelling by Dowell, who knows this "saddest story"—its original title—before he begins, having heard it twice before, as he confesses, from "the lips" of two of its principals: Edward, the good soldier whose adulterous affairs generate the narrative movement, and Leonora, Edward's wronged but commanding wife, who emerges as the victorious good soldier in a domestic warfare. The image of lips whispering a tale into an ear—a repeated image of the transmission of speech—emphasizes the seductive intimacy with which Dowell has received and will in turn now transmit the story to the listener-reader. Moreover, in the Dedicatory Letter to Stella that prefaces the second edition of the narrative, Ford, presumably speaking in his own voice, tells us his novel is a retelling of a true story he has heard. In thus inserting a story of the narrative as a repetition of a prior true story, Ford constructs an ambiguous frame around Dowell as narrator, one that confuses the relation between truth and fiction, between external author and surrogate speaker. Significantly, Ford tells us he had the story from the male voice only, from Ashburnham, the good soldier, omitting the role of Leonora as storyteller that Dowell gives us. Instead, the Dedicatory Letter as a frame providing the tale's origins makes a woman—Stella, the external recipient of Ford's story—the silent ear who gives it potential meaning.

Ford substantiates the importance of the male transmission of stories through a series of anecdotes which, like Conrad, figures intimacy as an act of talking and listening. First, Ford records that his friend, John Rodker, said in his "clear, slow drawl," "Ah yes. It is. . . the finest French novel in the English language" (1951, xx). The allusion to the "clear slow drawl" of his friend's voice, as in James' description of Ransom's Southern drawl in *The Bostonians,* associates the quality of languorous sensuality with speech. The association is then extended by the speaker's remark that *The Good Soldier* is more French than English: French because it is a narrative of adultery analogous to the story of courtly love within the novel—the story of the troubadour Peire Vidal that Dowell tells—and is set in Provence, original site of the troubadours and the rise of romance narrative. Moreover, the novel is itself like the French story of Peire Vidal, which Dowell calls the story of culture, in representing monogamy and fidelity as senti-mental rather than, as in the Protestant English novel, valorized as the source of morality and maturity. Following this "French" logic, Ford then tells the anecdote about the adjutant who looks sick because, having just gotten engaged to be married, he is now reading *The Good Soldier,* which tells and foretells of betrayal and infidelity. Similarly, Ford's book implicitly transmits a paranoid knowledge that will have unsettling effects on the reader.

Finally, Ford tells us that while he was on military parade, petrified with nervousness, "one of the elderly red hatbands walked close be-hind my back and said distinctly in my ear: 'Did you say The *Good* Soldier?' " (1951, xxi). This seductive whispering into his ear of a voice that questions the meaning of the "good" insinuates an interrogation of precisely those ethical certainties of English society—honor, virtue, strength, honesty—which the trope of the good soldier represents. Moreover, he does so through that familiar exchange of intimacy between voice and ear that foreshadows their insidious roles in this "French" version of the English novel.

Dowell stages his relation to the reader also as a tête à tête, specifi-cally invoking the talking cure by imagining the listener as a silent interlocutor sitting opposite him:[12] "So I shall just imagine myself for a fortnight or so at one side of the fireplace of a country cottage, with a sympathetic soul opposite me. And I shall go on talking, in a low voice while the sea sounds in the distance and over head the great black flood of wind polishes the bright stars" (12). This is soothing, seduc-tive talk, lulling the listener with the sounds and rhythms of a bedtime story. If the scene and sounds of intimacy suggest a basic trust is being established, the story Dowell tells the reader-listener reveals betrayal, as Dowell replays with his imagined interlocutor the two scenes of his disillusion: the unexpected confessions of Edward and Leonora. "I trusted in Edward and Leonora and in Nancy Rufford . . . as I had trusted in *my mother's love*. And that evening Edward spoke to me" (202, italics mine).

Certainly the text will suggest that mother-love is not to be trusted, nor father-love either. From both Edward and Leonora, Dowell learns the nature of the labyrinthine adulterous plot in which they have all been implicated and of his betrayal by all its significant figures. As listener to both Edward and Leonora, he has been forced "to get it full in the face" (105). Significantly, this trope recurs a few pages later as Dowell, retelling the scene of Florence's traumatic discovery of her own displacement, gives into an uncharacteristic outburst of rage: "Florence must have got it in the face, good and strong" (110). The sadistic pleasure he takes in this assaultive image and its repetition turns it into a kind of pornographic "money shot," a violent ejaculation from speaker to listener that reveals the sadomasochistic positionality of both in this text. Indeed, although Dowell begins his intimate disclosure with an image of trustful talking and listening— the lips speaking into an ear—it is increasingly replaced by this violent trope of linguistic assault that analogously threatens the reader-listener of Dowell's confessional tale.

If learning too much puts one at risk, not knowing is even more problematic, indeed is *the* problematic of this tale of passion. Dowell's repeated "I don't know," the classic psychoanalytic signifier of repression that punctuates his discourse, transmits his not-knowing to the reader who wants to know, even demands that the reader as ear supply the knowledge the narrator does not have. "Is all this digression or isn't it digression? Again I don't know. You, the listener, sit opposite me. But you are so silent. You don't tell me anything. I am at any rate trying to get you to see what sort of life it was I led" (14). By thus implicating the silent reader as a withholding, nonreflective source of truth, an imaginary analyst, Dowell, and Ford behind him, attempts to compel the reader to discover the meaning already in his speech. Thus, the reader is rhetorically enjoined to serve the narrator as an ear through which he can discern the implications of his speech.

Similarly, within the story's action, Dowell discovers his desire by hearing himself speak to another character. This is, of course, the very nature of the psychoanalytic dialogue: to provide what Silverman calls an acoustic mirror, to allow the voice to be freely heard by the Other, so that desire and unconscious knowledge can be acknowledged. The novel repeatedly stresses the need for an interlocutor; for example, Leonora, "like a person who is listening to the sounds in a sea shell held to her ear" (97), hears in Dowell's naive remark that Edward is "a good husband" and "good guardian to your ward" her own unconscious knowledge of Edward's illegitimate desire for Nancy, in great part because the repetition of the word *good* in the first phrase "good husband," a phrase Leonora knows to be false, casts doubts on the structural repetition, "good guardian"—and, of course, on "the good soldier." Similarly, when after Florence's death, Leonora says to Dowell, "You might marry her" (103), he had not thought of it before; "it made things plainer, suddenly" (104).

This articulation of a character's as yet unacknowledged desire through the ear of the other is most consequential in the case of Edward, in the scene of his sudden recognition of his feelings for Nancy: "It was as if his passion for her hadn't existed; as if the very words he spoke, without knowing that he spoke them, created the passion as they went along. Before he spoke, there was nothing; afterwards, it was the integral fact of his life. Well, I must get back to my story" (116). In the double irony that inhabits Dowell's last remark, in the "recollection" that is his story, as he remembers voices of those presumed to know, the story itself as he speaks it creates for the narrator "the integral fact of his life." Ironically, this "integral fact of his life," indeed, his life-story itself, is represented as the story of others. Like the true hysteric, Dowell is dissociated from his desire and from his story at the same time that he reveals it through the desire of the other. By the end of the novel, his story is everyone's story—"the story of culture," the archetypal narrative of adultery with which Western romance narrative began.

What is Dowell's desire? The text offers the attentive reader ample clues through its reliance on hysterical paradigms. Striking in this regard is Dowell's description of the disappearance, or repression, of Florence as the primary object: "You have no idea how quite extraordinarily for me that was the end of Florence. From that day to this I have never given her. . . so much as a sigh. . . . She just went completely out of existence, like yesterday's paper" (120). Yet it is Florence, the temptress-as-talker, who is the critical engine of the story's mobility, who seduces Edward through stories, who compels them all into the orgy of transgressive talk that the novel becomes. What does it mean that she so completely vanishes from Dowell's conscious repertory and that she is replaced—as Edward's lover and Dowell's patient—by Nancy, her silent and innocent counterpart?

The key scene that opens the story to these questions is the excursion to Marburg, where the corrupt Florence explains the significance of the Protest, the document that shaped British faith. As Carol Jacobs has remarked, this document, the Articles of Marburg, records an argument over the phrase, "This is my body"—over whether it is to be taken figuratively or literally (1978, 32–51). This historical-linguistic argument over the meaning of the body provides a resonant counterpoint to the action of this scene, which plays on the same question: What is the meaning of the body?

> And she laid one finger upon Captain Ashburnham's wrist.
>
> I was aware of something treacherous, something frightful, something evil in the day. I can't define it and can't find a simile for it. It wasn't as if a snake had looked out of a hole. No, it was as if my heart had missed a beat. It was as if we were going to run and cry out; all four of us in separate directions, averting our heads. In Ashburnham's face I know that there was absolute panic. I was horribly frightened and then I discovered that the pain in my left wrist was caused by Leonora's clutching it. (44–45)

What is happening? Whose body is at issue here? How are we to read these bodily connections? The passage is rich with unspoken ambiguities that represent a hysterical diffusion not unlike that of Eliot's hysteric. How similar is Dowell's inability to find a verbal referent for his inchoate terror, his projective identification with Ashburnham as he sees his own panic reflected on Ashburnham's face, as he feels on his own wrist the touch that Ashburnham receives, although somatically transformed from Florence's erotic touch to Leonora's painful clutch. "The panic again stopped my heart. I muttered, I stuttered—I don't know how I got the words out" (44–45). If, as Dowell puts it, "it wasn't that a snake had looked out of a hole," what is happening to cause such a shattering of the speaking subject? The enigma of Dowell's panic compels us to read his panic as well as the literal document that is its signifying backdrop, but Ford's text at this juncture remains resistant to interpretation. If "palpable shafts" of light break into the "heavily shuttered" chamber that houses the Protest, the narrative wants to keep us in the dark while allowing language to insinuate ambiguous meanings.

Certainly the text constructs Florence's touch, the literal and figurative articulation of her body on Ashburnham's wrist, as a perception whose meaning Dowell cannot acknowledge, the snake in the hole that he denies. Yet in representing Dowell's projective identification with Ashburnham's passive experience of a woman's touch, the text also points in another direction: to Florence's phallic power to actively control the circulation of desire. Put otherwise, Dowell's "craving for identity with the woman he loves" (115), which comes out of a context of heterosexual passion, paradoxically leads him to assume a feminine subject position in what Kristeva calls an amatory identification, in which *having* becomes *being* (1986a). Insofar as the hysteric's desire is the desire of the other, ultimately it is neither Florence nor Nancy but the object of *their* desire, the object of all the others' desire, Ashburnham, the good soldier, who is the true object of desire in this tale of passion.

> The lover is a narcissist with an object. . . . The lover, in fact, reconciles narcissism and hysteria. As far as he is concerned, there is an idealizable other who returns his own ideal image. . . . In amorous hysteria, the ideal other is a reality not a metaphor. . . . Endowed with the sexual attributes of both parents, and by that very token a totalizing, phallic figure. (Kristeva 1986a, 250)

At Marburg this opening up of desire as identification is quickly foreclosed by Leonora's cover-up and Dowell's grateful accession to it. Throughout the text Dowell will foreclose any intimation of desire, as he does at the very beginning, when he tells us he finds sex "nebulous" (12) and regards himself as "no better than a eunuch" (12). Indeed, although he finally admits toward the end of the novel that "I can't conceal from myself the fact that I loved Edward Ashburnham" (253), he does conceal that fact throughout his narrative, heading off not only for Florence but for himself any talk that might stimulate the "heart," any conversation about "what the English call 'things'" (16), those things that are the very matter of the French novel. As at Marburg, these "things"—Dowell's word itself functioning as an empty signifier repressing the body's particularities—keep surfacing in spite of, or perhaps because of, his vigilance.

The primary means of revelation is precisely through conversations about "things," through a sequence of scenes of overhearing that move the plot forward. Maisie Maiden overhears Edward and Florence talking about her and, realizing that she is no longer Edward's favorite, her heart literally succumbs to this inadvertent attack and she dies. Florence overhears Edward speak his love for Nancy—she "heard the words from behind the tree" (117)—and commits suicide. Nancy's scene of overhearing is more diffusely constructed, more metonymic, its meaning initially linked to overhearing her father's "booming" voice (128). In what seems an extratextual allusion to *Heart of Darkness,* Dowell and Nancy overhear her father talking of the Congo and of the proper treatment of natives: "Oh, hang humanity," he says, and these words immediately trigger Nancy's inexplicable terror.

Dowell's choice of words in describing the effects of the father's voice on his daughter are telling: "that peculiar note of his voice, used when he was overbearing or dogmatic, could *unman* her" (129, italics mine). This "unmanning" again suggests Dowell's own identification as "feminized" listener, as do his empathic descriptions, here of her disintegration under the violent voice of her father and subsequently of her willing submission to Edward's erotic voice. "The half-opened door opened noiselessly to the full. Edward was there. . . . 'I forbid you to talk about these things. . . . I am the master of this house' . . . And at the sound of his voice, heavy, male, coming from a deep chest, in the night, with the blackness behind him, Nancy felt as if her spirit bowed before him, . . . that she desired never again to talk of these things" (229–30). Nancy's compliance with Edward's command is followed by her rapture as Edward telephones to arrange for the care of her mother:

> She sat there in a blissful dream. She seemed to see her lover, sitting as he always sat, in a round-backed chair, in the dark hall—sitting low, with the receiver at his ear, talking in a gentle, slow voice, that he reserved for the telephone—and saving the world and her, in the black darkness. She moved her hand over the bareness of the base of her throat, to have the warmth of flesh upon it and upon her bosom. (231)

Edward's gentle telephone voice is a radical departure from the booming paternal voice as phallus, transmitting a more diffuse, maternally inflected sensuality, a pleasure kinesthetically reproduced when Nancy touches herself "to have the warmth of flesh. . . upon her bosom."[13] In contrast to the earlier touch of Florence and the clutch of Leonora, Nancy's self-touching enacts an imaginary union with Edward as the maternal father. Significantly, it is this gentle, slow voice that Dowell assumes at the novel's beginning when he imagines himself speaking softly to a trusting listener, suggesting that he as narrating subject would appropriate the voice of the good soldier as the voice of the text, would become himself—in an act of self-touching—the object of his desire. Instead, as we have seen, Dowell's maternal voice quickly becomes the voice of a hysteric, yielding "explosive sentences" (193) more like Leonora's lash than Edward's caress.

Finally, Ford's fiction, in constructing narrative intimacy through the speaking voice, accords the voice a fantasmatic power as both a caress and an assault. As a caress, the voice soothes us into an illusion of intimacy. Leonora takes Edward's whispering to her as a sign of his returning affection: "he whispered little jokes about the odd figures they saw up at the Casino. It was not much to make a little joke—but the whispering of it was a precious intimacy" (189). In such passages Ford, like Conrad, represents the speaking voice seducing through its sensuous evocations of half-forgotten sounds and rhythms.[14] These intimations of linguistic felicity can suddenly turn into that sadistically orgiastic explosion of knowledge "full in the face." From a novel that begins as a soothing eroticized exchange between talker and listener, Dowell structures a sadomasochistic orgy in which the worst offenders are precisely those who release repressed desire in and as speech. Even though Leonora "had been drilled to keep her mouth shut" (177), when she gives in to her desire for communication, "What had happened was just hell. Leonora had spoken to Nancy; Nancy had spoken to Edward. Edward had spoken to Leonora—and they had talked and talked" (201).

In this rondel of talking and listening, Edward's climactic scene of overhearing becomes a torment for Dowell as well. While earlier in the novel Dowell had referred with distaste to the world of male anecdotes and sexual jokes, in which the body of a woman is circulated in language, at the end he describes the female counterpart of this tendentious tongue-lashing talk: "It was as if Leonora and Nancy banded themselves together to do execution. . . upon the body of a man who was at their disposal. . . . Night after night he would hear them talking; talking. . . seeking oblivion in drink, he would lie there and hear the voices going on and on" (253).

Not surprisingly, then, Dowell ends up as nurse-caretaker to a silent woman, the narrator of her story as well as the story of the others. His story remains punctuated by denials, equivocations, forgettings, disordered chronologies, all means of keeping the reminiscences from which Freud said the hysteric suffers under erasure while at the same time confessing them. Indeed, ultimately Dowell shows himself, like Leonora, as suffering from "a desire for communicativeness" (192); behind him, so does Ford. The writer who positions himself as Dowell's double in the second edition, who in the prefatory Dedicatory Letter writes in his own voice of having heard the story from Ashburnham, and thus once again conflates what is inside and outside fiction, Ford places himself both inside and outside the text and its anxieties.

Yet there remains a significant difference between inside and outside. For while Dowell had to listen to the woman talking—he gets his knowledge full in the face from Leonora—Ford gets it only from Ashburnham. To have heard the story from Leonora's mouth, Ford implies by his foreclosure of Leonora as narrative source, would have effectively hystericized him, turned him into a Dowell. In ascribing the story's transmission to Ashburnham, Ford can imaginatively sustain a chain of male oral/aural transmission, a chain that we might see linking male modernist writers together in a defensive bond against the female voice.[15]

IN PLUMBING THE relation between voice and ear in these modernist experiments with dialogical form, I have been pointing to a reiteration of the trope of the fearsome woman with a big mouth that verges on paranoia. Whether she opens it to reveal a honeyed or a moneyed voice, the image of the woman's mouth as the entrance to a potent, invisible, and ultimately alien female interiority speaks to a fundamental male anxiety in these texts. I do not mean to conclude by invoking a simple essentialism of sexual difference that modernism itself challenged nor to reduce the meanings of these modernist texts to this simple fantasmatic origin. Certainly Conrad is not Marlow, nor Ford Dowell. Yet as my readings have incrementally suggested, both narrators are insistent textual indicators of a hysterical relation to the eroticized body that exceeds the text's frame and points to the authorial subject beyond it, a relation that demonizes the woman with a big mouth.

This should not be surprising; insofar as an author's gender identification places him or her in a particular relation to the symbolic order, it also places him or her in a relation to the body and to its inscribed meanings. As contemporary psychoanalysis reminds us, the body is always also the image of the body, already caught within a network of internally fueled projections, externally imposed inscriptions, always cathected by language processes at the same time that it exists in the real as a material presence. Clearly, hysteria means one thing to a woman inhabiting a contested female body while resisting its significations, another to a man for whom the female body represents an unutterable alterity that can un-man him. The hysteric, I have argued, refuses the body as constructed by the symbolic order, that is to say, refuses the body as a signifier of sexual difference. Thus the hysteric either lacks an image of the body or, what amounts to the same thing, has an image of the body as excess. Whether as excess or lack, as Freud concluded and these texts confirm, it is the female body and the feminine position, projected in the imaginary and inscribed by the symbolic, which figure a danger to the speaking subject and generate the passions of the voice.

What is particularly notable in this regard is that these early texts of Eliot, Conrad, and Ford point to a strategic use of hysteria as a defense, a form of mimicry through a first-person narrator that became part of the formal poetics of anxiety that was modernism. Of course, this strategy of mimicry and masquerade was not peculiar to twentieth-century writers. Recall, for example, that in *Villette,* Brontë's protomodernist construction of a hysterical narrative, Lucy Snowe finds her tongue liberated by donning male garb in a play. Analogously, I would argue, Lucy Snowe as hysterical narrator is a mask that enabled Brontë's text to perform a liberating excavation of the problematics of female identity while Brontë herself as authorial subject could remain defensively dissociated from its conflicts. Late-nineteenth- and early-twentieth-century writers seem increasingly to move toward this use of a first-person representation of hysterical anxiety as a masquerade through which they could both contain and also probe the darker corners of their own psychic space.

Indeed, masquerade and hysterical mimicry became an avowed area of interest in modernist aesthetics as well as in modern psychoanalysis.[16] Joan Rivière's "Woman as Masquerade," for example (see chap. 1), written during the period of high modernism, described masquerade as an unconscious enabling strategy for women, allowing them access to transgressive desire through disguise.[17] Rivière's intellectual woman felt compelled to put on a mask of flirtatious femininity after her lectures in order to ward off a feared retaliation for her phallic presumption in speaking. As Rivière concluded,

> Womanliness therefore could be assumed and worn as a mask, both to hide the possession of masculinity and to avert the reprisals expected if she was found to possess it. . . . The reader may now ask how I define womanliness or where I draw the line between genuine womanliness and the masquerade. My suggestion is not, however, that there is any such difference; whether radical or superficial, they are the same thing. (1986 [1929], 213)

Femininity is in these terms a representation based on an external demand that the hysteric attempts to satisfy.

More recently, Luce Irigaray has explained women's performance of a patriarchally defined femininity as an act of hysterical miming, but stresses its function in saving desire itself: "hysterical miming will be the little girl's or the woman's effort to save her sexuality from total repression and destruction. . . or hysteria" (1985a, 72). For Irigaray, the miming of a compulsory sexual identity is both a feature of hysteria and a strategic defense against it, a way of avoiding "total repression" and the debilitation of desire that is its consequence.[18] Although Irigaray, like Rivière, is describing hysterical miming as a particularly female strategy of self-rescue, their formulations can be taken as paradigmatic of the function of hysterical miming more generally.

In this context, modernist intentionality can be reformulated as a compulsive mimicry of hysterical form meant to ward off an even more threatening disintegration. Indeed, I would contend that for the authorial as well as the historical subject, hysteria was both real and unreal, that like Hamlet's antic play, hysteria as both paradigm and pathology offered Eliot, Conrad, and Ford a means of eluding "total repression." Or put more positively, it gave them a way of speaking through the Other in order to explore their own phobic involvement in the unsettling cultural ambiguities of desire and difference that characterized turn-of-the-century discourse.

In short, I am suggesting that hysterical mimicry as the mimicry of hysteria allowed these modernist writers to indulge an anxiety of identity—as representation, as masquerade, as alter ego—to play with lack of control, of voice, while simultaneously avoiding recognition of their complicity in its hysterical structure, remaining ostensibly behind the scenes. By this tactic of dissociation the author outside the text is allowed to keep his authority intact.[19] This is itself part of the fiction of fiction; as my close readings suggest, these texts perform not a transcendence of hysteria but a strategic implication in it. No more than their readers can Eliot, Conrad, and Ford be excluded as authorial writing subjects from the passions of their narrative voices.

Notes

Preface

Unless otherwise stated, citations from the works of Sigmund Freud are from the 1959 *Standard Edition of the Complete Psychological Works* (24 vols.), abbreviated in the text as *SE*.

1. For extended discussions of the subject of narrative voice to which I am strongly indebted, see Ferrer (1990), Silverman (1988), Cohan and Shires (1988), and Brooks (1984).

2. As feminist philosophers have contended, that supposedly disinterested universal subject of Western culture bears the typical attributes of the masculine subject. See, for example, Harding's (1986) discussion of gender and the universal subject.

3. See Showalter (1990), Ardis (1990), and DuPlessis (1985) for discussions of the impact of the New Woman on Victorian discourse and narrative structure.

4. See Armstrong (1987) for a different but complementary reading of the place of women in nineteenth-century narrative.

5. Although Freud interpreted Medusa as a figure of castration fear based on the absence of the maternal penis, many psychoanalysts interpret the Medusa head as a figure of the phallic and castrating mother. See, for example, Slater (1968, 20–21).

6. For an early theorization of that relation, see Klein, "The Importance of Symbol Formation in the Development of the Ego" (1931) in *The Selected Melanie Klein* (1986). A. Anzieu provides a clear articulation of the ways in which the orifices of the body become erogenous places of passage (1990, 137).

7. Certainly rage is an issue in his discussion of aggression and the death drive in *Beyond the Pleasure Principle* (1920, *SE* 18). See also Freud's papers on psychosexual development (1924, 1929, 1931, 1933), usefully collected in the Collier paperback under the title *Sexuality and the Psychology of Love* (1963).

8. See especially Mitchell's "The Question of Hysteria" in *Women: The Longest Revolution* (1984); Kristeva (1982, 1989); and Irigaray's remarks on hysteria and depression (1985a, 61–72). Klein's theories have obviously been an important influence in these more recent formulations.

9. Following Klein, such theorists as Fairbairn and Kernberg continued to theorize the relation of rage to drives and frustrations. See Fairbairn (1952) for more on aggression and rage; also Kernberg (1976), for whom, like Klein, rage is a primitive derivative of the aggressive drive.

10. For an interesting discussion of the relation between aggression and femininity that touches on hysteria, see Green, "Aggression, Femininity, Paranoia and Reality" (1972), reprinted in *On Private Madness* (1986a, 104–14).

11. Theodore Reik's use of the phrase, "listening with the third ear," in his book by that name—a phrase he took from Nietzsche's *Beyond Good and Evil* (pt. 8, 246)—has become a classic trope of psychoanalytic discourse.

12. Hartman points out that presence is an effect produced by words; "the reality of the effect is inseparable, in literature, from the reality of words that conduct voice-feeling" (1981, 121).

13. See Stewart's (1990) provocative discussion of the reader's involuntary corporeal mimicry of the text, a mimicry that ironically evokes a typical feature of hysteria. As he remarks, "the place of reading. . . is none other than the reading body" (1990, 1).

14. See Showalter's discussion of war neurosis as a form of male hysteria (1985, 167–94).

Chapter One. History/Hysteria

1. See Gay's extensive elaboration of the changes in Victorian life and their effects (1984).

2. *Physics and Politics* (1872, 1; quoted in Gay 1984, 52–53).

3. This characterization comes from Holbrook Jackson, *The Eighteen Nineties* (1913, 21–23; quoted in Gay 1984, 52).

4. See Gay (1984), Showalter (1990), and Ardis (1990) for extended discussions of the cultural anxieties provoked by the New Woman in Victorian England. I take the statistics that follow from Gay's text. For an analogous discussion of the New Woman in the United States, see Smith-Rosenberg (1985, 245–96).

5. Sensibar (1991) gives a good deal of useful historical information about hysteria and its medical context, claiming that it is essential to a reading of Henry James, *The Bostonians* (see my chap. 4). See also Showalter (1985); Sayers (1982).

6. See Smith-Rosenberg's highly informed and informative chapter, "The Hysterical Woman," in *Disorderly Conduct* (1985) for an excellent overview of this issue. Gay also records striking examples of Harvard medical professor Edward Clarke's subjectively processed science, as, for example, the spurious case of Miss D., "who had entered Vassar at 14 healthy, began menstruation at 15, continued to study, recite, [and as a consequence] began to have fainting fits during exercises [and] graduated with impaired physique" (1984, 214–15).

7. For refutations of such opinions as Darnell's and Clarke's, see Smith-Rosenberg's chapter "The New Woman as Androgyne" in *Disorderly Conduct* (1985).

8. Ardis heroinizes the New Woman by pointing out that "the New Woman refused to be assimilated into the iconography of the Victorian 'Womanhood'" (1990, 2–3). See also Showalter (1990) on the sexual challenge of the New Woman.

9. Showalter surveys the flourishing literature of female difference and emancipation in the final decades of the nineteenth century, including novels such as Gissing's *The Odd Women,* in which emancipation means the rejection of heterosexual marriage, and Walter Besant's *The Revolt of Men,* which represents a reversal of gender roles in a dystopian future.

10. *History of Woman Suffrage,* ed. Elizabeth Cady Stanton, Susan B. Anthony, and Matilda Joslin Gage, vol. 1 (quoted in Gay 1984, 194).

11. Interestingly, Henry James represents such a figure in the sexually ambiguous Dr. Prance in *The Bostonians,* but marks her as a sympathetic character by her taciturn alienation from feminist oratory.

12. See Krohn (1978) for a discussion of the psychological features of this epidemic. Showalter (1985) provides a more extensive discussion of the meaning of hysteria for women in its nineteenth-century historical context.

13. Hélène Cixous has been the most noteworthy feminist assuming this position; see her dialogue with Catherine Clément in *The Newly Born Woman* (1986).

14. Oral fixations are also responsible for a cathexis of speaking, of the throat and the voice: some of Dora's and Anna O.'s symptoms suggest orality as the preferred mode of nonsatisfaction and anxiety (A. Anzieu 1990, 140–43).

15. Heath (1986) has extrapolated from Rivière's case history a dynamic explanation of the problematics of femininity that also illuminates women's familiar ambivalence about public speaking.

16. Veith describes the *Malleus Maleficarum* of 1494 as a document that "reveals beyond doubt that many, if not most, of the witches as well as a great number of their victims described therein were simply hysterics who had suf-

fered from partial anesthesia, mutism, blindness, and convulsions, and above all, from a variety of sexual delusions" (1965, 61).

17. For an elaboration of the ambivalence of male identity, see Silverman (1992). For a fuller discussion of the ways in which hysteria in both men and women is linked to the primary relation to an imaginary mother, and to oral conflicts, see David-Ménard (1989). A. Anzieu writes that hysteria involves "the erogenous diffusion of a mode of oral excitation to other parts of the body. . . namely a cathexis of the orifices of the body as erogenous place of passage. Persistence of the mouth-genital confusion is connected with this. . . . In men it reveals a fixation to early feminine identifications and difficulties whose form makes one inevitably think of hysteria" (1990, 121).

18. Rousseau praises Sydenham for his "discovery" that hysteria imitates culture (1993, 102) and that the hysterical symptom was produced by stresses within the culture that it mimed. Rousseau presents a provocative historical reading of hysteria that explores the links between representation and pathology. See "A Strange Pathology" in Gilman et al. (1993).

19. Smith-Rosenberg's discussion of the relation of hysteria to femaleness, while in many ways an excellent summary, oversimplifies its formulation in psychoanalysis: "It was defined as an entity that was peculiarly female and has almost always carried with it a pejorative implication" (1985, 197). Like Charcot before him, Freud took great pains to assert that hysteria was not limited to women, classing himself as a "petit hysteric." Moreover, Smith-Rosenberg's statement that "more recently, psychoanalysts such as Elizabeth Zetzel have refined this Freudian hypothesis, tracing the roots of hysteria to a woman's excessively ambivalent preoedipal relation with her mother and to the resulting complications of oedipal development and resolution" is misleading; the importance of the mother in hysterical etiologies was emphasized by Freud after the Dora case (see "Hysterical Phantasies and Their Relation to Bisexuality" (1908, SE 9) and developed more fully by subsequent psychoanalytic theorists.

20. In his obituary notice of Charcot, Freud praised him for releasing the hysteric from the derogation to which she had been subject (SE 3:19).

21. Charcot's famous photographs (published in three volumes, "Iconographie photographique de la salpetrière") captured women in various stages of the *attitude passionelle,* and portrayed types of erotic body language that continued to bind hysteria to the spectacle of a disturbing female sexual excess not unlike the image of the possessed woman of an earlier time.

22. Woolf's essays on modernist writing, "Mr. Bennett and Mrs. Brown" and "Modern Fiction," can both be read as contrasting a visual mode of representation that focuses on perceived and bounded objects and a more

subtle subjective representation of "the atoms as they fall upon the mind" (1953, 155).

23. See Marcus (1990 [1974]) for a reading of Freud's case history as a great modernist novel.

Chapter Two. Freud's Passion/Dora's Voice

1. See "Hysterical Phantasies and Their Relation to Bisexuality" (1908, *SE* 9).

2. See Freud's discussion of unconscious repression in *The Ego and the Id*, *SE* 19:20–21.

3. "A hysterical attack is not a discharge, but an action; it retains the original character of every action—it being a means to the reproduction of pleasure" (Letter 52, *SE* 1:239).

4. See Silverman's (1988) brilliant discussion, "The Fantasy of the Maternal Voice" (72–100).

5. Barthes conjures a "vocal writing" that, like Kristeva's "semiotic," emphasizes the sensuous materiality of language: "its aim is not the clarity of messages. . . . What it searches for. . . are the pulsional incidents, the language lined with flesh, a text where we can hear the grain of the voice, the patina of consonants, the voluptuousness of vowels, a whole carnal stereophony; the articulation of the body of the tongue, not that of meaning, of language" (1975, 67).

6. Malcolm (1990) points out the double role of the analyst, who is both doctor-healer and scientist and who embodies both the father's cultural authority and the mother's nurturing intimacy. The doctor, like the omnipotent mother, transmits emotional connection through physical ministrations; the analyst, Malcolm notes, has a verbal closeness and emotional distance. The analyst's position is also strengthened by the material technique of analysis, which gives him or her the power of the gaze.

7. "As long as the face and mouth have not been revealed and the eye of the spectator has not 'verified' the coincidence of the voice with the mouth . . . the vocal embodiment is incomplete and the voice conserves an aura of invulnerability and magic" (Chion 1982, 32–33). See Silverman (1988, 49–50, 72–76) for a fuller discussion of Chion's work and its implications; the analytic setting itself, by placing the analyst outside the analysand's field of vision, allows the analyst's speech to be attached to the analysand's interior objects.

8. This internalization of the analyst's speech recapitulates the construction of the voice of conscience, the superego, which as Freud theorizes is an

internalization of the parental voice. For a full discussion, see *The Ego and the Id* (1923, *SE* 19).

9. The erotic play in the signifiers *dry* and *wet* has been the subject of a good deal of critical commentary; see Hertz (1990) and Gallop (1990).

10. Although Reik used this phrase long after Freud developed his talking cure, it is an apt metaphor for what Freud described as the free-floating attention of the analyst. Freud recommends that the analyst become a "telephone receiver. . . adjusted to the transmitting microphone" of the patient's unconscious in "Recommendations to Physicians Practicing Psycho-Analysis" (1912, *SE* 12:115–16). The place of the ear in fantasy has been the subject of a good number of psychoanalytically informed discussions: see, for example, Ernest Jones' essay on the fantasy of insemination through the ear in *Essays in Applied Psychoanalysis* (1964, 2:266–357); Derrida's comments in *The Ear of the Other* (1985); and Thomas G. Pavel's "In Praise of the Ear (Gloss's Glosses)" (1986). Kristeva notes that "with the female sexual organ changed into an innocent shell, holder of sound, there arises a tendency to eroticize hearing [and the] voice" (1986b, 173).

11. Heath (1981) invokes Lacan's position that the invocatory field is "nearest to the experience of the unconscious (the invocatory drive is 'not able to close': eyes shut but not ears)" (176–77). He takes this phenomenology of listening still further in elaborating the relations among inner speech, outer speech, and thought (201–3).

12. Freud emphasizes that all words were originally word-sounds whose traces remain in language in *The Ego and the Id* (1923, *SE* 19).

13. LaPlanche and Pontalis elaborate a primal scene of audition in which the voice "breaks the continuity of an undifferentiated perceptual field and at the same time is a sign (the noise waited for and heard in the night) which puts the subject in the position of having to answer to something," in which a subject hears a "spoken or secret discourse going on prior to [his/her] arrival, within which [s/he] must find her/his way" (1968, 10–11).

14. Kofman (1985) notes that the enigma is also deepened by the very riddle of communication: its demand for interpretation. Indeed, language itself carries the freight of enigma; verbalization is itself propelled into existence by unconscious fantasy, whose residue remains as the affect of the text. Thus, the formal quality of the text is fraught with intimations of unknown possibilities, a menace, a promise, contained within words themselves.

15. In "Early Stages of the Oedipal Complex" (1986), Melanie Klein specifically theorizes an epistemophilic drive; see also Moi's (1990) reading of the Dora case, "Representation of Patriarchy: Sexuality and Epistemology in Freud's Dora," which emphasizes the analogy between knowledge and the phallus.

16. Sprengnether has interpreted Freud's suppression of the mother from theory and its significance in *The Spectral Mother* (1990).

17. For an extended discussion of the prominence of oral mechanisms and symptoms in hysteria, see Marmor (1953) and A. Anzieu (1990). Anzieu points out that hysteria involves "the erogenous diffusion of a mode of oral excitation onto other parts of the body, especially the skin surface and the sensory orifices" (137).

18. On this point, see also Hertz (1990, 228–29).

19. In Freud's narrative construction of the origins of human sexuality, before humans had an erect gait, men were attracted to women intermittently through the smell of their menstrual periods. With "the diminution of the olfactory stimuli by means of which the menstrual process produced an effect on the male psyche. . . their role was taken over by visual excitations which. . . were able to maintain a permanent effect. . . . The diminution of the olfactory stimuli seems itself to be a consequence of man's raising himself from the ground. . . . The fateful process of civilization would thus have set in with man's adoption of an erect posture. . . proceeded through the devaluation of olfactory stimuli and the isolation of the menstrual period to the time when visual stimuli were paramount and the genitals became visible, and thence to the continuity of sexual excitement" (*Civilization and Its Discontents,* 1930 [1929], *SE* 21:99–100, n. 1).

20. "With the assumption of an erect posture by man and with the depreciation of his sense of smell, it was not only his anal eroticism which threatened to fall victim to organic repression, but the whole of his sexuality, so that this, the sexual function, has been accompanied by a repugnance which cannot further be accounted for, and which prevents its complete satisfaction and forces it away from the sexual aim into sublimations and libidinal displacements" (*SE* 21:106, n.3).

21. Sprengnether notes that in Freud's narrative "the nurse/invalid structure of sexual relations survives as a fantasy along with the surrender of an aggressive male role at the same time that it denies the power of the nurse by asserting a more culturally sanctioned role division in the structure of Herr K.'s relation to Dora" (1990, 259). Repeatedly in the history of hysteria, an "active" daughter in the role of powerful nurse and a passive invalid-father enact a scene of sexual reversal that undermines the phallic law and its constitution of gender positionality and provokes the daughter's hysteria.

22. Identification becomes increasingly important as Freud turns to issues of ego and object, beginning with "On Narcissism: An Introduction" (1914, *SE* 14) and "Mourning and Melancholia" (1917 [1914], *SE* 14); see especially the section on "Identification" in *The Ego and the Id* (1923, *SE* 19) and "Group Psychology and the Analysis of the Ego" (1921, *SE* 18).

23. In *The Ego and the Id* (1923, *SE* 19), Freud develops the complete oedipus complex as comprising contrasting positions of desire and identity. In the negative oedipus complex, which temporally precedes the positive, the girl actively desires the mother and wants to give her a child, a position that suggests her identification with the father. After recognizing maternal castration, she turns from the maternal object and enters the positive complex, in which she desires first the phallus and then the paternal object who possesses it. It is important to note, as Silverman points out, that "identification with the mother during the negative oedipus complex is at least in part an identification with activity. The equation of femininity and passivity is a consequence only of the positive oedipus complex and the cultural discourses. . . which support it" (1988, 103).

24. Gay points out that the brute in the bedroom is a scenario that repeatedly crops up in late nineteenth-century fiction, either overtly or in barely disguised displacement. Moreover, men also thought of themselves as brutal, since they were in the position to force women into their "duty" (1984, 283). Of course, in actual social fact, because sexual instruction to women was often lacking, women did not understand the nature of their "marital duties" until after marriage, and were not prepared properly for either the psychological or physical pain of heterosexual intercourse.

25. Freud also links hysteria and melancholia in his early writings; he writes to Fliess that "there really is such a thing as hysterical melancholia" and notes such features common to both pathologies as sexual anesthesia and anorexia nervosa. See *Extracts from the Fliess Papers* (*SE* 1:277, 200, respectively); also the letter to Fliess of January 16, 1899 (1985, 340–41). In "Mourning and Melancholia" (1917 [1915], *SE* 14), however, he tries to separate the two categories by noting that while hysteria maintains an object-cathexis, melancholia gives up any relation to the object per se.

26. In this context, we might recall Irigaray's comment on Dora:

So the enigma of the feminine seems, largely, to come down to that of the lips and to what she keeps hidden. This would explain the reaction of Dora—and many of her sisters—to Herr K.'s kiss. . . . The lips as such represent an important enough place of investment for the imposition of a kiss to be an almost unbearable sort of violation. To take a woman's lips would be like taking the fort-da away from a man. . . . The lips are the woman herself, the threshold of the woman, undistanciated by some object or other. To take a kiss from her is to take what is most virginal in her, what is closest to her feminine identity. To make her pregnant is, possibly, another violation, crossing another threshold. To force a woman to speak, what is more, to force a woman lying down to open her lips, to come out of herself, may represent an analytic violation. (1989, 136)

To force a woman to speak, indeed, to give her the words, is a fantasy of the virile father that underlies analytic mastery.

27. In a famous letter to Fliess that announces the birth of psychoanalysis Freud uses childbirth as a metaphor for his rivalrous creation:

"It was November 12, 1897; the sun was precisely in the eastern quarter; Mercury and Venus were in conjunction—" No, birth announcements no longer start like that. It was on November 12, a day dominated by a left-sided migraine, on the afternoon of which Martin sat down to write a new poem, on the evening of which Oli lost his second tooth, that, after the frightful labor pains of the last few weeks, I gave birth to a new piece of knowledge. Not entirely new, to tell the truth; it had repeatedly shown itself and withdrawn again, but this time it stayed and looked upon the light of day. (November 14, 1897, in *Letters to Fliess,* 1985, 278–79).

Interestingly, Irigaray's critique of the son's envy is similar to Klein's analysis of filial envy of the maternal body (1986). See also Sprengnether's (1990) analysis of the maternal figure in Freud's history and theory.

28. For a fuller discussion of the ways in which hysteria is linked to the primary relation to an imaginary mother, see A. Anzieu (1990, 121–45) and Irigaray (1985a, 62–73).

Chapter Three. Invalids and Nurses

1. Mitchell also constructs the daughter as a cultural position rather than an existential being (1984, 308–13).

2. See *Beyond the Pleasure Principle* (1920, *SE* 18) and Lecture 33, "Femininity," in the *New Introductory Lectures on Psycho-Analysis* (1933 [1932], *SE* 22), respectively.

3. See Kristeva's elaboration of these relations involving melancholy, masochism, and hatred in *Black Sun* (1989, 11–12). Freud argued that the loss of self-regard typical in melancholia was a result of rage directed against the incorporated lost object, now part of the self. Freud discusses rage at the lost object in "Mourning and Melancholia" (1917 [1915], *SE* 14); also, in *The Ego and the Id,* 1923, *SE* 19: "In melancholia the object to which the super-ego's wrath applies has been taken into the ego by identification" (51).

4. Freud's remarks on melancholia also support Irigaray's reading: "In melancholia," Freud had noted, "the object has not perhaps actually died, but has been lost. . . even if the patient cannot consciously perceive what [s]he lost" ("Mourning and Melancholia," 1917 [1915], *SE* 14:245). Freud's emphasis on *what* is lost turns the loss of the maternal object into a loss *in* the subject that cannot be represented.

5. Montrelay also argues that the female subject is prevented by her position as object of desire from effectively distancing herself from the body without hysteria. "From now on, anxiety, tied to the presence of this body, can only be insistent, continuous. This body, so close, which she has to occupy, is an object in excess which must be 'lost,' that is to say, repressed, in order to be symbolized" (1978, 91–92). French feminist critics in particular have elaborated the ways in which the male child can position himself at a greater distance from the body, while the female is compelled by virtue of her identification with the mother, to be the body.

6. See especially "Early Stages of the Oedipus Complex" (1928) and "Mourning and Its Relation to Manic-Depressive States" (1940), reprinted in *The Selected Melanie Klein* (1986).

7. In describing the importance of oral fixations in hysteria, A. Anzieu notes that in the cases of both Dora and Anna O., conflict is situated in the throat and the voice (1990, 141). For a more extensive discussion of this same point, see David-Ménard (1989, 64–104). "Dora experiences everything by way of her mouth," David-Ménard writes. "Dora's mouth and throat are thus the theatre where she tries to articulate the way things are between the sexes" (90–91).

8. It is well documented that both Henry and William suffered from physical ailments and effects no less mysterious and hysterical than Alice's. See especially Strouse (1980, 24–25, 110–11).

9. Alice James had been diagnosed variously as hysterical, neurasthenic, melancholic—all related, and extremely common, disorders among women of her class and time. See Strouse (1980, 248) and Yeazell, "Introduction" (1981). In her *Diary* entry for February 21, 1890, she writes, "I had to peg away pretty hard between twelve and twenty-four 'killing myself' as someone calls it—absorbing in the bone that the better part is to clothe oneself in neutral tints, walk by still waters, and possess one's soul in silence" (1964, 95). It is fascinating to note that in the months after her mother's death, she was suddenly no invalid, but nursed her demanding and depressed father until he starved himself and died less than a year after his wife.

10. Writing of a suffering English lady who was first married to a handsome cavalry officer by whom she had one daughter, and who after his death, married a stodgy curate by whom she had nine children, Alice James approvingly notes that the woman was berated by her daughter for her second marriage, and by her sister for having so many children and setting a bad example (October 12, 1890 [146–47]); see also the story of the daughter dying because of her father's remarriage, a story Henry James used as subject of "The Marriages" (April 22, 1891 [105]).

11. In this way one can understand why her criticism of Eliot's remarriage

is immediately followed by her unforgiving censure of Eliot's articulation of her pain:

> What an abject coward she seems to have been about physical pain, as if it weren't degrading enough to have headaches, without jotting them down in a row to stare at one for all time, thereby defeating the beneficient law which provides that physical pain is forgotten. If she related her diseases and her "depressions" and told for the good of others what armour she had forged against them, it would be conceivable, but they seem simply cherished as the vehicle for a moan. (40–42)

12. Paradoxically, Alice James welcomed her illness as giving her substance; when she finally discovered that she had a tumor, she was elated to be able to name her problem as real: "Ever since I have been ill, I have longed and longed for some palpable disease, . . . but I was always driven back to stagger alone under the monstrous mass of subjective sensations which that sympathetic being 'the medical man' had no higher inspiration than to assure me I was personally responsible for" (207).

13. See Swan (1974) for a full discussion of this complex maternal imaginary in Freud.

14. For additional relevant biographical material on Florence Nightingale, see Stark's introduction to *Cassandra* (1979) and Woodham-Smith's biography (1951).

15. In discussing motives for illness in the Dora case, Freud had pointed out that hysterical symptoms are typically "leveled at a particular person, and consequently vanish with that person's departure" (*SE* 7:61).

16. See Stark's introduction to *Cassandra* (1979); Allen (1981); Showalter (1985); and Poovey (1988).

17. Virginia Woolf similarly remarked that "Florence Nightingale shrieked aloud in her agony," and gave as footnote to this remark "See *Cassandra* by Florence Nightingale." See *A Room of One's Own* (1957, 57).

18. I first learned of the formless form of this document in conversation with Elaine Showalter. Subsequently, Katherine Snyder generously provided me with a copy of the original manuscript. I am greatly indebted to her transcription of Nightingale's first version of *Cassandra,* and her insightful and extensive discussion of manuscript changes in "From Novel to Essay: Gender and Revision in Florence Nightingale's *Cassandra*" (1993).

19. See Hirsch's discussion of this imaginary relation in *The Mother-Daughter Plot* (1989, 57–60).

20. Snyder (1993), in examining the social history behind the gendering of the essay as a masculine form, points out that nineteenth-century readers took the essay as a nonfictional and mimetic expression of the writer's actual self.

21. Snyder notes such other alterations as Nightingale's excision of details

that were autobiographical or too conventionally romantic, and her shortening of the heroine's fantasies (1993, 27–28).

22. Significantly, it was Nightingale's father who actually read aloud to her, not her mother, though the conflict in its underlying oral structure remains tied to the maternal figure. Thus, her father takes his place with a number of maternal father figures who appear in hysterical histories. See my discussion of Olive Schreiner in chap. 5.

23. As Silverman points out, "Since the voice is capable of being internalized at the same time as it is externalized it can spill over from subject to object and object to subject, violating bodily limits" (1988, 80).

24. Psychoanalytically speaking, cutting out the tongue is a trope of castration, in particular, an excision of the power of speech. Its relation to the nightingale myth was reinforced for me recently when Professor Lia Lerner, of the Department of Spanish and Comparative Literature at Fordham University, called my attention to one of Boccaccio's stories in which a woman is holding a nightingale that suddenly is transformed into a penis. Making a similar point, Silverman writes that the "female voice provides the acoustic equivalent of an ejaculation" (1988, 68).

25. See especially Showalter (1977, 285–90) and Gilbert and Gubar's chapter on Brontë (1979). For an admirable discussion of Woolf's fear of her own rage and its relation to her conviction that anger inevitably distorted art, see also Zwerdling (1986, 243–53).

26. John Kucich (1987) reads Brontë's texts through their oppositional tensions between expression and repression. As Kucich astutely points out, in Brontë's texts "not only latent rage and subversive sexuality, but also the exploration of repression and desire itself. . . serve a libidinal structure in which both gestures are affirmed, and are to some degree reversible" (38). See also Auerbach (1973, 328–42) for a discussion of Brontë's divided voice as a psychic conflict that remains unresolved, and which Auerbach characterizes as abnormal.

27. See, for example, Patrick Brantlinger on the confusion of the psychological with the social plot (1977, 124–27).

28. There have been a good number of excellent extended and psychoanalytically informed readings of *Villette*. See especially Jacobus, "The Buried Letter" (1986).

29. In a brilliant reading of *Villette's* lack of closure, Garrett Stewart notes that both the heroine's destiny and the death of M. Paul in a shipwreck are arrested. In the final passages, the present is read rather than the past and therefore the story is not past, not closed. As Stewart remarks, "The enunciation enjoins its own arrest" (unpublished manuscript). See also Garrett Stewart, "A Valediction For Bidding Mourning: Death and the Narratee in

Brontë's *Villette*," in *Death and Representation,* edited by Sarah Webster Goodwin and Elisabeth Bronfen (Baltimore: Johns Hopkins University Press, 1993), pp. 51–77.

30. See Athena Vrettos (1990) for a comparison of Lucy's psychology and the neurotic symptoms of hysteria as discussed in nineteenth-century medical literature.

Chapter Four. Medusa's Voice

1. In conversation with American historian Ellen DuBois.

2. Quoted in DuBois (1975, 68). Also see Mitchell's discussion (1984) of the relation between nineteenth-century feminism and hysteria.

3. For an excellent discussion of the American political scene and its representation in *The Bostonians,* see Sensibar (1991, 57–72).

4. Habegger claims that James' "critique derives from a censored vision of antebellum reformers" and is not reliable about "the Gilded Age" (1990, 226–27).

5. As Strouse points out, given the greater proportion of women to men after the Civil War, the "Boston marriage" became increasingly common among upper-middle-class single women (1980, 200). For a fuller discussion of such relationships, see Smith-Rosenberg's "The Female World of Love and Ritual" (1981), reprinted in *Disorderly Conduct* (1985); Strouse notes that James was made uncomfortable by the intensity of Alice's relation to Katherine (199–200) and observes the extent to which Boston "seemed a city of women" to James. "He felt himself in a 'deluge of petticoats' among the 'sisterhood of shoppers', writers, hostesses, visitors and suffragists then waging a campaign for the female vote" (215).

6. *The Bostonians,* ed. Alfred Habegger (Indianapolis: Bobbs-Merrill, 1976), 76. All subsequent page references are cited in the text and refer to this edition.

7. *Woman in the Nineteenth Century,* quoted in *The Norton Anthology of Literature by Women,* ed. Gilbert and Gubar (1985, 301–2).

8. Critics have noted how similar the opinions of Ransom and Henry James Sr. about women's place are. See, for example, Habegger (1986), who documents Henry James Sr.'s reactionary "philosophy of marriage" and how it "began to shape the novelist's fictions" (15). Given the proximity of his father's death to the composition of the novel, it is not unlikely that James would ambivalently incorporate some of his father's opinions in the process of mourning him.

9. See Strouse (1980, 249). James vehemently denied this intention, yet

many others besides William remarked on the similarity of description. Strouse also discusses Henry's encouragement of a relation between his sister and Elizabeth Peabody (135–36).

10. As Schmitz points out, the transcendentalist fathers of the previous generation—including his own father—held for James no patrimony that he wanted to claim (1985, 155–73).

11. Strouse claims that "it was Alice whose brittle nervousness and defensive championing of women can be traced in Olive's lineaments" (1980, 251).

12. Ian F. A. Bell (1990), among others, has discerningly pointed to James' dislike of publicity—of the values of advertising and self-promotion in the developing consumer culture of the late nineteenth century. Reading James in an Emersonian context, Bell notes that James took from Emerson the notion of disinterested self-expression as opposed to the pandering avidity of publicity-seekers like Selah Tarrant.

13. The pervasive homoerotic innuendoes in the depiction of the bond between Olive and Verena have already been remarked upon by a number of critics. See especially Faderman (1978) and Fetterly (1978). Clearly, the erotic quality of their connection allows Olive to appropriate Verena as her voice in a Boston marriage of the two as one. Indeed, Olive's desire to expose the unhappiness of women—"A voice, a human voice is what we want" (54)—by finding a voice outside herself to represent it, her vision of partnership with Verena as "an organic whole" (144) shows how fetishistically the voice functions in this novel as well as how much the contest between Olive and Ransom for Verena is also a contest for the phallus.

14. The imaginative identification between author and character has been eloquently elaborated by Hertz (1990); see chap. 2.

Chapter Five. From Dream to Night-Mère

1. Havelock Ellis, her suitor and subsequently lifelong friend and quasi-therapist, in writing Schreiner's case history, characterized her symptoms—eating disorders, unexplained illnesses, a terror of sexual involvement, masochistic fantasies—as those of a classic hysteric (July 29, 1884, *Letters,* 35–36, quoted in First and Scott 1990, 134).

2. Ralph Iron alludes to the name of one of Schreiner's idols, Ralph Waldo Emerson, and the Emersonian ideal of strength and self-reliance. Like the resistant identity that Alice James had named her "hard core," Schreiner's pseudonym both enshrined Emersonian self-reliance and gendered it as masculine.

3. Ardis points out that while Schreiner's Lyndall indicated "a new breed

of feminist. . . in the process of being born," the New Woman was not actually named as such until 1894, when Ouida "selected. . . the phrase from Sarah Grand's essay 'The New Aspects of the Woman Question' [March 1894, *North American Review*]. Before then she was Novissima, the odd woman, the wild woman" (1990, 10–11).

4. Lyndall's unhappy ending recalls Florence Nightingale's failed *Cassandra* and the politics of exhaustion that its dying woman articulates, as well as Olive Chancellor's morbid fantasies of a sea of suffering women in *The Bostonians*. For a discussion of this ending, see especially DuPlessis (1985). DuPlessis also reads Schreiner's novel for its fundamental splittings of character and plot, although her emphasis is somewhat different: "In Lyndall, Schreiner has made a character who must fight against herself within herself. She is split between her sensual needs and her feminist ideals" (27).

5. The biographical material is taken from Berkman (1989).

6. Although I am less interested in constructing a psychobiography than in focusing on Schreiner's text, her physical performance of an impossible utterance, her method of articulating through the body what she could not express in verbal language, points to a habit of hysterical performance in her transactions with experience, and suggests a connection between her various inexplicable illnesses and utterance. In this context, Schreiner's lifelong battle with respiratory ailments, especially asthma, recalling both Nightingale's metaphors of suffocation and Charcot's descriptions of blocked orality, suggests also a psychosomatic suffocation by internalized demands common to the profile of nineteenth-century hysteria. Ironically, as Schreiner grew older, the mother-daughter relationship reversed itself: her mother increasingly turned to Schreiner for emotional support, so much so apparently that later in writing her history, Schreiner remarked, "It is I who have always had to think for, guide and nurse her since I was a tiny child" (Berkman 1989, 18). This rewriting, a fantasmatic reversal of the relation between mother and child that sustains the power of the nurse as a dominant figure, was central to the power relations in *The Story of an African Farm*.

7. *The Story of an African Farm* (Harmondsworth, Eng.: Penguin Books, 1986), 170. All subsequent page references appear in the text and refer to this edition.

8. In this context, Schreiner's father's name, Gottlieb (god-love), linguistically suggests the object of Waldo's quest.

9. DuPlessis (1985) discusses Schreiner's novel as a disruption of old narrative conventions; Showalter (1977) describes it as succumbing to an old notion of feminine defeat.

10. Contemporary feminist critiques often heroinize hysteria rather than seeing it as a debility; see especially the argument between Cixous and

Clément (1986). The concept of the subject-in-process is Kristeva's, but she distinguishes between the hysteric and the subject-in-process:

> Since the violence of drive charges is not halted, blocked, or repressed, what takes the place of the bodily, natural, or social objects. . . is not just a representation, memory, the sign. In contrast to the hysteric, the subject in process/on trial does not suffer from reminiscences, but rather from obstacles that tend to transform the facilitation. . . into reminiscences. Unlike hysteria, where the subject visualizes past experience and represents those "memories. . . in vivid visual pictures," this process breaks up the totality of the envisioned object. (1984, 102)

11. Schreiner's letters to Havelock Ellis dramatically articulate a dilemma that had been expressed by Nightingale a generation earlier. Idealizing the figure of the sympathetic male, desiring the kind of symbiotic relationship that Victorian marriage institutionalized, Schreiner represented herself as at the same time driven by an antipathy toward marriage: "I can't marry, Henry, I can't. . . . I must be free you know, I must be free," she wrote to Ellis. Although she dismissed him as a husband, she continued to write to him as a "Sweet brother soul"; her words recall Nightingale's desire for an imaginary male twin: "for so many years I have longed to meet a mind that should understand me. . . . Now I have found it. . . . In that you are myself, I love you, and am near to you, but in that you are a man I am afraid of you, I shrink from you" (July 29, 1884, *Letters,* 35–36; quoted in First and Scott 1990, 134).

Although Schreiner shrank from the erotic male as object, she frequently identified herself as more man than woman and, like Nightingale, deprecated those characteristics she associated with femininity. First and Scott note the extent to which she engaged in an uncritical use of the term *virile* to describe what was admirable in the New Woman, who was "not the always fainting and always weeping. . . Emily or Sophia" (278). If "Emily or Sophia" was the proper name of the proper Victorian heroine, the androgynously named Lyndall in *Story of an African Farm* signified a new kind of heroine.

12. Freud explained the gendered variations of masochistic desire in "A Child Is Being Beaten." In his narrative, the girl, repressing her passive desire for the father, replaces herself in fantasy with either a boy or a child of indeterminate sex who is being beaten by the father. Since, as Freud points out, "the children who are being beaten are almost invariably boys, in the phantasies of boys just as much as in those of girls. . . . this characteristic. . . points to a complication in the case of girls. When they turn away from their incestuous love for their father, with its genital significance, they easily abandon their feminine role" (1919, *SE* 17:191).

13. Deleuze characterizes masochism as an affair between a male masoch-

ist and a cold and severe mother. The son, stripped of virility, is reborn as a sexless man; the mother is invested with the phallus (1991, 58). See also Silverman's extended discussion of Deleuze on masochism (1992, 56ff.).

14. Schreiner's own masochistic passions have been described by her biographers: for example, of a romantic attachment, Schreiner remarked to Havelock Ellis, "I would like him to tread on me and stamp me fine into powder" (Calder-Marshall, *Havelock Ellis,* 1959, 91; quoted in First and Scott, 1990, 132). Similarly, Lyndall, her feminist heroine, remarks: "I too could love so, that to lie under the foot of the thing I loved would be more heaven than to lie in the breast of another" (232). Even the narrative voice of her novel echoes this desire: "The road to honor is paved with thorns; but on the path to truth, at every step you set your foot down on your heart" (148).

15. Gregory Rose's mystical exaltation of love for the punishing woman— "Who am I, what am I, that she should look at me? It was right that she left me; right that she should not look at me" (248)—is bizarrely represented as the source of his redemption. How similar is this rhetoric to that of the hero of Masoch's *Venus in Furs,* who declaims, "To love and be loved, what joy! And yet how this splendour pales in comparison with the blissful torment of worshipping a woman who treats one as a plaything, of being the slave of a beautiful tyrant who mercilessly tramples one underfoot" (1991, 155). See also Studlar (1988) for an excellent formulation of the masochistic aesthetic.

16. The difference between mourning and melancholia in Freud's text is elusive, one concept continually slipping into the other: Mourning is the process of working through the detachment from a once loved object of loss; melancholia differs primarily in that the work of mourning remains unaccomplished and is accompanied by a masochistic diminution in self-regard. Both can derive from the loss of an actual object through death or absence. "In one set of cases it is evident that melancholia too may be the reaction to the loss of a loved object" or a lost ideal, "some abstraction. . . such as one's country, liberty, an ideal, and so on" (1917 [1915], *SE* 14:243). In either case, the ambivalence toward the lost object when internalized produces a loss of self-regard that is particularly relevant to Lyndall.

17. In this regard, melancholia differs from hysterical desire and rage: "The difference . . . between narcissistic and hysterical identification may be seen in this; that whereas in the former the object-cathexis is abandoned, in the latter it persists and manifests its influence" (1917 [1915], *SE* 14:250).

18. See Kristeva's discussion of metaphor (1993), to which I return in chap. 6. As Kristeva points out, through a displacement of sensation into language "metaphor achieves the feat of transsubstantiation dreamed of by the novelist" (58).

19. Woolf uses a similar structure to represent negativity in the "Time

Passes" section of *To the Lighthouse,* as she attempts to present an uncanny world without a subject, "eyeless and so terrible." "Nothing stirred in the drawing room. . . . Nothing now withstood them, nothing said no to them" (1927, 203, 208, respectively).

20. This fact of childhood speech research was pointed out to me in conversation with Professor Judith Duchan of the Department of Communicative Disorders and Sciences, State University of New York−Buffalo.

21. See especially "The Importance of Symbol Formation in the Development of the Ego" (1930) rpt. in *The Selected Melanie Klein* (1986).

22. See Parkin-Gounelas (1991) for more on this aspect of Schreiner's work.

23. In a complementary passage earlier in the novel the pregnant Lyndall had articulated a desire that rests on the same problematic trope: "I like to feel that strange life beating up against me. . . . I like to realize forms of life utterly unlike mine" (214). After a long Whitmanesque catalogue evoking other lives, she concluded with imagining "the voices of women and children; a mother giving bread and milk to her children in little wooden basins and singing the evening song. I like. . . to feel it run through me—that life belongs to me; it makes my little life larger; it breaks down the narrow walls that shut me in" (215). While few would quarrel with the desire to constitute the family of man, here the increasingly sentimentalized rhetoric is an index of its infantile desire.

24. See especially Higonnet (1986). While ultimately my conclusion coincides with Gilbert and Gubar's, that Schreiner identified "the woman primarily with the womb," and that the novel "continued to deny women either tactical strategies for resistance to male domination or psychological strategies for coming to terms with female eroticism" (1988, 82), it is also true, as DuPlessis argues, that Schreiner is a pivotal figure in a liberatory modernism, her work breaking the sequence of oedipal narrative (1985). For additional views on this formalist aspect of Schreiner's work, see also First and Scott (1980) and Berkman (1989).

Chapter Six. The Great Refusal

1. See Zwerdling (1986, 170); Bazin (1973); Fromm (1979); and DeSalvo's introduction to *Melymbrosia* (1982). In DeSalvo's comprehensive tracing of the making of *The Voyage Out* (*Virginia Woolf's First Voyage*) she discusses Woolf's ambivalence about getting married at the time of writing the novel: "She was revising scenes describing how ambivalent Rachel and Terence are about loving one another, and Rachel's death, which can be interpreted as an escape from marriage through death, while she herself was preparing to accept

Leonard Woolf's proposal of marriage!" (1980, 7). Discussions of *The Voyage Out* that overlap with my own are DuPlessis (1985); Froula (1986); and Friedman (1992).

2. DeSalvo points out that in Woolf's juvenile prose piece, *The Experience of a Paterfamilias,* significantly written from the father's point of view, rivalry exists between the father and child for the attention of the mother; when the mother inexplicably hides the baby from her husband, her "motive in hiding the baby from me was to find out if I was really as brutal as I seemed." This early piece explores the nature of familial brutality; as DeSalvo remarks, on two facing pages of *Paterfamilias* there are four overt acts of brutality that threaten the baby's well-being (1980, 147–55).

3. *The Voyage Out* (New York: Harcourt, Brace & World, 1948), 326. Subsequent page numbers refer to this edition and are cited in the text.

4. This is not to say that a desire for the same necessarily entails a psychotic refusal of difference. Undifferentiated merging, the desire to lose the boundaries between subject and object, self and other, is not the same as the desire for the same erotic body as one's partner. As a relation between two differentiated women, a desire for the same in lesbian sexuality, for example, assumes that the object of desire is differentiated, though sexual difference as marked by the phallus may be repudiated. And as we know, the problematics of merging, and the regressive connections with the maternal figure, also inform heterosexual relations.

5. Among contemporary theorists Kristeva has most elaborated the relation between language and maternal loss. See especially chapter 2 of Kristeva's *Black Sun* (1989); also, Melanie Klein's "Mourning and Its Relationship to Manic-Depressive States" (1940, rpt. 1986).

6. In her excellent study of the use of silence in Woolf's texts, Laurence (1991) distinguishes three kinds of silence: what is thought but left unsaid, what is still inchoate and thus unspoken, what is unsayable because of social taboos. Laurence develops a useful lexicon of silence—pauses, nothingness, emptiness, blanks, absence, gulfs—which are relevant to my discussion of hysterical effects. Although I think Laurence mistakenly conflates the semiotic with the feminine—it is Kristeva's project precisely to disentangle the semiotic-maternal from the feminine—her use of Kristeva's categories of the semiotic and the symbolic overlaps with my own. In a related approach, Ruotolo (1986) uses interruption as a category to explore the nuances of silence as they interrupt the narrative movement. Minow-Pinkney (1987) also uses Kristeva to discuss the embodiment of silence in a reading of the semiotic that closely approaches my own concerns in *The Voyage Out,* although she deals minimally with this particular text.

7. These remarks are suggested by Kristeva's discussion of metaphor in

"Apologia for Metaphor" (1993); as Kristeva points out, through a displacement of sensation into language "metaphor achieves the feat of transubstantiation dreamed of by the novelist" (58).

8. In the legend of St. Euphrosyne, as DeSalvo points out, she escapes the marriage demanded by her father by cross-dressing, disguising herself as a man and becoming a venerated ascetic (1980, 60). The names of the male characters also suggest previously inscribed subject positions that are gendered: Terence, the poet; Ambrose, the saint who introduced the practice of reading silently; and the ascetic St. John, who in Brontë's *Jane Eyre* articulates the thematics of self-denial.

9. Edvard Munch, who was interested in the relation between perception and imagination, "included the effect of his own fluttering eyelashes in some versions of 'The Sick Child'" Tom Lubbock (1992) notes. "In later life he suffered from a very obstructive 'floater' in the vitreous humor of one eye—shaped like a bird—and recorded that. . . hovering in the middle of his field of vision." Lubbock remarks that Munch's "optical problems might be charged with a significance equal to his hallucinations"; he made "no attempt to distinguish between imaginative and optical vision, between 'the mind's eye' and the retina" (1992, 19).

10. Ferguson points out that rape parodies the formal features of happier sexual relations by disposing the same sets of body parts, so that it is not the physical act but the attitude that is crucial in distinguishing marriage from rape. Thus, Hebraic law could recast rape as a misunderstanding that could be rectified by marriage (1987, 92). Similarly, in strictly Catholic countries where the raped woman is considered damaged goods, there is strong pressure on the rapist to marry his victim and thus atone for his sin and recuperate her value. If Richardson's Clarissa refused this logic in a new Christian narrative which, privileging the word over the body, allowed the woman to say No even though she had been sexually assaulted, *The Voyage Out* seems in its deep structures to adhere to the older logic—men are brutes; marriage is rape—while trying to evade it. As Ferguson notes, Andrea Dworkin also reconstitutes rape as the paradigm of heterosexual relations by equating sexual ability with intention; men, given their biological capacities, are the natural violators of women.

11. DeSalvo points out that in an earlier manuscript version of the novel, the heroine is fascinated with *Religio Medici* and its image "of the labyrinth of dark interior channels," an image connected to "Browne's belief in the inherent perversity of 'this trivial and vulgar way of coition'" (xxxii). Rachel's dream is a later version of this "inherent perversity," and the little man inside the damp vault a hysterical representation of the penetrating and disgusting phallus. Indeed, a loathsome "little man" is a recurrent character in Woolf's

text, entering first as Mr. Pepper, and later as Dr. Rodriguez, a "hairy" little man. The hairy little man is a particularly repulsive male figure for Woolf: for example, in a letter to Vanessa, she writes: "I could not write, and all the devils came out—hairy black ones. To be 29 and unmarried, to be a failure—childless—insane too, no writer" (#570, quoted in DeSalvo 1980, 72).

12. See DeSalvo (1980, 53–56) for an extended discussion of Rachel's disgust and ambivalence about sexuality and maternity. *Melymbrosia* is much more open about Rachel's sexual fears (1980, 40–44, 62–63). See also the discussion of rape in Garrard (1982, 163–64).

13. The passage alludes to the Apocalypse: "I John, saw the holy City, the new Jerusalem, coming down from God out of heaven, prepared as a bride adorned for her husband." St. John's vision at the end of the novel changes the metaphor of the new Jerusalem from bride to mother.

14. For another related view of the relation between narcissism and masochism in Woolf's texts, see Bernheimer (1990b).

15. David-Ménard points out that the hysterical voyeur of the primal scene desires to be included, to participate in the parental sexual relationship; excluded from that relation, he or she must find *jouissance* through his or her symbolization of sexual difference (1989, 102). Rachel's inability to symbolize difference is precisely the problem; she can only find her *jouissance* by a regressive retreat into the body.

16. In *Tales of Love*, Kristeva remarks that the representation of an erotic scene between two women is used by the male voyeur as a safeguarding strategy. "In order not to be swallowed up by one of them, the egotist grants himself at least two. . . . The single passion is deadly and leads to confinement and unrepresentable confusion" (1987b, 359). This dynamic seems also to be at play for the various voyeurs of *The Voyage Out,* who themselves are doubled in the act of looking.

17. DeSalvo, comparing an earlier version of the hero and heroine with Terence and Rachel, points out that each hero "is exceedingly passive, incapable of quieting a woman's fears; each would prefer not to be in love with a woman; each would rather be by himself or, in Terence's case, involved in a friendship with another man. Each would rather remain celibate, so each chooses a woman who is the feminine complement of himself. Yet both couples seem locked to one another in relationships which vacillate between desire and avoidance" (1982, xxvii). What DeSalvo does not say is that each is in some way essentially a woman himself, in the dress of a masculine counterpart.

18. "The mechanism of poetical creation is the same as that of hysterical fantasies" (*Letters*, Freud to Fliess, May 31, 1897).

19. In a later scene, the rivalry between Helen and Terence is explicit:

So you're going, Rachel?" Helen asked, "You won't stay with me?"
She smiled, but she might have been sad.
Was she sad, or was she really laughing? Rachel could not tell, and she felt
for the moment very uncomfortable between Helen and Terence. Then she
turned away, saying merely that she would go with Terence, on condition
that he did all the talking. (311)

20. In this context, the pitiless sun of Schreiner's novel, which bears great
similarity to Woolf's maternal stare, can also be read as a phallic maternal gaze.

21. Abel's discussion of Woolf's interest in anthropology (1989, 21–29)
concerns primarily the 1920s, in which there was a proliferation of anthropological publications that were central to the contemporary discussions of
gender. Her remarks are also relevant to *The Voyage Out,* published more than
a decade earlier. The first volume of *The Golden Bough* appeared in 1907 and
included documentation on the worship of mother goddesses and matrilineal
societies. Abel mentions especially the importance of J. J. Atkinson's *Primal
Law* (1903), which projects the mother into the myth of the primal horde's
murder of the father. In this version of origins, the mother intervenes to
protect her sons and is thus the source of oedipal law.

22. Anthropological inquiries into totemism suggested that the totem
animal who is revered and also often devoured is associated with the maternal
body. One recalls the wise chickens at the end of *Story of an African Farm.*
Interestingly, as Abel points out (1989, 23), in a case history Freud labeled "the
little Chanticleer," a child began imitating poultry after a chicken snapped at
his penis. Freud interprets the chicken as a totem animal that stands in for his
father, but Abel argues that the chicken is embedded in a dynamic of eating
and being eaten that is preoedipal, and that the gender of the chicken is at the
least ambiguous. DeSalvo notes that in an earlier manuscript version, Rachel is
literally called "the spring chicken" (1980, 55).

23. This conversion is not unlike Freud's account of melancholia, in which
an object-cathexis is replaced by an identification, a conversion that he extended as a general occurrence in *The Ego and the Id* (1923, *SE* 19).

24. In a later essay, "On Being Ill" (1930), Woolf again privileged illness as
a royal road to another form of representation: "English has no words for the
shiver and the headache. . . . A sufferer. . . is forced to coin words himself,
and taking his pain in one hand and a lump of pure sound in the other (as
perhaps the people of Babel did in the beginning), so to crush them together
that a brand new word in the end drops out" (1966, 194). Pain and a lump of
sound: the cry in a new language, a new discourse forged from "illness," is
what Woolf's narrative voice moves toward as it joins forces with Rachel's
feverish consciousness in *The Voyage Out.*

25. Interestingly, however, Woolf offered as model of this new form of

representation neither Dorothy Richardson's novel, which had first provoked the phrase "stream of consciousness," nor her own experiments in prose, but Joyce's, casting the debate between old and new modes of writing as a debate among male authors, between Bennett and Galsworthy on the one hand, and Joyce and Conrad on the other. That Woolf, a novelist experimenting with a new voice, should reach for male rather than female writers as exemplary figures has only recently seemed worthy of interrogation. It suggests the familiar barring of the woman writer who can never be the representative subject—"she" is the "woman writer" while Joyce is the writer—an exclusion that contributed to women's hysteria.

Chapter Seven. Male Modernists and the Ear of the Other in *Heart of Darkness* and *The Good Soldier*

1. In this context, Marcus's (1990) description of Freud as a modernist writer seems to me mistaken; the Dora text is a great modernist narrative but it is so in spite of Freud's intention to make the story cohere.

2. Insofar as it is paranoid, however, this fear is a projection of his own aggressive desires.

3. Ford, "Heart of Darkness," from *Portraits from Life* (1936, 1937), reprinted in the 3rd Critical Edition of Conrad's *Heart of Darkness* (1988, 212–13). All subsequent page references to the novel are from this edition and appear in the text. Ford reveals the importance of sound to Conrad's technique, and his own, when he writes of the ending of the tale: "The last paragraph of a story should have the effect of what musicians call a coda—a passage meditative in tone, suited for letting the reader or hearer gently down from the tense drama of the story, in which all his senses have been shut up, into the ordinary workaday world again" (213).

4. Although Marlow's voice initially seems different from the voice of the outer frame narrator, his diction more Anglo-Saxon than Latinate, Marlow, too, will regularly yield to a melancholy romanticism that he overtly disclaims. The convergence of the two voices in the melancholy register tells us that *Heart of Darkness* remains in part a romance quest even as it ironically denigrates the quest for the ideal.

5. In Conrad's manuscript version, the phrase "in the unseen" appears here, reiterating Conrad's subversion of vision as the medium of truth (1988, 9).

6. See Slater (1968, 87–115) for a suggestive discussion of the serpent as a symbol of devouring maternity.

7. Meyer points out that "in [Conrad's] fiction the love of a man for a

woman is so fused with fantasies of nursing as to confer upon all masculine aggression the significance of unrestrained biting" (1967, 182).

8. Shakespeare also played with the repetition of this particular phoneme in Desdemona's "I cannot say 'whore.' It does abhor me now I speak the word" (*Othello*, act 4, scene 2, ll. 161–62).

9. Brooks uses this as the epigraph to *Reading for the Plot* (1984).

10. For a discussion of the interweaving of their fictional and personal lives, and their eventual estrangement, see Moser (1980).

11. *The Good Soldier* (New York: Alfred A. Knopf, and Random House, 1951), 115. All subsequent page references appear in the text and refer to this edition.

12. My gratitude to Deborah Kloepfer, who pointed out the analogy between the hysterical narrative of *The Good Soldier* and the psychoanalytic dialogue in an unpublished paper, "The Presence in the Pauses: Hysterical Narrative in *The Good Soldier.*"

13. Green points out that a typically feminine wish is "to have constantly at her side the man of her desire in a double role—protecting and virile like the father, and at the same time being used as if he were the mother" (1986a, 110). This is the wish of both Nancy and Dowell.

14. See Felman (1983) who remarks, "To seduce is to produce felicitous language" (28).

15. In this regard, Gubar and Gilbert's (1988) thesis, which deals with a war between male and female writers for textual authority, has psychoanalytic resonance.

16. André Breton's *The Surrealist Manifesto* (1924) made clear to what extent psychoanalysis provided modernist art with an aesthetics of the unconscious. As Breton explained its origins, he had been engaged in an experiment with a writer friend:

> Preoccupied as I. . . was with Freud, and familiar with his methods of investigation. . . I resolved to obtain from myself what one seeks to obtain from patients, namely a monologue poured out as rapidly as possible over which the subject's critical faculty has no control—the subject himself throwing reticence to the winds—and which as much as possible represents *spoken thought*. . . . By the end of the first day of the experiment we were able to read to one another about fifty pages obtained in this manner and to compare the results we had achieved. The likeness was on the whole striking. There were similar faults of construction, the same hesitant manner, and also, in both cases, an illusion of extraordinary verve, much emotion, a considerable assortment of images. (1965, 601–2)

17. See Irigaray (1985b) and Montrelay (1978).

18. "To play with mimesis is thus, for a woman, to try to recover the place

of exploitation by discourse. . . . It means to resubmit herself. . . to ideas about herself that are elaborated in/by a masculine logic but so as to make visible by an effect of playful repetition, what was supposed to remain invisible" (Irigaray 1985b, 76).

19. Later modernist texts make other moves to remove any trace of authorial presence: one thinks of Joyce's desire to play the indifferent god behind the scenes of *Ulysses,* his text giving the illusion of unmediated first-person consciousness through interior monologues; of Eliot's elusive fragmentation of alien voices in *The Wasteland,* his original title, *He Do the Police in Different Voices,* indicating and yet covering over his self-dispersion.

Works Cited

Abel, Elizabeth. 1989. *Virginia Woolf and the Fictions of Psychoanalysis*. Chicago: University of Chicago Press.

Allen, Donald R. 1981. "Florence Nightingale: Toward a Psychohistorical Interpretation." In *Florence Nightingale: Saint, Reformer, or Rebel?* edited by Raymond G. Herbert. Malabar, Fla.: Robert E. Krieger.

Anzieu, Annie. 1990. "The Hysterical Envelope." In *Psychic Envelopes*, edited by Didier Anzieu. London: Karnac Books.

Anzieu, Didier. 1976. "L'enveloppe sonore du soi." *Nouvelle revue de psychanalyse* 13:173.

———, ed. 1990. *Psychic Envelopes*. London: Karnac Books.

Ardis, Ann. 1990. *New Women, New Novels*. New Brunswick, N.J.: Rutgers University Press.

Armstrong, Nancy. 1987. *Desire and Domestic Fiction: A Political History of the Novel*. New York: Oxford University Press.

Auerbach, Nina. 1973. "Charlotte Brontë: The Two Countries." *University of Toronto Quarterly* 42:328–42.

———. 1982. *Woman and the Demon: The Life of a Victorian Myth*. Cambridge: Harvard University Press.

Barthes, Roland. 1975. *The Pleasure of the Text*. Translated by Richard Miller. New York: Hill & Wang.

———. 1977. "The Grain of the Voice." *Image-Music-Text*. Translated by Stephen Heath. New York: Noonday Press.

Bazin, Nancy Topping. 1973. *Virginia Woolf and the Androgynous Vision*. New Brunswick, N.J.: Rutgers University Press.

Bell, Ian F. A. 1990. "The Personal, the Private, and the Public in *The Bostonians*." *Texas Studies in Literature and Language* 32(2): 240–55.

Bemporad, Jules R. 1988. "Hysteria, Anorexia and the Culture of Self-Denial." *Psychiatry* 51.

Benjamin, Jessica. 1986. "A Desire of One's Own: Psychoanalytic Feminism and Intersubjective Space." In *Feminist Studies/Critical Studies,* edited by Teresa DeLauretis. Bloomington: Indiana University Press.

Berkman, Joyce. 1989. *The Healing Imagination of Olive Schreiner.* Amherst: University of Massachusetts Press.

Bernheimer, Charles. 1990a. Introduction to Part I. In *In Dora's Case: Freud-Hysteria-Feminism,* edited by Charles Bernheimer and Claire Kahane. 2d ed. New York: Columbia University Press.

———. 1990b. "A Shattered Globe: Narcissism and Masochism in Virginia Woolf's Life Writing." In *Psychoanalysis Annual.* New York: Routledge.

Bernheimer, Charles, and Claire Kahane, eds. 1990. *In Dora's Case: Freud-Hysteria-Feminism.* 2d ed. New York: Columbia University Press.

Bjorhovde, Gerd. 1987. *Rebellious Structures: Women Writers and the Crisis of the Novel, 1880–1900.* Oslo: Norwegian University Press.

Bollas, Christopher. 1978. "The Aesthetic Moment and the Search for Transformation." *Annual of Psychoanalysis* 6:385–94.

Boone, Joseph. 1986. "Modernist Maneuverings of the Marriage Plot." *Publications of the Modern Language Association* 101:374–88.

Brantlinger, Patrick. 1977. *The Spirit of Reform: British Literature and Politics, 1832–1867.* Cambridge: Harvard University Press.

Breton, André. [1934] 1965. *What Is Surrealism?* Translated by David Gascoigne, London, 1936; quoted in *The Modern Tradition: Backgrounds of Modern Literature,* edited by Richard Ellman and Charles Feidelson. New York: Oxford University Press.

Brodhead, Richard. 1986. *The School of Hawthorne.* New York: Oxford University Press.

Brontë, Charlotte. 1960. *Jane Eyre.* New York: New American Library.

———. 1974. *Shirley, a Tale.* Edited by Andrew and Judith Hook. Penguin English Library. Harmondsworth, England: Penguin Books.

———. 1979. *Villette.* Edited by Mark Lilly with an introduction by Tony Tanner. Penguin English Library. Harmondsworth, England: Penguin Books.

Brooks, Peter. 1984. *Reading for the Plot.* New York: Random House.

Brumberg, Joan Jacobs. 1988. *Fasting Girls: The Emergence of Anorexia Nervosa as a Modern Disease.* Cambridge: Harvard University Press.

Burgin, Victor, James Donald, and Cora Kaplan, eds. 1986. *Formations of Fantasy.* New York: Methuen.

Butler, Judith. 1990. *Gender Trouble: Feminism and the Subversion of Identity.* New York: Routledge.

Chion, Michel. 1982. *Le voix du cinema.* Paris: Éditions de l'Étoile.

Chodorow, Nancy. 1978. *The Reproduction of Mothering.* Berkeley: University of California Press.

Cixous, Hélène. 1981. "Castration or Decapitation." *Signs* 7(1):41–55.

Cixous, Hélène, and Catherine Clément. 1986. *The Newly Born Woman.* Translated by Betsy Wing. Minneapolis: University of Minnesota Press.

Cohan, Steven, and Linda M. Shires. 1988. *Telling Stories: A Theoretical Analysis of Narrative Fiction.* New York: Routledge.

Conrad, Joseph. [1902] 1988. *Heart of Darkness.* Edited by Robert Kimbrough. 3rd Norton Critical Edition. New York: W. W. Norton.

Cummings, Katherine. 1991. *Telling Tales: The Hysteric's Seduction in Fiction and Theory.* Stanford: Stanford University Press.

David-Ménard, Monique. 1989. *Hysteria from Freud to Lacan.* Ithaca: Cornell University Press.

Davis, Sara deSaussure. 1978. "*The Bostonians* Reconsidered." *Tulane Studies in English* 23:39–60.

Decker, Hannah S. 1991. *Freud, Dora, and Vienna 1900.* New York: Free Press.

DeKoven, Marianne. 1989. "Gendered Doubleness and the 'Origins' of Modernist Form." *Tulsa Studies in Women's Literature* 8 (Spring): 19–42.

DeLauretis, Teresa. 1984. *Alice Doesn't: Feminism, Semiotics, Cinema.* Bloomington: Indiana University Press.

Deleuze, Gilles. 1991. *Coldness and Cruelty.* In *Masochism.* Translated by Jean McNeil. New York: Zone Books.

Derrida, Jacques. 1985. *The Ear of the Other: Otobiography, Transference, Translation: Texts and Discussions with Jacques Derrida.* Edited by Claude Levesque and Christie V. McDonald; translated by Peggy Kamuf; "Otobiographies," translated by Avital Ronell. New York: Schocken Books.

DeSalvo, Louise. 1980. *Virginia Woolf's First Voyage.* Totowa, N.J.: Rowman & Littlefield.

———. 1982. Introduction to *Melymbrosia: An Early Version of "The Voyage Out,"* by Virginia Woolf. New York: New York Public Library.

Douglas, Ann. 1973. "The Fashionable Disease." *Journal of Interdisciplinary History* 4:25–52.

DuBois, Ellen. 1975. "The Radicalism of the Woman Suffrage Movement: Notes toward the Reconstruction of Nineteenth-Century Feminism." *Feminist Studies* 3 (Fall).

DuPlessis, Rachel Blau. 1985. *Writing beyond the Ending: Narrative Strategies of Twentieth Century Women Writers.* Bloomington: Indiana University Press.

Eliot, George [Mary Anne Evans]. 1966. *The Mill on the Floss.* Riverside Editions. Boston: Houghton Mifflin.

Eliot, Thomas Stearns. [1917] 1952. "Hysteria." In *Prufrock and Other Obser-*

vations. Reprinted in *The Complete Poems and Plays: 1909–1950.* New York: Harcourt, Brace & World.

Evans, Martha Noel. 1992. *Fits and Starts: A Genealogy of Hysteria in Modern France.* Ithaca: Cornell University Press.

Faderman, Lillian. 1978. "Female Same-Sex Relationships in Novels by Longfellow, Holmes, and James." *New England Quarterly* 51:309–32.

Fairbairn, W. Ronald D. 1952. *An Object Relations Theory of the Personality.* New York: Basic Books.

Felman, Shoshana. 1977. "Turning the Screw of Interpretation." *Yale French Studies* 56:94–207.

———. 1983. *The Literary Speech Act: Don Juan with J. L. Austin, or Seduction in Two Languages.* Translated by Catherine Porter. Ithaca: Cornell University Press.

Ferguson, Frances. 1987. "Rape and the Rise of the Novel." *Representations* 20 (Fall): 88–112.

Ferrer, Daniel. 1990. *Virginia Woolf and the Madness of Language.* Translated by Geoffrey Bennington and Rachel Bowlby. London: Routledge.

Fetterly, Judith. 1978. "*The Bostonians:* Henry James's Eternal Triangle." In *The Resisting Reader: A Feminist Approach to American Fiction.* Bloomington: Indiana University Press.

Fiedler, Leslie. 1960. *Love and Death in the American Novel.* New York: Criterion Books.

First, Ruth, and Ann Scott. [1980] 1990. *Olive Schreiner.* New Brunswick, N.J.: Rutgers University Press.

Flexner, Eleanor. 1975. *Century of Struggle.* Rev. ed. Cambridge: Harvard University Press.

Ford, Ford Madox. [1927] 1951. *The Good Soldier: A Tale of Passion.* Vintage Books. New York: Alfred A. Knopf, and Random House.

———. [1936, 1937] 1988. "Heart of Darkness." In *Portraits from Life.* Reprinted by permission of Houghton Mifflin in Joseph Conrad, *Heart of Darkness.* Edited by Robert Kimbrough. 3rd Norton Critical Edition. New York: W. W. Norton.

Forrester, John. 1990. *The Seductions of Psychoanalysis: Freud, Lacan, and Derrida.* Cambridge: Cambridge University Press.

Foucault, Michel. 1978. *The History of Sexuality.* Vol. 1. Translated by Robert Hurley. New York: Pantheon.

Freud, Sigmund. 1959. *Standard Edition of the Complete Psychological Works.* Translated under the general editorship of James Strachey in collaboration with Anna Freud, assisted by Alix Strachey and Alan Tyson. 24 vols. London: The Hogarth Press and the Institute of Psychoanalysis.

———. 1985. *The Complete Letters of Sigmund Freud to Wilhelm Fliess, 1887–*

1904. Translated and edited by Jeffrey Moussaieff Masson. Cambridge: Harvard University Press.

Friedman, Susan Stanford. 1992. "Virginia Woolf's Pedagogical Scenes of Reading: *The Voyage Out, The Common Reader,* and Her 'Common Readers.'" *Modern Fiction Studies* 38(1):101–25.

Fromm, Harold. 1979. "Virginia Woolf: Art and Sexuality." *Virginia Quarterly Review* 55:441–59.

Froula, Christine. 1986. "Out of the Chrysalis: Female Initiation and Female Authority in Virginia Woolf's *The Voyage Out.*" *Tulsa Studies in Women's Literature* 5(1):63–90.

Gallop, Jane. 1990. "Keys to Dora." In *In Dora's Case: Freud-Hysteria-Feminism,* edited by Charles Bernheimer and Claire Kahane. 2d ed. New York: Columbia University Press.

Garrard, Mary D. 1982. "Artemisia and Susanna." In *Feminism and Art History: Questioning the Litany,* edited by Norma Broude and Mary D. Garrard. New York: Harper & Row.

Gay, Peter. 1984. *The Bourgeois Experience.* 2 vols. Vol. 1, *Education of the Senses.* Oxford: Oxford University Press.

Gilbert, Sandra, and Susan Gubar. 1979. *The Madwoman in the Attic: The Woman Writer and the Nineteenth-Century Literary Imagination.* New Haven: Yale University Press.

———. eds. 1985. *The Norton Anthology of Literature by Women: The Tradition in English.* New York: W. W. Norton.

———. 1988. *No Man's Land: The Place of the Woman Writer in the Twentieth Century.* 2 vols. Vol. 1, *The War of the Words.* New Haven: Yale University Press.

Gilligan, Carol. 1982. *In a Different Voice.* Cambridge: Harvard University Press.

Gilman, Sander L., et al., eds. 1993. *Hysteria beyond Freud.* Berkeley: University of California Press.

Green, André. 1986a. "Aggression, Femininity, Paranoia, and Reality." In *On Private Madness.* Madison, Conn.: International Universities Press.

———. 1986b. "Potential Space in Psychoanalysis." In *On Private Madness.* Madison, Conn.: International Universities Press.

——— 1986c. "Passions and their Vicissitudes." In *On Private Madness.* Madison, Conn.: International Universities Press.

Habegger, Alfred. 1986. "The Lessons of the Father: Henry James Sr. on Sexual Difference." *Henry James Review* (7).

———. 1990. *Henry James and the "Woman Business."* Cambridge: Cambridge University Press.

Haller, John S., and Robin M. Haller. 1977. *The Physician and Sexuality in Victorian America.* New York: W. W. Norton.

Harding, Sandra. 1986. *The Science Question in Feminism*. Ithaca: Cornell University Press.

Hartman, Geoffrey H. 1981. *Saving the Text: Literature, Derrida, Philosophy*. Baltimore: Johns Hopkins University Press.

Heath, Stephen. 1981. *Questions of Cinema*. London: Macmillan.

———. 1986. "Joan Rivière and the Masquerade." In *Formations of Fantasy*, edited by Victor Burgin, James Donald, and Cora Kaplan. New York: Methuen.

Hertz, Neil. 1983. "Medusa's Head: Male Hysteria under Political Pressure." *Representations* 4 (Fall): 27–54.

———. 1990. "Dora's Secrets, Freud's Techniques." In *In Dora's Case: Freud-Hysteria-Feminism*, edited by Charles Bernheimer and Claire Kahane. 2d ed. New York: Columbia University Press.

Higonnet, Margaret. 1986. "Speaking Silences." In *The Female Body in Western Culture*, edited by Susan Robin Suleiman. Cambridge: Harvard University Press.

Hirsch, Marianne. 1989. *The Mother-Daughter Plot: Narrative, Psychoanalysis, Feminism*. Bloomington: Indiana University Press.

Hunter, Dianne. 1985. "Hysteria, Psychoanalysis, and Feminism: The Case of Anna O." In *The M/Other Tongue: Essays in Feminist Psychoanalytic Criticism*, edited by Shirley Garner, Claire Kahane, and Madelon Sprengnether. Ithaca: Cornell University Press.

Irigaray, Luce. 1985a. *Speculum of the Other Woman*. Translated by Gillian C. Gill. Ithaca: Cornell University Press.

———. 1985b. *This Sex Which Is Not One*. Translated by Catherine Porter with Carolyn Burke. Ithaca: Cornell University Press.

———. 1989. "The Gesture in Psychoanalysis." Translated by Elizabeth Guild. In *Between Feminism and Psychoanalysis*, edited by Teresa Brennan. London: Routledge.

Jacobs, Carol. 1978. "*The* (too) *Good Soldier:* 'A Real Story' " *Glyph* 3 (Spring): 32–51.

Jacobus, Mary. 1986. "The Buried Letter." In *Reading Woman: Essays in Feminist Criticism*. New York: Columbia University Press.

James, Alice. 1964. *The Diary of Alice James*. Edited with an introduction by Leon Edel. New York: Dodd, Mead. Reprinted 1982: Penguin American Library. Harmondsworth, England: Penguin.

James, Henry. 1947. *The Notebooks of Henry James*. Edited by F. O. Matthiessen and Kenneth S. Murdock. New York: Oxford University Press.

———. 1966. "Turn of the Screw." Edited by Robert Kimbrough. Norton Critical Edition. New York: W. W. Norton.

————. 1976. *The Bostonians.* Edited by Alfred Habegger. Indianapolis: Bobbs-Merrill.

Jones, Ernest. 1964. *Essays in Applied Psychoanalysis.* 2 vols. New York: International Universities Press.

Kahane, Claire. 1985. "Gothic Mirrors and Feminine Identity." In *The M/Other Tongue: Essays in Feminist Psychoanalytic Criticism,* edited by Shirley Garner, Claire Kahane, and Madelon Sprengnether. Ithaca: Cornell University Press.

————. 1991. "The Aesthetic Politics of Rage." *Literature/Interpretation/Theory* 2:1–13.

Keller, Evelyn Fox. 1985. *Reflections on Gender and Science.* New Haven: Yale University Press.

Kernberg, Otto. 1976. *Object Relations Theory and Clinical Practice.* New York: Jason Aronson.

Klein, Melanie. 1986. *The Selected Melanie Klein.* Edited by Juliet Mitchell. Harmondsworth, England: Penguin Books.

Koestenbaum, Wayne. 1989. *Double Talk: The Erotics of Male Literary Collaboration.* New York: Routledge.

Kofman, Sarah. 1985. *The Enigma of Woman: Woman in Freud's Writings.* Translated by Catherine Porter. Ithaca: Cornell University Press.

Kristeva, Julia. 1980. *Desire in Language.* Translated by Leon S. Roudiez. New York: Columbia University Press.

————. 1982. *Powers of Horror.* Translated by Leon S. Roudiez. New York: Columbia University Press.

————. 1984. *Revolution in Poetic Language.* Translated by Margaret Waller with an introduction by Leon S. Roudiez. New York: Columbia University Press.

————. 1986a. "Freud and Love: Treatment and Its Discontents." Translated by Leon S. Roudiez. In *The Kristeva Reader,* edited by Toril Moi. New York: Columbia University Press.

————. 1986b. "Stabat Mater." Translated by Leon S. Roudiez. In *The Kristeva Reader,* edited by Toril Moi. New York: Columbia University Press.

————. 1986c. "Women's Time." Translated by Alice Jardine and Harry Blake. In *The Kristeva Reader,* edited by Toril Moi. New York: Columbia University Press.

————. 1987a. *In the Beginning Was Love.* Translated by Leon S. Roudiez. New York: Columbia University Press.

————. 1987b. *Tales of Love.* Translated by Leon S. Roudiez. New York: Columbia University Press.

————. 1989. *Black Sun: Depression and Melancholia.* Translated by Leon S. Roudiez. New York: Columbia University Press.

————. 1993. "Apologia for Metaphor." In *Proust and the Sense of Time*. Translated with an introduction by Stephen Bann. New York: Columbia University Press.

Krohn, Alan. 1978. *Hysteria: The Elusive Neurosis*. New York: International Universities Press.

Kucich, John. 1987. *Repression in Victorian Fiction: Charlotte Brontë, George Eliot and Charles Dickens*. Berkeley: University of California Press.

Lacan, Jacques. [1952] 1982. "Intervention on Transference." Translated by Jacqueline Rose. In *Feminine Sexuality: Jacques Lacan and l'Ecole Freudienne*, edited by Juliet Mitchell and Jacqueline Rose. New York: W. W. Norton.

————. 1977. *Écrits: A Selection*. Translated by Alan Sheridan. New York: W. W. Norton.

Lanser, Susan. 1992. *Fictions of Authority: Women Writers and Narrative Voice*. Ithaca: Cornell University Press.

LaPlanche, Jean, and J.-B. Pontalis. 1968. "Fantasy and the Origin of Sexuality." *International Journal of Psychoanalysis* 49:1–18.

Laqueur, Thomas. 1986. "Orgasm, Generation, and the Politics of Reproductive Biology." *Representations* 14 (Spring): 1–41.

————. 1990. *Making Sex: Body and Gender from the Greeks to Freud*. Cambridge: Harvard University Press.

Laurence, Patricia Ondek. 1991. *The Reading of Silence: Virginia Woolf in the English Tradition*. Stanford: Stanford University Press.

Lecourt, Edith. 1990. "The Musical Envelope." In *Psychic Envelopes*, edited by Didier Anzieu. London: Karnac Books.

Linker, Kate. 1984. "Sexuality and Representation." In *Art after Modernism*, edited by Brian Wallis. Boston: D. R. Godine.

London, Bette. 1990. *The Appropriated Voice: Narrative Authority in Conrad, Forster, and Woolf*. Ann Arbor: University of Michigan Press.

Lubbock, Tom. 1992. "Edvard Munch: Propaganda of the Soul." *Modern Painters* 5 (Winter): 16–19.

Lukasher, Ned. 1989. "The Epistemology of Disgust." Foreword to Monique David-Ménard, *Hysteria from Freud to Lacan*. Ithaca: Cornell University Press.

Malcolm, Janet. 1990. "Reflections: J'appelle un chat un chat." In *In Dora's Case: Freud-Hysteria-Feminism*, edited by Charles Bernheimer and Claire Kahane. 2d ed. New York: Columbia University Press.

Marcus, Steven. 1990. "Freud and Dora: Story, History, Case History." In *In Dora's Case: Freud-Hysteria-Feminism*, edited by Charles Bernheimer and Claire Kahane. 2d ed. New York: Columbia University Press.

Marmor, Judd. 1953. "Orality in the Hysterical Personality." *Journal of the American Psychoanalytic Society* 1(4):656–71.

Masoch, Leopold von Sacher-. 1991. *Venus in Furs*. In *Masochism*. Translated by Jean McNeil. New York: Zone Books.

Meyer, Bernard C. 1967. *Joseph Conrad: A Psychoanalytic Biography*. Princeton: Princeton University Press.

Miller, Nancy K. 1986. *The Poetics of Gender*. New York: Columbia University Press.

———. 1988. *Subject to Change: Reading Feminist Writing*. New York: Columbia University Press.

Minow-Pinkney, Makiko. 1987. *Virginia Woolf and the Problem of the Subject*. Brighton, England: Harvester.

Mitchell, Juliet. 1984. *Women: The Longest Revolution*. New York: Pantheon.

Moi, Toril. 1990. "Representation of Patriarchy: Sexuality and Epistemology in Freud's Dora." In *In Dora's Case: Freud-Hysteria-Feminism*, edited by Charles Bernheimer and Claire Kahane. 2d ed. New York: Columbia University Press.

Montrelay, Michele. 1978. "Inquiry into Femininity." *m/f* 1:83–101.

Moser, Thomas. 1980. *The Life in the Fiction of Ford Madox Ford*. Princeton: Princeton University Press.

Nightingale, Florence. 1979. *Cassandra*. New York: Feminist Press.

Parkin-Gounelas, Ruth. 1991. "Olive Schreiner's Organic Art." In *Fictions of the Female Self: Charlotte Brontë, Olive Schreiner, Katherine Mansfield*. New York: St. Martin's Press.

Pavel, Thomas G. 1986. "In Praise of the Ear (Gloss's Glosses)." In *The Female Body in Western Culture*, edited by Susan Robin Suleiman. Cambridge: Harvard University Press.

Poovey, Mary. 1988. *Uneven Developments*. Chicago: University of Chicago Press.

Rimmon-Kenan, Shulamith, ed. 1987. *Discourse in Psychoanalysis and Literature*. London: Methuen.

Rivière, Joan. [1929] 1986. "Womanliness as Masquerade." In *Formations of Fantasy*, edited by Victor Burgin, James Donald, and Cora Kaplan. New York: Methuen.

Rosolato, Guy. 1974. "La voix: entre corps et langage." *Revue française de psychanalyse* 37:1.

Rousseau, George S. 1993. "A Strange Pathology." In *Hysteria beyond Freud*, edited by Sander L. Gilman et al. Berkeley: University of California Press.

Ruotolo, Lucio P. 1986. *The Interrupted Moment: A View of Virginia Woolf's Novels*. Stanford: Stanford University Press.

Sayers, Janet. 1982. *Biological Politics: Feminist and Anti-Feminist Perspectives*. London: Tavistock; New York: Methuen.

Schiesari, Juliana. 1993. *The Gendering of Melancholy*. Ithaca: Cornell University Press.

Schmitz, Neil. 1985. "Mark Twain, Henry James, and Jacksonian Dreaming." *Criticism* 27:155–73.

Schreiner, Olive. 1976. *The Story of an African Farm*. New York: Schocken Books.

Sedgwick, Eve Kosofsky. 1990. *Epistemology of the Closet*. Berkeley: University of California Press.

Segal, Naomi. 1989. "Freud and the Question of Women." In *Freud in Exile: Psychoanalysis and Its Vicissitudes*, edited by Edward Timms and Naomi Segal. New Haven: Yale University Press.

Sensibar, Judith. 1991. "The Politics of Hysteria in *The Bostonians*." *South Central Review (Journal of the SCMLA)* (Summer): 57–72.

Shorter, Edward. 1988. "Paralysis: The Rise and Fall of a Hysterical Symptom." In *Expanding the Past*, edited by Peter Stearns. New York: New York University Press.

Showalter, Elaine. 1977. *A Literature of Their Own: British Women Novelists from Brontë to Lessing*. Princeton: Princeton University Press.

———. 1985. *The Female Malady: Women, Madness, and English Culture, 1830–1980*. New York: Pantheon.

———. 1990. *Sexual Anarchy*. New York: Viking.

———. 1993. "Hysteria, Feminism, and Gender." In *Hysteria beyond Freud*. Edited by Sandor Gilman et al. Berkeley: University of California Press.

Silverman, Kaja. 1988. *The Acoustic Mirror*. Bloomington: Indiana University Press.

———. 1992. *Male Subjectivity at the Margins*. New York: Routledge.

Slater, Philip E. 1968. *The Glory of Hera: Greek Mythology and the Greek Family*. Boston: Beacon.

Smith-Rosenberg, Carroll. 1985. *Disorderly Conduct: Visions of Gender in Victorian America*. New York: Oxford University Press.

Snyder, Katherine. 1993. "From Novel to Essay: Gender and Revision in Florence Nightingale's *Cassandra*." In *The Politics of the Essay*, edited by Ruth-Ellen Boetcher Joeres and Elizabeth Mittman. Bloomington: Indiana University Press.

Sprengnether, Madelon. 1985. "Enforcing Oedipus: Freud and Dora." In *The M/Other Tongue: Essays in Feminist Psychoanalytic Criticism*, edited by Shirley Garner, Claire Kahane, and Madelon Sprengnether. Ithaca: Cornell University Press.

———. 1990. *The Spectral Mother: Freud, Feminism, and Psychoanalysis*. Ithaca: Cornell University Press.

Stark, Myra. 1979. Introduction to *Cassandra*, by Florence Nightingale. New York: Feminist Press.

Stewart, Garrett. 1990. *Reading Voices*. Berkeley: University of California Press.

———. 1993. "A Valediction For Bidding Mourning: Death and the Narratee in Brontë's *Villette*." In *Death and Representation,* edited by Sarah Webster Goodwin and Elisabeth Bronfen. Baltimore: Johns Hopkins University Press.

Strachey, Lytton. 1918. *Eminent Victorians.* New York: Harcourt, Brace.

Strouse, Jean. 1980. *Alice James: A Biography.* New York: Houghton Mifflin.

Stubbs, Patricia. 1979. *Women and Fiction: Feminism and the Novel, 1880–1920.* Totowa, N.J.: Barnes & Noble.

Studlar, Gay Lynn. 1988. *In the Realm of Pleasure: Von Sternberg, Dietrich, and the Masochistic Aesthetic.* Urbana: University of Illinois Press.

Suleiman, Susan Robin, ed. 1986. *The Female Body in Western Culture.* Cambridge: Harvard University Press.

Swan, Jim. 1974. "Mater and Nannie." *American Imago* 31(1): 1–64.

Veith, Ilza. 1965. *Hysteria: The History of a Disease.* Chicago: University of Chicago Press.

Vrettos, Athena. 1990. "From Neurosis to Narrative: The Private Life of the Nerves in *Villette* and *Daniel Deronda*." *Victorian Studies* 33(4):551–79.

Wardley, Lynn. 1989. "Women's Voice, Democracy's Body and *The Bostonians*." *ELH* 56(3):639–66.

Welter, Barbara. 1966. "The Cult of True Womanhood: 1820–1860." *American Quarterly* 18 (Summer).

White, Allon. 1981. *The Uses of Obscurity: The Fiction of Early Modernism.* London: Routledge.

Whitford, Margaret. 1991. *Luce Irigaray: Philosophy in the Feminine.* London: Routledge.

Wilt, Judith. 1987. "Desperately Seeking Verena: A Resistant Reading of *The Bostonians*." *Feminist Studies* 13(2):293–316.

Winnicott, D. W. [1953] 1971. "Transitional Objects and Transitional Phenomena." In *Playing and Reality.* London: Tavistock.

———. [1967a] 1971. "The Location of Cultural Experience." In *Playing and Reality.* London: Tavistock.

———. [1967b] 1971. "Mirror-Role of Mother and Family in Child Development." In *Playing and Reality.* London: Tavistock.

———. [1969] 1971. "The Use of an Object and Relating through Identifications." In *Playing and Reality.* London: Tavistock.

———. 1971. "Creativity and Its Origins." In *Playing and Reality.* London: Tavistock.

Woolf, Virginia. 1948. *The Voyage Out.* New York: Harcourt, Brace & World.

———. 1953. "Modern Fiction." In *The Common Reader.* First Series. Harvest Books. New York: Harcourt, Brace & World.

———. 1955. *To the Lighthouse.* New York: Harcourt, Brace & World.

———. 1957. *A Room of One's Own*. New York: Harcourt, Brace.

———. 1966. *Collected Essays*. 4 vols. London: Hogarth.

———. 1979. *The Letters of Virginia Woolf, Volume Four (1929–1931)*. Edited by Nigel Nicolson and Joanne Trautmann. 1st American edition. New York: Harcourt Brace Jovanovich.

———. 1982. *Melymbrosia: An Early Version of "The Voyage Out."* Edited with an introduction by Louise DeSalvo. New York: New York Public Library.

Wyatt, Jean. 1990. *Reconstructing Desire*. Chapel Hill: University of North Carolina Press.

Yeazell, Ruth Bernard. 1981. Introduction to *The Death and Letters of Alice James*. Berkeley: University of California Press.

Zwerdling, Alex. 1986. *Virginia Woolf and the Real World*. Berkeley: University of California Press.

Index

Abel, Elizabeth, on Woolf and anthropology, 120, 172nn. 21, 22
Abjection, 41, 111–13. *See also* Disgust; Kristeva, Julia
Adams, Henry, 72
Ambivalence: and female oedipus complex, 35, 174n.13; and hysterical symptom, xi, 8, 9; and language, 90; and male identity, 64–65, 154n.17; and marriage, 100; and maternal power, 125–26; and melancholia, 89–90; and narrative, 55, 82. *See also* Bisexuality; Identification
Androgyny: and feminist speakers, 6–7; and naming, 80–81
"Angel in the House," 5, 61
Anna O., x, 15–16, 46
Anzieu, A., on erogenous body, 151n.6, 154n.17, 157n.17; on cathexis of speaking, 153n.14, of mouth, 160n.7
Anzieu, D., on maternal voice, 17
Ardis, Ann, xv, 3, 86, 153n.8, 164–65n.3
Armstrong, Nancy, 151n.4
Atkinson, J. J., 120
Audition: in *The Bostonians*, 75–76; in *The Good Soldier*, 145–47; and primal scene, 19–20; in psychoanalytic dialogue, 20–21; in the texts of Conrad and Ford, 131–32;

in *The Voyage Out*, 115–16; and words, xiii. *See also* Hysteria; Oratory; Primal scene; Talking Cure
Auerbach, Nina, 5
Austen, Jane, *Emma*, ix
Authorial subject: 53, 129–30, 148–49

Bagehot, Walter, on the new physics, 1–2
Barthes, Roland: and figuration, viii, ix; and voice, viii, 17, 133; on vocal writing, 155n.5
Bell, Ian F. A., 164n.12
Bennett, Arnold, 13
Bernheimer, Charles, 9, 171n.14
Binary model of difference, 3–5
Bisexuality: Freud on, xi; and identification, 8, 86. *See also* Ambivalence; Hysteria; Identification
Bluebeard, 101, 107
Bostonians, The, 64–79, 80; Boston marriage, 163n.5, 164n.13; critique of transcendentalism in, 68–70, 164n.10; and female hysteria in, 73; and feminism, 65–66, 73; homoerotic innuendo in, 76, 77, 79, 164n.13; hysterical narrator of, 65–66, 68; male hysteria in, 64, 70, 75–76; morbidity in, 73–77, 79; phallic imagery in, 66, 71–72, 75; primal scene of audition in, 75–76;

Bostonians, The (*continued*)
rage in, 67, 69; rape in, 75–76, 78–79; ridicule in, 69–71; sadomasochistic relations in, 75, 77–78; sexual difference as structuring trope of, 67, 72; voice as fetish, 66, 70, 72; xenophobia in, 70
Breton, André, and *Surrealist Manifesto*, 174n.16
Breuer, Josef, and Anna O., x, 15–16. *See also* Anna O.
Brönte, Charlotte: rage and, 37, 53–54. Works: *Jane Eyre*, ix, 53, 54, 58, 60; *Shirley*, xiv, 3, 37, 53–57, 58, 62, 82; *Villette*, xii, xiv, 37, 57–63, 148
Brooks, Peter, 134, 138, 151
Butler, Judith, 9

Carlyle, Thomas, 71, 96
Cassandra: and Christ as prophet, 52, 73; on danger of passivity, 50; on desire to talk, 51; on imaginary counterpart, 51; manipulation of narrative voice in, 48–50, 52, 73; melancholy in, 48; on maternal voice, 50–51; on rage and invalidism, 51–54; textual revisions of, 47–50. *See also* Nightingale, Florence
Castration anxiety, 7–8, 25, 121; and speech, 162n.24
Charcot, Jean, x, 11, 92; *globus hystericus*, 11, 92; *lecons du Mardi*, 11–12; photographs of hysterics, 154n.21
Chion, Michel, and maternal voice, 16, 155n.7. *See also* Maternal voice
Civilization and Its Discontents: origins of disgust in, 24, 157nn. 19, 20
Clarissa, 107
"Comus," 101, 122–23. See also Rape; *Voyage Out, The*
Conrad, Joseph, xiv, 127; and narrators, 130; and hysterical mimicry,

148, 150. Works: *Heart of Darkness*, xiv, 120, 125, 132–38; *Lord Jim*, 138; *Nigger of the Narcissus*, 133
Countertransference, xiv, 20. *See also* Transference
"Cult of True Womanhood," 5
Cummings, Katherine, xvi

Darwin, Charles, and *The Descent of Man*, 5
David-Menard, Monique: on disgust, 24–25; on primary maternal relation, 99, 154n.17; on cathexis of mouth, 160n.7
Davis, Sara de Saussure, 65
Death drive, 34
DeLauretis, Teresa, and oedipal narrative, ix
Delueze, Gilles, on masochism, 85, 166–67n.13. *See also* Masochism
DeSalvo, Louise, 168–69n.1; on *Melymbrosia*, 170n.11, 171nn. 12, 17; on *Paterfamilias*, 169n.2
Disgust: and abjection, 41, 111–13; in the Dora case, 24–26; and Alice James, 41; in *The Voyage Out*, 108–109, 112–13. *See also* Dora case
Dora case, x, xii, 14–33; and bisexual identification, 22; and cathexis of the voice, 32, 37, 132; defloration fantasy, 29; disgust in, 24–26; Dora's dreams, 26–32; fellatio fantasy, 22–24; homosexuality in, 25–26, 28, 109; and maternal object, 30–32, 99, 102; and melancholia, 30; and oedipal narrative, ix, 21–22; orality in, 22, 25, 32; and primal scene listening, 26; and transference, xiv. *See also* Freud, Sigmund; Hysteria
DuPlessis, Rachel Blau: on narrative endings, 165n.4; 165n.9; on Schreiner's subversion of oedipal narrative, 168n.24

Edel, Leon, 38
Eliot, George: Alice James's rage at,
40–42, 161n.11; *Letters*, 40–42;
Mill on the Floss, 37, 39. *See also*
James, Alice
Eliot, T. S.: and "Hysteria," xiv, 134,
128–29; hysterical mimicry, 148,
150; and mimesis of hysteria, 129;
xenophobia of, 70. *See also* Authorial subject; "Hysteria"
Ellis, Havelock, on Olive Schreiner,
164n.1, 166n.11, 167n.14
Emerson, Ralph Waldo, 44, 164n.2

Felman, Shoshana, 130
Female body: and ambivalence, 100,
148; and female sexuality, 26, 101;
and hysteria, 148; identification
with, 160n.5; and Alice James, 41–
46; medical discourse on, 4–5;
rage at, 36–37; and voice, 59
The Female Malady, xv
Femininity: as masquerade, 8–9,
149; and passivity, 9–10, 29, 86;
and rage, 35, 46. *See also* Riviere,
Joan
Feminism, ix, xv; American feminist
movement, 6, 65; androgyny and,
6–7, 80–81; hysteria and, 6–9,
64–67; Henry James and, 64–66;
modernism and, xv–xvi; and New
Woman, ix; Florence Nightingale
and, 53; oratory and, 6–9, 64–67;
rage and, 67–70; Olive Schreiner
and, 80–81. *See also Bostonians,
The*; New Woman; Oratory; *Story
of an African Farm*
Ferguson, Frances, 170n.10
Fictions of Authority, xvi
Ford, Ford Madox: on aural technique, 173n.3; and first-person narrator, 63, 130–31; 139–40; *The
Good Soldier*, xii, xiv, 63, 128, 131,

138–47; and hysterical voice, 127,
147, 148, 150
Frazer, James, 120
Freud, Sigmund: on bisexual identification, xi, 15, 22, 35; on Charcot,
11–12, 154n. 20; definition of hysteria, x, 14–15; and Dora case, x,
xii, xiv, 14; 20–31; and envy of maternal power, 32, 159n.27; on femininity, 9–10; on link between
hysteria and melancholia, 158n.25;
primal scene of audition, 19–20;
on rage, xii, 14, 35, 151n.7, 159n.3;
on romantic fantasies, 68; and
transference, xiv, 20; and voice in
psychoanalytic dialogue, 12, 16–
20, 155–56n.8. Works: "Beyond
the Pleasure Principle," 151n.7;
"Creative Writers and Daydreaming," ix, 68; "Ego and the Id,"
156nn. 8, 12; "Femininity," 35;
"Fragment of an Analysis of a
Case of Hysteria," xiv, 15, 17; "On
the History of the Psychoanalytic
Movement," 18; "Hysterical
Phantasies and their Relation to
Bisexuality," xi, 154n.19; *The Interpretation of Dreams*, 31–32;
"Mourning and Melancholia,"
159nn. 3, 4; "Recommendations
to Physicians Practicing Psychoanalysis," 156n. 10; *Studies on Hysteria*, 15, 103; *Totem and Taboo*,
135. *See also Civilization and Its
Discontents*; Disgust; Dora case;
Hysteria
Freudian switchword, 58, 86, 137
Fuller, Margaret, 67

Galsworthy, John, 13
Gay, Peter: on male brutality,
158n.24; on Victorian bourgeois
culture, 2, 4, 152n.4, 153n.6

Gilbert, Sandra, and Susan Gubar:
  on feminism and modernism, xv;
  on Schreiner's dysphoric endings,
  168n.24
Gilman, Sander, xvi
Good Soldier, The: and amatory identification, 144; dissociation of desire in, 143; erotics of talking and
  listening, 140–46; and *Heart of
  Darkness*, 145; maternal betrayal
  in, 141; maternal father in, 146; as
  psychoanalytic dialogue, 139; sadomasochism in, 146–47
Green, André, 14, 129, 152n.10

Habegger, Alfred, 65, 163n.8
Hartman, Geoffrey, 152n.12
Heart of Darkness, xiv, 120, 125; aural
  writing in, 132; critique of idealism
  in, 136–38; homosociality in, 136;
  orality in, 134–35, 137–38; primal
  scene of hearing, 131–33; voice as
  phallus, 133, 134, 136
Heath, Stephen, 12–13, 20, 153n.15,
  156n.11
Hertz, Neil: on male hysteria 7, 64,
  79; on Freud, 20, 132
Hirsch, Marianne, 47, 62, 161n.10
Hypatia, 79
Hypnosis, 11–12
Hysteria: and ambiguities of sexual
  difference, xi, 5; body as site of
  meaning, x; Charcot's phases of,
  11–12; as daughter's disease, 34–
  35; as defense, 129–48; definition
  of, x; and displacement, 22; etiology of, 8, 34; and female emancipation, viii–x, 2–4, 64–65; and
  feminine ideal, 9; and feminism,
  6–9, 165n.10; Freud's, x, xi; historical change and, 1–5; history of, 7,
  9–13; and homoerotic desire, 22,
  26, 28, 35, 73, 102; as language disorder, 15–16; male, x, 9–10, 64,

70, 127; and melancholia, 30–31,
  36, 124, 167n.17; mimicry and
  masquerade in, 147–50; and modernism, xiv, xv, 127, 147–50; mutism, 9; and nurse-figure, 46; and
  paranoia, 1, 128–29; and passivity,
  34; psychopoetics of, xiv, 127, 129,
  147–50; and public speaking, 8, 65,
  149; rage and, xii, 35–37, 39–40,
  45; seduction fantasy in, 18, 34;
  suffrage movement and, 4; Victorian age and, 1–7, 9–13. *See also*
  Ambivalence; Bisexuality; Disgust;
  Nurse-figure; Rage; Sexual
  difference
"Hysteria" (Eliot), xiv; implicit authorial subject in, 128–29; and
  paranoia, 129; as poetic mimesis of
  hysteria, 129
Hysteria beyond Freud, xvi

Idealization, 41, 44, 110
Identification, xi, xiv, 8, 40, 79,
  157n.22; amatory, 144; Dora's, 22,
  28–29; Freud's with Dora, 21;
  Henry James with female protagonist, 79; with maternal body,
  46, 112; and melancholia, 172n.23;
  in mourning, 89; and narcissism,
  40, 144; and oedipus complex, 28,
  35, 158n.23; and paranoia, 129; in
  primal scene, 19–20, 116, 145; and
  splitting, 87–88
Imaginary counterpart: in *Cassandra*, 51–52; and Alice James,
  40; and Florence Nightingale, 46;
  in *Story of an African Farm*, 82
In Dora's Case, 21
Irigaray, Luce, xii, 152n.8; on Freud's
  theory of feminine development,
  30; on hysterical melancholia, 30–
  31, 36; on hysterical mimicry, 149;
  on sadomasochism, 32

Jacobs, Carol, 143
James, Alice, xii, xiv, 87; *Diary*, 37–
46; desire for death, 45–46, 48;
on George Eliot, 40–42; and
Ralph Waldo Emerson, 44; as
hysteric, 37–38; and hysterical inhibition, 40, 59; and Henry
James, 66, 79; and William James,
40; and Katherine Loring, 38, 45,
66; on marriage, 41–42; and paternal voice, 44–45, 52; and rage
at maternal body, 43–46
James, Henry, xii, xiv, 9, 18, 38; attitude toward publicity, 164n.12;
The Bostonians, 64–79, 80, 140;
and fear of aphanisis, 66; and feminization of culture, 67, 71; and
Alice James, 66, 79; and narration
of *The Turn of the Screw*, 130–31;
and Elizabeth Peabody, 69, 163–
64n.9. *See also Bostonians, The*
James, Sr., Henry, 68, 163n.8
James, William, 40, 69
Jane Eyre, ix, 53, 58
Janet, Pierre, x
Jeune, Mary, 7
Joke theory, 44, 132

Klein, Melanie, xii, 36, 151n.6; epistemophilic drive, 95; on etiology
of rage, 36
Kofman, Sarah, on enigma of language, 156n.14
Kristeva, Julia: abjection, 111–12, 123;
and amatory identification, 144;
on Dora's jouissance, 123; on homosexual erotics and idealization,
110; on metaphor, 103, 167n.18,
169–70n.7; *Powers of Horror*, 111;
rage as narcissistic crisis, xii, 35–
36, 103; semiotic and symbolic, 17;
subject-in-process, 166n.10; on
temporality and syntax, 15; voyeurism, 171n.16

Krohn, Alan, 9, 153n.12
Kucich, John, on Charlotte Brönte
and repression, 162n.26.

Lacan, Jacques, xi, 23–24, 90
Lanser, Susan, xvi
Laplanche, Jean, and J.-B. Pontalis, on
primal scene of audition, 156n.13
Laqueur, Thomas, 3
Laurence, Patricia Ondek, 102; on
Woolf's uses of silence, 169n.6
Lecourt, Edith, 17
Linton, Eliza Lynn, 6
Loring, Katherine, 38, 45, 66
Lukasher, Ned, 24

Malcolm, Janet, 155n.6
Marcus, Steven, 173n.1
Marriage plot, x, 3, 62, 76, 78–79,
100, 104, 124
Masochism, xii, xiv; "A Child Is Being Beaten," 83–85, 166n.12; and
death drive, 34–35; Gilles Deleuze
on, 85, 166n.13; hysteria and, 93, 98;
as narrative resolution, 84, 89; rage
and, 34–35, 37; Olive Schreiner
and, 167n.14; *Venus in Furs*,
167n.15. *See also* Rage; Schreiner,
Olive; *Story of an African Farm*
Maternal body: abjection of, 25, 111–
13, 120–22; ambivalence toward,
100, 112, 125–26; disavowal of, 35;
envy of, 32, 159n.27; and idealization, 44, 91, 97, 125; and language,
32, 90, 94, 102; rage at, 36–37, 95,
122; recuperation of, 123–24. *See
also* Abjection; Ambivalence; Klein,
Melanie; Kristeva, Julia
Maternal gaze, 120, 172n.20
Maternal loss, 88, 90, 102, 110, 122;
and melancholia, 89–98, 124–25,
159nn. 3, 4. *See also* Masochism;
Melancholia

Maternal power: in *Heart of Darkness*, 134–38; in *Story of an African Farm*, 91, 94–95; in *To the Lighthouse*, 119–26; in *The Voyage Out*, 101. *See also* Ambivalence

Maternal voice, 16–17, 32, 43–44, 50

Maternity, 3–4

Medusa, x, 7, 151n.5

Melancholia, xii, xiv, 6, 30–31, 48–49; hysterical, 36, 167n.17; and identification, 172n.23; and mourning, 88–90, 124, 159n.4, 167n.16; and rage, 122, 159n.3, 167n.17. *See also* Hysteria; Maternal loss; Rage

Mesmerism, 18

Mill on the Floss, The, 37, 39–40

Miller, Nancy, 98

Mitchell, Juliet, xii, 34

Modernism: and authorial absence, 129–30, 175n.19; and Joseph Conrad and Ford Madox Ford, 127; and dialogical form of novel, 147; and feminism, xiv–xvi; and hysteria, xv, 13, 63, 127, 148–50; and masquerade, 148; and New Woman, xv–xvi; and sexual difference, 147; Virginia Woolf on, 13, 154–55n.22, 172–73n.25; and *The Voyage Out*, 125–26

Moi, Toril, 156n.15

Montrelay, Michele, 160n.5

Munch, Edvard, 104, 170n.9

Napoleon, 82, 83, 94

Narrative voice: disruptions of, xiv, 51–52, 53, 57, 67–69; use of first-person vs. third-person, vii, 47–50, 63, 148–49; focalization of, 104; frame narrators and, 130–33; Freud's manipulation of, 26–27; hysteria and, viii–xvi, 139, 147; and speaking subject, vii–viii, x, xiii

New Woman: appearance of, ix, 2, 5–6, 64–66, 164–65n.3; Olive

Schreiner and, 80, 84, 166n.11; response to, xv, 2–7. *See also Story of an African Farm*

New Women, New Novels, xv

Nightingale, Florence, xii, xiv, 37; *Cassandra*, 47–53; as feminist, 53; and nursing, 46–47; and women's suffering, 73. *See also Cassandra*

Nightingale myth, 52, 76, 79, 162n.24

No Man's Land, xv

Nurse-figure, 26, 46, 147, 157n.21

Oedipus complex, ix, 27, 29, 35, 158n.23; and father-daughter relations, 93, 107, 123; and heterosexual plot, ix, 21–22, 28, 68, 78, 110; and oedipal law, 27–28, 76

Oneida community, 74

Orality: and cannibalism in *Heart of Darkness*, 134–38; and fellatio, 22–23, 26; as privileged hysterical zone, 22, 25, 160n.7; and rage, xii; in *Story of an African Farm*, 92, 94; and woman's mouth in "Hysteria," 128; and woman's mouth in *The Good Soldier*, 147–48. *See also* Hysteria; Klein, Melanie

Oratory: 6–9, 62, 64–67. *See also Bostonians, The*

Passivity: and femininity, 10, 29; medical promotion of, 10; and passion, 14; pathogenic, 50; and rage, 14, 37; and *The Romance of the Rose* and "The Sleeping Beauty," 86. *See also* Femininity

Paternal seduction, 23, 107–8, 145

Patmore, Coventry, 5

Peabody, Elizabeth, 69, 163–64n.9

Phallus: indeterminacy of, in Dora case, 26; mockery of, 94, 125; and phallic mother, 26, 151n.4; and rage, 35: rivalry for, 8–9; voice as,

9, 146, 164n.13; Woolf's disgust with, 170–71n.11. *See also* Riviere, Joan; Voice

Pinel, Phillipe, 10–11

Poovey, Mary, 3

Pound, Ezra, 70

Primal scene: of audition, 19–20, 75–76; 115–16, 145; of castration, 120–21; and identification, 116; and sexual indeterminacy, 26; as structuring trope, 113–15; 145; and voyeurism, 116, 171n.15

Projection, xi; and projective identification, 19; of interiority, 93; and rage, 59

Queen Victoria, ix

Rage: and aggression, 151n.7; body as object of, 42, 45, 59; Charlotte Brönte and, 53–54; Dora and, 28; and female bildungsroman, 124; and hysteria, xii, xiii; Alice James and, 40–45; and masochism, 37; at maternal object, 36–37; and melancholy, 36, 122, 159n.3; narrative voice and, 37, 53–54, 67–69, 141; as passion, 14; and sexual ambivalence, 35. *See also* Klein, Melanie; Melancholia

Rape: analytic violation as, 29, 158n.26; in *The Bostonians*, 75, 76, 78–79; in the Dora case, 28–29; and marriage, 170n.10; maternal rape, 118; in *The Voyage Out*, 101, 107, 109–10, 170n.10. *See also* Nightingale myth

Rape of Lucrece, 101, 105

Realism, viii, 13, 126

Reik, Theodore, listening with the third ear, 18, 152n.11, 156n.10

Riviere, Joan, "Womanliness as Masquerade," 8–9, 149

Rosalato, Guy, 16

Rousseau, George, 10, 154n.18

Sadomasochism, 31–32; in *The Bostonians*, 75, 77–78; in *The Good Soldier*, 141, 146–47; in *Story of an African Farm*, 95. *See also* Masochism; Rape

Schiesari, Juliana, 48

Schmitz, Neil, 164n.10

Schreiner, Olive, xiv, 3, 37, 80–81, 124; and Havelock Ellis, 166n.11, 167n.14; as hysteric, 164n.1, 165n.6; and Rebecca Lyndall, 81; and masochism, 84–86, 93, 95, 167n.14; *Story of an African Farm*, 80–98, 99, 124. *See also Story of an African Farm*

Seduction: in conversation, 139–41; maternal, 118–19; paternal, 23, 107–8, 145; in psychoanalytic dialogue, 17–22; theory, 34

Semiotic: and symbolic, 17. *See also* Kristeva, Julia

Sensibar, Judith, 4, 152n.5

Sexual Anarchy, xv

Sexual difference: binary model of, 2; challenge to, ix; and feminism, ix, 64–66, 89; as masquerade, 57; negation of, xi, 25–27, 84, 169n.4; and primal scene, 116; and speaking subject, viii–x, 58; as structuring trope, 66–67, 81–82; Victorian discourse on, 5–6; and writing, 58, 77. *See also* Bisexuality; Riviere, Joan

Shirley: narrative voice in, 57; rage in, 54–55; splitting in, 53, 55–56

Showalter, Elaine, xv, 6, 7, 10, 47, 153nn. 9, 12, 161n.18, 165n.9

Silverman, Kaja, 16, 85, 129, 154n.17, 155n.7, 158n.23, 162nn. 23, 24

Slater, Philip, 151n.5., 173n.6

Smith-Rosenberg, Carroll, 4–5, 156nn. 6, 7, 154n.19

Snyder, Katherine, 161nn. 18, 20, 21
Speaking subject, vii, xi, 32, 50, 98
Splitting, as narrative technique, 53, 56, 63, 82–83, 87–88, 111
Sprengnether, Madelon, 26, 157nn. 16, 21
Stewart, Garrett: on lack of closure in *Villette*, 162–63n.29; on voicing, xiii; 32, 152n.13
Story of an African Farm, xiv, 80–98; feminism in, 80, 82, 84; first person singular vs. first person plural in, 83; ironies of narrative voice, 94–95; Lyndall as the New Woman, 80, 84; masochistic structuring, 84–86, 93, 95, 98; and maternal voice, 94–98; and melancholia, 90–98; rage in, 81; splitting in, 82, 87–88
Stowe, Harriet Beecher, 3
Strachey, Lytton, 47
Strouse, Jean, 40, 160n.8, 163n.5, 164n.11
Suffrage, 2, 65–66
Sydenham, Thomas, 10

Talking cure, 13, 16–21; as literary technique in *The Good Soldier*, 140–42
Telling Tales, xvi
Transference, xii; and counter-transference xiv; in the Dora case, 20; as literary strategy in *The Good Soldier*, 141
Turn of the Screw, The, 130

Veith, Ilza, 9, 153n.16
Villette, 39, female body vs. female voice, 57, 58–63; hysterical strategies in, 57–58, 63; and masquerade, 148; modernist voice of, 63, 148; rage in, 58, 59–61
Voice: definition of, vii, xiii; hysteri-cal, viii, 47; identification and, 19–

20, 50–51, 136; internalization of, xiii, 155–56n.8; maternal, 16–17, 44, 50; and miscegenation, 72; passion for, 49–50; as phallus, x, 66, 70, 136, 146, 164n.13; rivalry for, 33, 66–67; seduction and, 51, 72, 76, 140, 146; and the talking cure, 12, 16–20. *See also* Maternal voice; Narrative voice; Nightingale myth
Voyage Out, The, xiv, 99–126, 128: ab-jection in, 111–13, and the Dora case, 102; focalization of voice, 104, 114; lesbian erotics in, 110–13, 116, 118–19, 170n.17; function of metaphor in, 102–3, 107; names in, 103; paternal seduction in, 106–8; primal scene in, 114–21; splitting in, 111; use of silence, 169n.6. *See also* Kristeva, Julia; Woolf, Virginia
Voyeurism, 20, 116, 171n.15

Winnicott, D. W., 17
Woolf, Virginia: on Brönte's anger, 53; on modernism, 13, 154–55n.22, 172–73n.25; on power of words, vii; on silence, 102. Works: "Modern Fiction," 13; *Mrs. Dalloway*, 114; "A Room of One's Own," 100; *To the Lighthouse*, 114, 119; *The Voyage Out*. xiv, 99–126, 128. *See also Voy-age Out, The*

Xenophobia, 70

Zwerdling, Alex, 162n.25